Religion and Global Culture

Religion and Global Culture

New Terrain in the Study of Religion and the Work of Charles H. Long

Edited by Jennifer I. M. Reid

LEXINGTON BOOKS
Lanham • Boulder • New York • Oxford

LEXINGTON BOOKS

Published in the United States of America
by Lexington Books
A Member of the Rowman & Littlefield Publishing Group
4501 Forbes Boulevard, Suite 200, Lanham, MD 20706

PO Box 317
Oxford
OX2 9RU, UK

British Library Cataloguing in Publication Information Available

Library of Congress Cataloging-in-Publication Data

Religion and global culture: new terrain in the study of religion and the work of
    Charles H. Long / edited by Jennifer I. M. Reid
        p. cm.
    Based on a conference held Apr. 5–7, 2001 at the University of Maine at
Farmington.
    Includes bibliographical references (p.) and index.
    ISBN 0-7391-0552-3 (cloth: alk. paper). — ISBN 0-7391-0810-7 (pbk. : alk. paper)
    1. Globalization—Religious aspects. 2. Religion and culture. 3. Long,
Charles H. I. Reid, Jennifer, 1962–

BL65.C8 R444 2003
200'.9—dc21   2002035734

Printed in the United States of America

⊖™ The paper used in this publication meets the minimum requirements of American National Standard for Information Sciences—Permanence of Paper for Printed Library Materials, ANSI/NISO Z39.48–1992.

For Charles H. Long

Contents

Acknowledgements

I wish to acknowledge the many individuals and groups who have contributed to this book. First and foremost, I must express my debt to Charles H. Long, without whom this project could not have transpired. Throughout a distinguished career during which he has advanced the field of the general history of religions in the United States (as initiated by Joachim Wach), Charles Long has impacted upon the lives and work of an incalculable number of students and colleagues. His influence can be discerned in an expansive corpus of work that is unified in its concern for the location of *origins* in the study of religion. Scholars who have contributed to this volume reflect both the Wachian tradition represented by Charles Long, and the shift in the notion of *origins* from an arena of the speculative or primordial to that of contacts and relations of, especially, the colonial and neocolonial eras. The work of Charles Long has been a seminal influence in this hermeneutical trajectory; and this book is a result of this work. In a more immediate sense, it is also a product of a number of years of discussion and support, both intellectual and practical, that I have been fortunate to have with Professor Long. For this I am deeply grateful.

I must also express my gratitude to the Maine Humanities Council and the New Century Community Program which, with support from the National Endowment for the Humanities, provided a major grant that made possible Religion, Global Culture, and the University, a conference held at the University of Maine at Farmington in April of 2001. In addition to being a success in its own right, the conference was the springboard from which this book emerged. I express my debt also to the University of Maine at Farmington for generously supporting the conference and, subsequently, for awarding me a sabbatical during which I was able to accomplish this project.

I wish to thank all the individuals, too many to name, who assisted in the completion of this book. In particular, I am grateful to Davíd Carrasco, whose comments and insights both at the 2001 conference and in its wake provided me with a constructive sense of direction in approaching this volume. I thank also Erik Jorgenson of the Maine Humanities Council; Daniel Gunn, Doug Rawlings, and Valerie Huebner, my colleagues at UMF; Kristin McLaren, Bruce McKee, Sean Bolduc, Andrew Bryant, Richard Cote, Matthew Fulkerson,

Timothy LeBeau, Philip McCormick, and Jennifer Toth; and, finally, Mark L. McPherran, Kate Reid, and Margaret Reid, without whom this book would certainly have remained only an intriguing possibility.

In addition, I wish to acknowledge *Journal of Religion* (University of Chicago) for generously granting me permission to republish Jim Perkinson's "Ogu's Iron or Jesus' Irony: Who's Zooming Who in Diasporic Possession Cult Activity?" 81:4 (2001).

Jennifer I. M. Reid

Introduction

Jennifer I. M. Reid

In his plenary address at a conference on globalization and religion held in the spring of 2001,[1] Charles H. Long related an anecdote about a Buddhist monk who, upon meeting Alexander the Great, is said to have asked him three questions. The first was "Who are you?" the second, "Do you not have a home?" and the third, "Why are you not at home?" The issues raised by these questions permeate the chapters included in this volume; broadly speaking, each is concerned with the problem of human origins and orientation, in respect to both religion and the study of religion.

Together, the authors of these chapters employ the comparative methods of the general history of religions, a field that owes its existence in North America to Joachim Wach and the students he taught at the University of Chicago between 1945 and 1955. As Kees Bolle points out, Wach's primary concern was with hermeneutics in the study of religion. He infused his students with a consciously reflexive approach to the study of religion, an approach that assumed as its point of departure regard for the authenticity of religious expressions and institutions, and stressed in its methodology the systematic study of these expressions in order to arrive at a sound theory of religion. For Wach, the historian of religion had the dual task of better understanding the cultural significance of religion and the nature of religion itself.[2] More than this, he assumed a hermeneutical position best represented, perhaps, by the term elasticity. For Wach, understanding required a dialectical relationship between the scholar and the religious subject.[3] He described this relationship (one made possible by what Philip Arnold calls the cipher of religion) in a classic chapter on Mahāyāna Buddhism:

> If the reader can acquire the inner composure and stillness that will permit him to penetrate the spirit of this literature, to understand it and to enjoy it, then he will also be able to understand the style of thinking and speaking that the Indians created for themselves. Whoever wishes to become familiar with Mahāyāna must simply accept a much bigger criterion; he must become broader and more

1

open—I might say more elastic—so that he can acquire the inner momentum
that will enable him to think, feel, and move with his subject.[4]

Following in this tradition, the contributors to this volume assume this reflexive
stance, seeking to understand the religious significance of origins and orientation within the historical context from which the study of religion emerged.

In the context of these chapters, the conversation about origins is located
primarily within the framework of what Charles Long has called a new arche, a
term that at once invokes Mircea Eliade's formative work on the religious construction of consciousness, and signals a distinct trajectory within the study of
religion. Eliade claimed that interactions and exchanges between archaic human
beings and the natural world were the religious context out of which human beings came to know themselves and their various modes of being human.[5] Building on such a notion of a "religious imagination of matter," Long has argued
further that the history of colonialism must be regarded as an environment that
religiously impinged on humankind: its mercantilism, enslavement, genocides,
and new hierarchies of power together constitute an originary structure—a second arche—that human beings perforce have had to undergo, and in relation to
which new modes of being human have been engendered. In his chapter, "Asking the Question of the Origin of Religion," Tatsuo Murakami begins by exploring the notion of the origin of religion as a problematic epistemological foundation of the study of religion; and taking a cue from Long, Murakami argues that
in a modern global culture, the space in which the "materiality of empirical others" is concomitantly acknowledged (others as historical subjects) and denied
(others as "primitive" and as a negative structure in relation to which "civilized"
has meaning) is the location of the origin of religion and, consequently, the point
of departure in the construction of an adequate hermeneutic.

The various chapters in this volume explore the religious significance of this
new arche within a variety of historical and geographical arenas. In one manner
or another, each chapter begins by asking the Buddhist monk's first two questions of Alexander: Who are you? and, Do you not have a home? and it is the
material structure of religious consciousness that provides each writer with a
portal through which these issues of identity and location are approached. My
chapter on Louis Riel examines the way in which material crisis (land loss and
game depletion) gave rise to prophetic visions, redefinition of community, and
rebellion in the nineteenth-century Canadian Northwest. Philip Arnold discerns,
in sweetgrass and ash baskets, a relationship with landscape within which the
deepest meanings of being Onondaga in central New York state are articulated.
Jacob Olupona suggests that the material imaginations of African immigrant
communities in the United States allow not only for cultural adaptability but for
creative reciprocal political, educational, and economic reconstructions of the
culture in which they find themselves; and Chirevo Kwenda explores the correspondences between literal and metaphorical meanings of heat and coolness, as
he writes of a "spirituality of distance" within which human existence remains

viable in the face of the homogenizing and hegemonizing properties of global-ization. Julian Kunnie argues that, confronted with the devastating human and ecological consequences of modernity, indigenous cultures the world over have maintained religious practices and ethical systems based upon intimate relation-ships with the natural environment, which alone are capable of ameliorating the devastating effects of Western industrialization; and Jim Perkinson discerns, within the bodies of Haitian possession cultists, alternative meanings of power and of modernity founded in fundamental contradiction. Assuming a slightly different vantage point, David Chidester suggests that despite multinational cor-porations' recourse to frankly religious language, large-scale exchanges, and an expressed aim of transcending national borders, it may well be that the arbitra-tion of their commodities is occurring at a much more restricted cultural level, where they are being legitimized under localized strata of signification.

Weaving its way through these chapters is a common concern for human be-ings' relationships with the material structures (landscapes, other humans, and so on) of their worlds and the mediations of these relationships. These media-tions—or exchanges—operate under differing signs of God or of the sacred from which they derive their legitimacy and by means of which identity-in-location are authenticated. Yet, by virtue of their situations in the neocolonial era, the spaces in which all these mediations occur are complex arenas of cul-tural contact and reciprocities where negotiations of identity, location, and the sacred are contested. In a sense, these are zones in which substantial numbers of people are compelled to confront the Buddhist monk's third question, Why are you not at home? In my chapter, the nineteenth-century Canadian Northwest presents itself as such an arena; Philip Arnold maps out central New York state and, in particular, Onandaga Creek, as a similarly contested zone; Chirevo Kwenda writes of *mthunzini*—a place in the shade—as an alternative to the heat of globalization; and Jim Perkinson reflects upon the figure of Ogu as a dias-poric space in which religious and cultural negotiations that are endemic of the Atlantic world are resolved. For Jacob Olupona, Julian Kunnie, and David Chidester, the contested zones assume global proportion. Olupona writes of an African diasporic space in the United States; Kunnie argues that geographically disparate communities are linked in the postcolonial period by virtue of their religious relationships to their worlds—relationships that preclude Western co-lonial, industrial, and ecological modes; and Chidester suggests that multina-tional attempts to religiously link similarly disparate communities for the sake of profit are shaped by the very communities they seek to penetrate.

In each of these arenas we find human beings actively mediating issues of identity and location both in ultimate terms and in respect of the material struc-tures of their situations. Together these various arenas create a global web of religious modalities within which a number of common threads can be dis-cerned. Predominant among these threads is what Charles Long calls a "dynamic of concealment," a Western stylization of the colonial and neocolonial experi-

ences through which non-European peoples have been rendered silent in respect
of dominant discourses concerning the meaning of the human in modernity. As
these chapters point out, it is this dynamic that has allowed for the portrayal of
revolutionary leaders such as Louis Riel as mad; of a nation such as Haiti as
AIDS-infected and demonic; of Native American traditions as mystical and
clothed in impenetrable otherworldliness; of indigenous peoples generally as
"uncivilized."

An equally consistent thread within these religious modes has been the critique of Western cultural and epistemological structures—structures that themselves have made this dynamic possible. Modern culture is a product of formative associations among cultures, landscapes, raw materials, and commodities;
and each of the zones is one of contest precisely because, repeatedly, Western
Europeans and their descendants have recoiled from acknowledging these reciprocal associations. In these chapters, the material structures in relation to which
non-Europeans negotiate their situations include dominant communities that
preside over matter for the purposes of social, political, and economic ascendancy; and while the people of these latter communities imagine that their identities remain insulated from their material situations, those who must undergo
their dominating presence cannot do so. In their zeal to control matter, these
insulated peoples transform landscapes and other human beings into raw materials that are never recognized as part of a mutual enterprise; and dominant discourses relating to these contested zones have generally served to reify this lack
of mutuality.

In concert with the work of Charles Long, these chapters together raise a
number of issues concerning fundamental assumptions that are at stake in a viable modern global culture as well as in the study of religion. We can speak of
global culture as an entity only because what is referred to as the West successfully undertook the occupation of all regions of the planet. Rationality, scien-
tism, and secularism were the self-affirming banners that the West carried into
all parts of the world, establishing the Western mode of being human as legitimate—and normative—under the sign of its own technological prowess. Bolle
and Olupona point out that globalization has been understood from this perspective as the ultimate Westernization of the entire planet; or, as Kwenda puts it, the
homogenization of the world's cultures. Yet, those communities of human beings who have undergone the West and its exercise in self-affirmation have experienced the limits of rationality most obviously in terms of human and ecological waste. Drawing on this experience, their own traditions, and the authority
of different signs of the sacred, they have created alternate modes of being modern people, modes that are at once critical of, and firmly situated within, this
historical experience of the cultural and epistemological structures of modernity.
These modes, or multiple meanings, as Perkinson points out, represent alternatives for considering what it means to be modern humans in this global environment.

In respect to the study of religion, the explorations of the meaning and nature of modernity contained within these chapters point, first, to the fact that at a profound level, matter is not inert but signifies a structure in relationship to which not only the archaic human beings of Eliade's researches were compelled to carry on the work of orienting themselves in ultimate terms. Second, the colonial period ushered into existence a complex alteration in the material structure of the human world, in the wake of which most of the world's people have of necessity redefined both individual and social bodies. Third, this redefinition has repeatedly been enacted under signs of the sacred that both account for this material alteration and pose a critique of Western religious and epistemological constructions. Non-Western peoples have religiously confronted a new arche, and their modes of doing so suggest to the contributors to this volume that, in order to speak of religion in modernity, scholars would be well served to do the same.

This volume begins with Tatsuo Murakami's discussion of the intellectual tradition of searching for the origin of religion. The closing chapter by Charles Long locates this abiding pursuit within the terrain mapped out by the volume's other contributors—within what we have termed a new arche. In inviting a reconsideration of the meaning of religion in a post-Enlightenment, globalized human situation, Long confronts our contributors (and the reader) with the array of historical and epistemological meanings implicated within the vocabulary of these chapters. For Long, religion, matter, indigeneity, and creolization are conceptual and empirical conditions that undergird the formation of the Atlantic world and the modern West. They are at once traces of modes of human existence that are irrecoverable, and possible constituents of a new form of global community conceived apart from the binary relations that these terms all too often signify. Propitiously, Charles Long continues to be, as David Chidester admiringly suggested a decade ago, *NguZanengxaki* (a Bringer of Problems.)[6]

Notes

1. The conference was titled "Religion, Global Culture and the University: An Institute on the Impact of Globalization on Religion and the Study of Religion," and was held at the University of Maine at Farmington, April 5-7, 2001.

2. Wach believed that the goal of the study of religion should be to understand "the whole from the parts, and then again . . . the parts from the whole." See Joachim Wach, *Introduction to the History of Religions*, ed. Joseph M. Kitagawa and Gregory D. Alles, with the collaboration of Karl W. Luckert (New York: Macmillan, 1988), xv; see also Joachim Wach, *Sociology of Religion* (Chicago: University of Chicago Press, 1944), 2, 5.

3. Wach suggested in his essay "On Understanding" that *verstehen* involved both the individual and social body: understanding of the past, of the scope of possible human "cultural activity," and of one's own "thoughts and actions." This kind of understanding

would ultimately be the foundation for a coherent theory of religion. See Joachim Wach, "On Understanding," in *Chapters in the History of Religions,* ed. Joseph M. Kitagawa and Gregory D. Alles (New York: Macmillan, 1988), 184; and Joseph Kitagawa's "Introduction" in the same volume, xix.

4. Wach, "Mahāyāna Buddhism," in *Chapters in the History of Religions,* 34-35.

5. Mircea Eliade, *Patterns in Comparative Religion,* trans. Rosemary Sheed (Lincoln: University of Nebraska Press), 1999.

6. David Chidester, *Savage Systems: Colonialism and Comparative Religion in Southern Africa* (Charlottesville: University Press of Virginia, 1996), xvii.

1

Asking the Question of the Origin of Religion in the Age of Globalization

Tatsuo Murakami

In his 1882 *Lectures on the Origin and Growth of Religion*, Friedrich Max Müller makes the following observation.

> If you consulted any of the books that have been written during the last hundred years on the history of religion, you would find in most of them a striking agreement on at least one point, viz. that the lowest form of what can be called religion is *fetishism*, that it is impossible to imagine anything lower that would still deserve that name, and that therefore fetishism may safely be considered as the very beginning of all religion.[1]

Ever since Charles de Brosses established the theory of fetishism it has served as the designation of the oldest form of religion, and has thus also tended to refer to the origin of all religions. We must first acknowledge, however, that in the background of Müller's statement is the impact of the theory of evolution and the idea of progress. Even before Charles Darwin's *The Origin of Species* (1859), evolutionism had a strong foothold in the European intellectual community. By the middle of the nineteenth century, evolutionism was the dominant theory in both natural and social sciences. The study of religion was no exception. In fact, Eric Sharpe declares that it was the advance of the "evolutionary method" that established the study of religion as a legitimate academic discipline. Marking the decade from 1859 to 1869 as the revolutionary era for the study of religion, he states that "comparative religion (at first a synonym for the science of religion) did not exist in 1859; by 1869 it did."[2] The "striking agreement" Müller mentions above, however, did not last beyond the nineteenth century. Toward the end of the nineteenth century, as the evolutionary theory of religion received criticisms from all directions, the issues concerning the historical origin of religion were dismissed all together. Since then, the origin of religion has hardly been taken as a serious topic of concern in the study of religion.

This chapter, however, proposes that writing off the question of the origin of religion at the same time that evolutionary theories of religion are discarded is a premature and ill-advised approach since its roots are much deeper than that. When we look back over the history of the history of religions (*religionswissenschaft*), we find that the question of origins has been a major preoccupation for many scholars of religion from its inception. As we try to assess the nature of the field, it is crucial to examine how the issues concerning the origin of religion were addressed in the past. Focusing on the fact that the question of the origin of religion was the initial mode of inquiry in the study of religion, we first examine the historical significance of this question for the modern academic study of religion. Such inquiry inevitably brings out important methodological issues including the essentialist–reductionist debate, the epistemological turn and hermeneutics, and the civilized–primitive dichotomy. This essay argues that these issues need to be readdressed even, or in fact especially, in this age of globalization, since globalization itself is predicated on the modern conditions that gave birth to the study of religion: that is, the Enlightenment, colonialism, and humanism. In what manner, then, can we raise the question of the origin of religion in a global context?

Ninety years after Müller's remark on the origin of religion, at the American Academy of Religion annual meeting in Chicago, Charles Long introduced the study of cargo cults as a new way of approaching religion.[3] In this presidential address, Long defined cargo cults as the product of the cultural contact between the West and non-West, the colonizer and the colonized. Cargo cults are not, he argued, a product of a simple process of the Western culture dominating and subjugating another culture. Rather, cargo cults show, in Long's wording, "the possibility of creating new human beings, neither New Guineans nor Westerners."[4] Long's suggestion was to locate the origin of religion somewhere between New Guineans and Westerners, and he construed cargo cults as an imaginative creation emerging from concrete interactions and exchanges between them. Long's approach to cargo cults is indeed an attempt to raise the question of the origin of religion in the global context. In the second half of this chapter, I delineate theoretical issues that Long underscores in his formulation of the question of the origin of religion.

The Question of the Origin of Religion Revisited

In the past decade or two there have been some signs of renewed interests in the question of the origin of religion. One recent work that argues for the importance of reconsidering the question of the origin of religion is J. Samuel Preus's *Explaining Religion*. Preus laments that although the origin question is the most fundamental one for the academic study of religion, scholars of religion have been shying away from this "original" question. In the introduction of his book, Preus expresses his dissatisfaction with the current state of the academy as follows:

> That their study ought to be conceived and organized amounts to evidence of an
> identity crisis in the field; yet there is little indication today that the question of
> the cause and origin of religion is, or even should be, a topic of interest. It is
> worth reflecting on this remarkable and unfortunate fact. For about a hundred and
> fifty years, from David Hume to Emile Durkheim and Sigmund Freud, the issue
> was pursued and debated with the greatest urgency. Now it is virtually ignored,
> and even demeaned as a futile question or worse.[5]

Preus attempts to establish a lineage of the "origin"-minded theorists of religion, starting from Jean Bodin, peaking with David Hume, and closing with Sigmund Freud. Preus designates this tradition as the "naturalist" approach and distinguishes it from the "theological" or "essentialist" approach.[6] Preus contends that, while theologians and essentialists need to postulate the transcendental source (be it "God," "the sacred," "the power," and so on) as the source of religion, naturalists concern themselves only with the natural cause of religion. He further asserts that he wants to account for the existence of religion in a nontranscendental "naturalistic" fashion. For Preus, examining the origin of religion means looking for this "natural" cause.

Now whether one uses the term *natural* or not, the question of the origin of religion presupposes that one can describe and/or explain religion as a coherent system unified by a single origin. One may view this origin positively or negatively, favorably or unfavorably, with awe or with contempt; the common denominator is the desire and confidence to know this origin. In this sense, although Preus describes his method as antithetical to the "essentialists," he may resemble his enemy more than he would hope. Both naturalists and essentialists are origin-oriented: what distinguishes the two approaches is their different orientation to the question of origin. For example, for Otto it is "the Holy," for Hume it is "man's fear of future," and for Durkheim it is "society."

Another way Preus characterizes the question of the origin of religion is its homocentric orientation and subsequent turn to epistemology. According to Preus, David Hume is the one who made this shift most consciously and explicitly. In Preus's words, Hume "stands in this account as the pivotal figure, being our clearest exemplar of the self-conscious turn from a theological to a scientific paradigm for the study of religion."[7] According to Preus, by placing the origin of religion in human nature, Hume asserts that human beings rather than God create (and maintain) religion. In this sense Hume brought religion from the domain of God into that of humans, or from the arena of theology to that of epistemology.

If we talk about the turn to human consciousness, however, Hume was not the first one to take this path. Peter Harrison calls our attention to Nicholas of Cusa (1401-64) whom Max Müller considered as "the first to study non-Christian religions in the independent spirit of a scholar and historian."[8] Harrison summarizes Cusanus's argument as follows:

Cusanus believed that the apparent contradictions between the claims of various traditions could be ameliorated by locating the whole discussion of religious diversity within the larger context of epistemology. Accordingly, his theological reflection began not with the traditional question of God's nature, but rather with an inquiry into the possibility of knowledge of God. Different modes of faith, for Cusanus, were not the result of different objects of worship, but of the conditions of human knowledge.[9]

Cusanus differed from other theologians of his time, since he addressed the question of religion in terms of human knowledge rather than of an understanding of the nature of God. Once we start to think of religion in terms of what we know and how we know, the study of religion begins to focus on epistemology, not theology. Cusanus was a theologian, but his methodological orientation makes him a contemporary of Hume. Cusanus's example shows us how it is possible to make the epistemological turn without discarding God in the process. Following the path paved by Cusanus, Hume, and others in the modern study of religion, religion is now viewed and discussed from the standpoint of human knowledge rather than from the standpoint of reflection on God's nature.

So far the question of the origin of religion presents two basic premises of the modern study of religion. First, religion is deemed a coherent system with a single origin. Second, it needs to be examined and understood with a human-oriented approach. We can view, for example, that the quest for the historical origin of religion was founded upon these premises. Following the same premises, the question of the origin of religion was next raised in terms of the structure of consciousness in its postevolutionist phase. That is to say, instead of seeking the origin in history, scholars of religion now theorize human consciousness as the origin of religion. Rudolf Otto and Gerardus van der Leeuw are representatives of this phase, and to a certain extent, Freud and Durkheim also fall into this category. This structural approach in the question of the origin of religion was a predominantly twentieth-century enterprise; however, there was one theorist of religion who paid special attention to the structural aspect of the origin of religion already in the nineteenth century. In the middle of the nineteenth century, when the origin of religion was discussed in terms of evolutionary theory, Ludwig Feuerbach sought the origin of religion in nonevolutionary terms. One year after Comte's publication of the last volume of *Cours de philosophie positive* in which he outlined his evolutionist theory of fetishism, Feuerbach wrote *The Essence of Christianity* (1841), where he argued that the origin of religion is in human consciousness rather than in the progressive history of human development. Let us now briefly examine Feuerbach's theory of religion and probe the meaning of the origin of religion for the study of religion.

Ludwig Feuerbach and the Question of the Origin of Religion

Ludwig Feuerbach's best-known contribution to modern philosophy is in the development of modern "materialism." Feuerbach's criticism of Hegel's idealism and Christianity's other-worldliness had a great influence on the young Karl Marx and became a platform for Marx's materialist critique of Hegel and religion. In his effort to reconstrue religion from a materialist perspective, Feuerbach sought the origin of religion not in God's nature but in human consciousness. In this sense, we can add Feuerbach to the list of seekers of the origin of religion and, furthermore, view him as someone whose primary concern was epistemology rather than theology. Now how did Feuerbach approach the origin of religion epistemologically?

In *The Essence of Christianity*, Feuerbach first asserts that what makes us humans is self-consciousness, that is, the subject being conscious of oneself as an object. "Man is nothing without an object," states Feuerbach, "but the object to which a subject essentially, necessarily relates, is nothing else than this subject's own, but objective, nature."[10] For Feuerbach, the essential characteristic of human beings is their ability to objectify themselves. How does this apply to religion? Feuerbach defines religion as human's consciousness of the infinite originating in the subject's own consciousness. "The consciousness of the infinite," states Feuerbach, "is nothing else than the consciousness of the infinity of the consciousness; or, in the consciousness of the infinite, the conscious subject has for his object the infinity of his own nature."[11] For Feuerbach, religion results from the subject realizing the infinity of its own consciousness. In traditional Christian theology, human beings are believed to mirror the nature of God; in Feuerbach's theory, on the contrary, God mirrors human beings. Feuerbach brings up the following example to illustrate this mechanism. There is only one sun in the solar system, but this sun appears different to respective planets in the solar system due to their different positions. In this respect, each planet perceives the sun according to its own positionality. Feuerbach thus argues:

> The relation of the Sun to the Earth is therefore at the same time a relation of the Earth to itself, or to its own nature, for the measure of the size and of the intensity of light which the Sun possesses as the object of the Earth is the measure of the distance which determines the peculiar nature of the Earth. Hence each planet has in its sun the mirror of its own nature.[12]

Feuerbach then applies this example to human consciousness and its object:

> In the object which he contemplates, therefore, man becomes acquainted with himself; consciousness of the objective is the self-consciousness of man. We know the man by the object, by his conception of what is external to himself; in it his nature becomes evident; this object is his manifested nature, his true objective ego.[13]

Feuerbach's approach is clearly epistemological rather than theological.

Furthermore, he seems to be articulating a hermeneutical relation between the subject and the object. Namely, through knowing (i.e., interpretation) of the object, the subject finds itself. Applying this relationship to God and a human, he states: "Consciousness of God is self-consciousness, knowledge of God is self-knowledge. By his God thou knowest the man, and by the man his God; the two are identical."[14] Van Harvey clarifies this point by contrasting Feuerbach with Hegel.

> Instead of saying that the Absolute Spirit (God) achieves self-knowledge by objectifying itself in the finite world, he [Feuerbach] argued that the finite spirit comes to self-knowledge by externalizing or objectivizing itself in the idea of God. Religion is not, as Hegel thought, the revelation of the Infinite in the finite; rather, it is the self-discovery by the finite of its own infinite nature. God is the form in which the human spirit first discovers its own nature.[15]

That we do not recognize this identification of God and a human is problematic according to Feuerbach. That is to say, human beings mistakenly see God outside of themselves. In fact, human beings not only separate themselves from this object (God) but also reify it. Feuerbach asserts: "Man—this is the mystery of religion—projects (*vergengenstandlicht sich*) his being into objectivity, and then again makes himself as an object to this projected image of himself thus converted into a subject."[16] In this projection, the subject first projects its nature and then misconstrues this projection as an independent object, and submits to it. Feuerbach finds this process of reification problematic, since it leads to a state of alienation. He states:

> Religion is the disuniting of man from himself; he sets God before him as the antithesis of himself. God is not what man is—man is not what God is. God is the infinite, man the finite being; God is perfect, man imperfect; God eternal, man temporal; God almighty, man weak; God holy, man sinful. God and man are extremes: God is the absolutely positive, the sum of all realities; man the absolutely negative, comprehending all negations.[17]

To the extent that Feuerbach considers such reification and alienation problematic, his view on the origin of religion becomes negative. Due to this critical view on the origin of religion, Feuerbach is sometimes considered someone who reduces religion to something else and is labeled as a "reductionist." It is interesting to note, however, that Feuerbach is also accused of initiating the "essentialist" approach in the study of religion.

In *The Meaning and End of Religion*, Wilfred Cantwell Smith contends that, with publications of *The Essence of Christianity* and *The Essence of Religion*, Feuerbach set the search for "the essence of religion" as a goal in the study of religion. "The important point," states Smith, "is not what he [Feuerbach] considered the essences to be, so much as the fact that he was suggesting that religion, and a religion, have an essence. Ever since the hunt has been on."[18] Is Feuerbach an essentialist or not? The confusion derives from the different usages of the term *essence*. In the essentialist/reductionist context, the "essence" of religion usually means its transcendent, supernatural, or superhuman source. Feuerbach is not an essentialist in this respect. He may, however, be considered an essentialist to the extent that the essence signifies the origin, as outlined in the work of W. C. Smith. Smith contends that the search for the essence is accompanied by the process of reification. If one is in search of the essence of religion, one naturally reifies religion. "[T]he concept of 'religion,' then," states Smith, "in the West has evolved. Its evolution has included a long-range development that we may term a process of reification: mentally making religion into a thing, gradually coming to conceive it as an objective systematic entity."[19] We have argued earlier that to raise the question of the origin of religion presupposes a coherent system or entity whose origin one tries to seek. That is to say, all origin-oriented approaches in the study of religion, both essentialist and naturalist, require reification. If that is the case, Feuerbach was certainly not the one who started the hunt. In fact, Feuerbach's position is rather similar to that of W. C. Smith to the extent that they both view reification negatively. As we have observed above, Feuerbach problematized the reification of self-consciousness as the origin of religion. Rather than accusing Feuerbach for reifying "religion," we should recognize Feuerbach's real contribution to the study of religion in his attempt to spot the negative characteristic in the origin of religion: the question of the origin of religion embraces the concept of negativity.

Another aspect of the reification process that relates in significant ways to the question of the origin of religion is the reification of negative ideas. That is, humans tend to reify or essentialize what they intend to criticize. Continuing on his discussion on the essence of religion, W. C. Smith observes that the notions of "religion" and "the religions" were first used in Western discourse to criticize or express the negative aspects about other people's religions. "I find it not insignificant," states Smith, "that the phrase 'religions of the World' is first used in a treatise in which these are presented as such in order to be refuted."[20] The idea of "religion" was initially formulated in order to be criticized and dismissed, yet in the process it was inadvertently reified. As we further examine the discourse on the origin of religion, we learn that both negative reification and the reification of the negative present themselves as crucial features of our discussion.

The Logic of Origination and the Study of Religion

So far we have tried to illustrate how deeply the question of the origin of religion is rooted in the modern study of religion. One significant work that deals directly with this issue is Tomoko Masuzawa's *In Search of Dreamtime: The Quest for the*

Origin of Religion. In this critical study she addresses the importance of the question of the origin of religion, and examines its ambiguous status in the field. Masuzawa sees her project as being "an archaeology of the present."[21] She sets out to assess the current state of the history of religions by examining the discipline's past. With this aim in mind Masuzawa focuses on the ambivalent attitude toward the question of the origin of religion among contemporary scholars of religion. Masuzawa observes that today's scholars of religion claim to renounce their search for the origin of religion for the sake of scientific objectivity, while vicariously participating in precisely that quest under the guise of studying "the origin-oriented" people (i.e., the "primitive" and the "archaic"). Masuzawa suspects that these "primitive," "archaic," or "religious" people may be a mere mouthpiece through which "Western man" speaks the "truth" about the origin of religion.

Furthermore, beneath this "obsession" with the origin question among scholars of religion, Masuzawa uncovers the assumption that "religion is said to be essentially concerned with origins and with the need to represent—and thus making it *present again*—an absolute beginning."[22] Masuzawa states:

> In the abode of learning generally, the origin-obsessed principles still hold sway: the preeminence of cosmogonic myths (that is, the myth of creation as the most paradigmatic of all myths), the notion of ritual as a repetition and reactualization of axial (mythic) events, or, more sociologically, ritual as representation of the ideal social paradigm projected into a mythic narrative. In short, all these notions are predicated on the economy of origination and its correlative, the ideology of representation, which the foregoing postmodern criticisms have put into question and exposed, precisely, as mythic and probably repressive.[23]

Masuzawa finds this logic of origination problematic and criticizes it by analyzing Mircea Eliade's *The Myth of the Eternal Return* as its prime example.

In Masuzawa's reading, Eliade's articulation of "the myth of the eternal return" is a closed, monotonous cycle, a "paradisiac confinement" for an "archaic man." In this confinement they are destined to ritually enact their cosmogonic myth over and over, since that is the only way they can orient themselves in an otherwise chaotic world. "Reading Eliade," observes Masuzawa, "we are duly struck by the image of archaic man's violent conservatism—his 'revolt' against the unprecedented occurrence, his demand for the 'abolition' of nonparadigmatic temporality."[24] Masuzawa then sums up:

> [A]rchaic man forever suffers from cosmic nostalgia; his life is an endless series of ceremonials performed on the brink of chaos. Terrorized by the continual threat of the new and the meaningless, he resorts to compulsory and compulsive repetition; through birth, marriage, war, commerce, healing, death and mourning, he repeats, and he refers, time and time again, to the self-identical beginning.[25]

Masuzawa contends that we need to question this image of archaic man and the logic of origination that he embraces. She suggests that the space for such questioning be "in the purported 'gap' between the archaic and the modern." She continues:

> The archaic, the other of the modern, is at once the other of us, the contemporary scholars of religion. But the other of oneself is always a double of oneself, a mirror image, a picture in reverse, a representation that doubles and couples the self and the other. This other—the archaic—is presented as peculiarly marked by a singular obsession with the moment of origin.[26]

Masuzawa raises an important issue here. Prior to her work there was no critical study that focused on the methodological significance of the question of the origin of religion for the study of religion. She also acutely points out the dual nature of the archaic/modern opposition as the locus of the origin of religion question. First, it is an opposition between two modes of existence called the modern and the archaic; second, it is a relation between the modern *subject* (i.e., scholars of religion) and the archaic *object* (i.e., "archaic" people or culture). When we approach the origin question, it is very important to recognize this duality. Having acknowledged these contributions, we must also point out some shortcomings of her analysis.

First, Masuzawa's delineation of Eliade is as much "paradigmatic" as Eliade's alleged depiction of "archaic man." While Masuzawa claims that she engages in "discourse analysis," her reading of Eliade remains quite literal. It is clear, for example, that "the archaic man" for Eliade is not just a concrete historical other, but also the structural other which constitutes part of a modern subject. By employing the term *the archaic man*, Eliade expresses the dilemma of the split self in the modern subject. Masuzawa seems to overlook or, to stick to her preference for Freudian language, "repress" this very crucial supposition by Eliade.

Second, Masuzawa's articulation of the logic of origination does not encompass the full meaning of the origin question. With her postmodern sensitivity, Masuzawa sets as her task the examination of the contemporary study of religion and to expose the logic of origination as one of "the covert operations of its metaphysical assumptions."[27] For Masuzawa, the logic of origination is a peculiar kind of "religious" logic which Western man projects onto archaic people and culture. Masuzawa thus characterizes the logic of origination as Western man's "cosmic nostalgia and a universal craving for an absolute origin" and suspects that the scholar of religion indirectly fulfills this desire through his double, the archaic.[28] Referring to Eliade's article, "The Quest for the 'Origins' of Religion," Masuzawa contends that the text expresses Eliade's renouncement of the origin of religion question, and yet his covert desire to retain it. We need to first point out that her reading of the text is inaccurate, since Eliade does not in fact renounce the search for the origin of religion. On the contrary, Eliade stresses the importance of asking the origin question. Let us now look at Eliade's article as another platform for articulating the logic of origination.

In "The Quest for the 'Origins' of Religion," Eliade illustrates how scholars of religion were once interested in the origins of religion but this search for origins was no longer possible after the emphasis on historical contexts was introduced to their methodology. This shift from "Nature to History," Eliade observes, was not necessarily "a negative, sterilizing experience"; however, it poses a serious question for historians of religion. Eliade states:

> So, after more than a century of untiring labor, scholars were forced to renounce the old dream of grasping the origin of religion with the aid of historical tools, and they devoted themselves to the study of different phases and aspects of religious life. Now, we may ask, is this the last word in the science of religion? Are we condemned to work indefinitely with our religious materials, considering them to be nothing more than historical documents, that is to say, expressions of different existential situations during the ages? Does the fact that we cannot reach the *origin* of religion also mean that we cannot grasp the *essence* of religious phenomena?[29]

Underneath Eliade's lament is the desire to know "what religion is." Eliade is implying that, just because one cannot attain the historical origin of religion, one should not give up on the search for the essence of religion, namely the "what is religion" question. This "what is religion" question is the same question raised by Enlightenment thinkers when they began asking about the origin of religion, and precisely the same question raised by both "essentialists" and "reductionists." Contrary to Masuzawa's understanding, we can see here that Eliade is not shy or "covert" at all about asking this question. He believes that this question of the origin of religion runs throughout the history of the study of religion, and he tries to demonstrate it in his article.

One observation Eliade makes in "The Quest for the 'Origins' of Religion" is that there is a curious union between the study of religion and the natural sciences in the nineteenth century. "[T]he beginnings of comparative religions," he states, "took place during the middle of the nineteenth century at the very height of the materialistic and positivistic propaganda." [30] Here Eliade refers to various efforts in social theories strongly influenced by natural sciences, especially those derived from Darwinian evolutionary theory. Eliade then observes that, while Auguste Comte and Herbert Spencer approached the origin question from a natural scientific paradigm, Max Müller and E. B. Tylor raised the same issue by focusing on so-called primitive religion. Calling our attention to this "synchronicity between materialistic ideologies on the one hand and the growing interest in oriental and archaic forms of religion on the other," Eliade contends that both "denote a sort of nostalgia for the primordial, for the original, universal *matrix*." "Matter, Substance," he continues, "represents the *absolute origin*, the beginning of all things."[31] Eliade is, first of all, stressing the significance of the origin question in the nineteenth century. Whether one deals with religious data or data concerning Nature, the logic of origination organizes all data. In this sense, the logic of origination is much more than "religious" logic or we might say logic expresses a religious point of view.[32] The logic of origination is a principle of identity, be it in a historical term (i.e., the identity of a nation, of a tradition, or an idea) or in an epistemological term (i.e., the identity of self-consciousness); it defines whatever it is in terms of the origin as "given." Any inquiry on identity which presupposes "the origin" as the source of value and meaning draws explanatory power from the logic of origination.

Furthermore, Eliade also points out how the origin was sought in terms of "matter" in the nineteenth century. While critics attack Eliade for being an essentialist (or even an ideologue), we need to recognize that he also demonstrates great interest in the material nature of religion. His concern for materiality in religion is a clear break from his predecessors such as Rudolf Otto and Gerardus van der Leeuw, who saw the origin of religion in terms of the structure of consciousness. Referring to Eliade's "imagination of matter" Charles Long observes regarding *Patterns in Comparative Religion*:

> In this text Eliade attempts to account for the inner structure of the consciousness of *homo religiosus* from an examination of the sacred symbols of archaic cultures. In this regard, the text begins from the other side of Otto, who attempted first to give us an account of consciousness and then to show how it expresses itself through religious forms. *Eliade's work shows how the forms of matter (nature) evoke modes of consciousness and experience* (hierophanies).[33]

In *Patterns in Comparative Religion*, Eliade illustrates how one becomes aware of "the supra-terrestrial" and "the infinite" when impressed by the depth of the sky and experiences "permanence" and "strength" when confronted with the hardness of a majestic rock.[34] Long's reading of *Patterns in Comparative Religion* suggests that Eliade sees the origin of religion in human confrontations with material environments as religious symbols. Following this line of inquiry, Long further develops a theory of religious hermeneutics, "the archaism of the subject."[35]

The first point Long wants to establish with his idea of archaism is that the origin of religion question needs to be readdressed in terms of hermeneutics. We have already seen this inclination in Feuerbach, but at that time the origin of religion was considered principally in terms of evolutionary history. By making this archaism a hemeneutical process, Long locates the origin of religion not in the distant past, but between the subject and the world surrounding it. For Long, "the archaic" does not imply "the ancient" or "the primitive" in a historical sense; rather, it reflects a hermeneutic mode in which human beings orient and realize themselves in the world. In religious hermeneutics, human beings define themselves through their interaction with, and interpretation of, religious symbols. Quoting Paul Ricoeur, Long asserts the priority of the symbol as the basis for a new archaism: "*Le symbole donne a penser*" (Symbol invites thought).[36] In this sense, Long's archaism as hermeneutics primarily expresses not a historical, but a structural origin of religion in a philosophical sense. Since this type of philosophical hermeneutics is best illustrated by Paul Ricoeur's works, I turn briefly to an examination of his theory of hermeneutics in relation to the question of the origin.

Hermeneutics and the Origin of Religion

According to Paul Ricoeur, what makes things "symbolic" is their equivocal nature.[37] In *Freud and Philosophy* Ricoeur illustrates a symbol as the source of interpretation, imbued with dual meaning. This book is first and foremost a study on interpretation, drawing material from Freud and his psychoanalysis. In Freudian psychoanalysis, asserts Ricoeur, the dream has a double meaning; it means something other than what it says. This double meaning, according to Ricoeur, defines "symbolic"; and this duality is not that of semantics (i.e., of the signifier and the signified), but that of signification (intentionality). Consequently, symbols require interpretation or hermeneutics. In his definition, symbols and interpretation constitute each other. In order to approach symbols, one must first understand hermeneutics.

In the hermeneutics of symbols, Ricoeur argues, there are two polarized oppositions. "According to one pole," states Ricoeur, "hermeneutics is understood as the manifestation and restoration of a meaning addressed to me in the manner of a message, a proclamation, or as is sometimes said, a kerygma." "[A]ccording to the other pole," he continues, "it is understood as a demystification, as a reduction of illusion."[38] These two conflicting vectors in hermeneutics are often called "hermeneutics of restoration" and "hermeneutics of suspicion." Although these two hermeneutics appear to negate each other, Ricoeur argues that they in fact work in tandem. He demonstrates this relationship by analyzing philosophical reflection on the Cartesian cogito as a hermeneutical process.

As quoted earlier, Ricoeur contends that "symbols give rise to thought."[39] Consequently, for Ricoeur, symbols are supposed to be at the core of philosophical reflection. Ricoeur, however, begins his argument by stating how the interpretation of symbols is at odds with philosophical reflection. "Philosophy, born in Greece," states Ricoeur, "introduced new demands in contrast to mythical thought; first and foremost it established the idea of a science, in the sense of the Platonic *episteme* or the *Wissenschaft* of German idealism." "In view of this idea of philosophical science," he continues, "the recourse to symbols has something scandalous about it."[40] First, symbols are specific and particular to respective cultures and languages. They are deeply rooted in those specific contexts while philosophical science seeks universality. Second, philosophy as a science requires univocality in meaning. Symbols, on the other hand, are equivocal and opaque. Ricoeur states that "the double meaning that gives them concrete roots weights them down with materiality."[41] Third, an interpretation of symbols allows multiple, often competing, interpretations while philosophical science seeks one truth. In what manner, then, can a philosophy of reflection be a hermeneutic?

Ricoeur begins his argument by defining philosophical reflection as "self-reflection." Self-reflection means the positing of the self, that is, a Cartesian cogito positing itself in reflection. Ricoeur argues, however, that this self-reflection is not intuition; it requires "work" on the part of the ego of ego cogito to establish itself. And this "work," Ricoeur argues, is hermeneutics. Ricoeur asserts: "The first truth—*I am, I think*—remains as abstract and empty as it is invincible; it has to be 'mediated' by the ideas, actions, works, institutions, and monuments that objectify it. It is in these objects, in the widest sense of the word, that the Ego must lose and find itself."[42] Since the Cartesian cogito is not the result of direct intuition but rather of *reflection*, Ricoeur detects the gap between "I" of *I am* and "I" of *I think*. Philosophical reflection, then, has to be an appropriation or rather *re*appropriation of the estranged "I" of *I am* by the "I" of *I think*. Ricoeur explains this process as follows:

> I must recover something which has first been lost; I make "proper of me" what has ceased being mine. I make "mine" what I am separated from by space or time, by distraction or "diversion," or because of some culpable forgetfulness. Appropriation signifies that the initial situation from which reflection proceeds is "forgetfulness." I am lost, "led astray" among objects and separated from the center of my existence. . . . Whatever the secret of this "diaspora," of this separation, it signifies that I do not at first possess what I am. . . . That is why reflection is a task, an *Aufgabe*—the task of making my concrete experience equal to the positing of "I am." Such is the ultimate elaboration of our initial proposition that reflection is not intuition; we now say: the positing of self is not given, it is a task, it is not *gegeben*, but *aufgegeben*.[43]

In Freudian psychoanalysis, the posited self in reflection is consciousness and the "lost self" is in the realm of the unconscious. The interpretation of dreams is consciousness's "task" to appropriate the "forgotten" (or "repressed") self in the unconscious. In psychoanalysis, the certitude of consciousness first has to be questioned and what follows is an interpretation of symbols. In Eliade's religious hermeneutics, as well as in Long's new archaism, the first step is also to acknowledge that the subject is initially lost and forgotten and needs to work (i.e., to interpret) to find who he or she really is. Eliade expresses this lost and forgotten self as "the archaic man" and urges us to recover it through the interpretation of religious symbols. Long also stresses the priority of religious symbols for constituting the self as the archaism of the subject.

In hermeneutics, as we observe above, there are two conflicting approaches: a hermeneutics of suspicion and a hermeneutics of restoration. For Ricoeur, these two vectors can be one and the same thing. He contends:

> Two enterprises which we at first opposed to one another—the reduction of illusions and the restoration of the fullness of meaning—are alike in that they both shift the origin of meaning to another center which is no longer the immediate sub-

ject of reflection: "consciousness"—the watchful ego, attentive to its own presence, anxious about self and attached to self. Thus hermeneutics, approached from
its most opposite poles, represents a challenge and a test for reflection, whose first
tendency is to identify itself with immediate consciousness.[44]

To the extent that they both lead to the decentering of consciousness and give rise to
a new locus of meaning, a hermeneutics of suspicion and a hermeneutics of restoration work the same. In other words, even though hermeneutics aims at recovering
the lost original self, it never really gets to grasp its "true" self. All one can do is to
try to bridge the gap between "I" of *I am* and "I" of *I think*, and that is why hermeneutics is regarded as a task. If we put the question of the origin of religion in this
light, we may be able to argue that the origin must be sought not as a given but a
task. In Eliade's religious hermeneutics, the origin of religion may represent the
modern man's attempt to recover (or recollect) oneself as the archaic man. In this
sense, "the archaic man" is no more than a memory of the modern man's forgotten
self. To simply equate an *internal or structural* archaic man with *external or historical* Australian aborigines is therefore not accurate in Eliade's hermeneutics. On
the other hand, however, it is also true that modern man remembers its forgotten
self (that is, oneself as the archaic man) by knowing Australian aborigines. Between
the archaic man and Australian aborigines there is certainly a gap and also a projection, but there is also some sense of resonance. Eliade is often criticized precisely
because he puts too much weight on this resonance as the locus of the problem of
the origin of religion. Charles Long, on the other hand, addresses another aspect of
this relation, that is the gap and the projection, as he introduces his key concept of
"primitive/ civilized."
    In his article on primitive religion, Long states:

> Primitive religions do not constitute self-conscious authentic religious historical
> traditions in the same manner as Christianity, Hinduism, Buddhism, and so on.
> In other words, there are no people who refer to themselves as practitioners of
> primitive religions. Primitive religion is thus a phrase referring to a constructed
> Western mode of categorizing certain kinds of cultural historical religious tradi-
> tions. As such the phrase itself raises a constitutive methodological issue. It is
> as much a cultural methodological category of the modern West as it is a way
> of describing certain kinds of religious data. [45]

First and foremost, Long establishes that the primitive/civilized is a methodological construct and thus structural in nature. On the other hand, however, Long also
acknowledges that the primitive does have a historical and concrete dimension to
the extent that it designates actual practice, people, objects, and so on. In the historical context, the primitive as the empirical other is a counterpart to its pair, the
civilized. By situating the modern subject and its other in a historical context, Long
demonstrates that there are two dimensions to the origin of religion question that
were not clearly differentiated by Eliade. Moreover, he also makes the origin of

religion question a contemporary issue, rather than that of the past, by calling our attention to the continuing hermeneutical relationship between the primitive and the civilized.[46] While Eliade never articulated the complex relationship between archaic man and its counterpart in history, Long tries to elaborate on that relationship in a concrete historical manner. In other words, Long locates the origin of religion somewhere between the civilized and the primitives. In *Significations*, Long discusses the primitive–civilized dichotomy in relation to the idea of religion as follows:

> Since the beginning of the modern period in the West the primitives have been understood as religious and empirical "others," empirical from the point of view of those disciplines and sciences which take these peoples and their cultures as the data of their inquiry—for example, anthropology, ethnology, and history of religions. These "others" are religious in two senses. In the first sense, the primitives form one of the most important bases of data for a non-theological understanding of religion in the post-Enlightenment West. In the second sense, the "primitives" define a vague "other"; their significance lies not in their own worth and value but in the significance this other offers to civilization when contrasted with it. The primitives operate as a negative structure of concreteness that allows civilization to define itself as a structure superior to this ill-defined and inferior "other."[47]

As we observe above, we would not have a modern study of religion without the Enlightenment speculation on the possible origin of religion in the primitive religions. The modern definition of religion, in this sense, cannot be articulated without the concrete and historical data of "primitive others." The "primitives" are, in this sense, the *material* origin of religion. This materiality of empirical others, however, is obscured since it only operates negatively as "a negative structure of concreteness." Long is also asserting that precisely because of this negative structure of concreteness the "others" are religious.

The Negative Structure of Concreteness

One central issue that Long addresses with the concept of the negative structure of concreteness is the ambiguous relation that the civilized has with its other. That is, the civilized has to maintain its structural relationship with the primitive, but simultaneously denies the concreteness or materiality of that relationship. One historical illustration of this relationship is found in Henri Baudet's *Paradise on Earth*.[48] In this book, Baudet examines Europeans' attitude toward, and experience of, non-Europeans; and he demonstrates how Europeans have developed two distinct ways of dealing with "others" since the beginning of their history. Baudet first observes that, as Europe engaged in a territorial battle with Asia, Europeans began to build fear and hostility against Asia and simultaneously developed a fascination and fantasy about Asia. Considering these ambiguous attitudes, Baudet characterizes two general tendencies in Europeans as they interacted with Asia and other non-European cultures and societies more generally. The first tendency is the realm of concrete relations with non-European countries, peoples, and worlds. In this realm the European and the non-European engaged in actual political, military, and socioeconomic exchanges. In contrast to this empirical level, Baudet next introduces the realm of imagination. This realm is filled with images derived not from observation, experience, and perceptible reality but from the Europeans' "psychological urge." Baudet stresses that this urge creates its own realities which are totally different from the political realities of the first category. In this imaginative realm, the non-Europeans were often fantasized as "noble savages."

Baudet argues that initially Europeans sought the image of the noble savage in their mythical, archaic time. The noble savage represented the Golden Age, the original innocence, and Adam and Eve before the Fall. This noble savage as a historical other, however, was later replaced by a contemporary, spatial other, namely, the natives of the non-European world. In the European imagination, these non-Western peoples were "not yet" corrupted like the European, and were "still" in a practically paradisiacal state. This transition from the original ancestor as noble savage to the non-European as noble savage was a critical shift in the European consciousness. Instead of reflecting upon their distant ancestors, Europeans began fantasizing about their actual contemporaries. Oddly enough, however, in the European's consciousness, the non-European existed outside history, just as the original human beings lived in "no time," or outside history.

When Europeans came across the Atlantic Ocean and "discovered" the New World, they naturally saw it as the Edenic Paradise. After their initial encounter, Europeans started to engage in concrete, material interactions with Native Americans, including military and commercial as well as more personal interchanges. They fought, killed, traded, befriended, and mixed their blood with the "others." At the same time, however, Europeans were able to imagine Native Americans as noble savages or abstract others, which existed only in their imaginations. The myth of the noble savage that derived from the imaginative realm was effectively used to obscure the actual material relationships between Europeans and the non-Europeans. By separating these two realms of reality, Europeans could split the others into two, that is, the ideal and the material, and deal with them separately; but never as a unified whole. This split itself was a prerequisite for the negative structure of concreteness.

Something more that can be adduced from the theory of the negative structure of concreteness is that in this dichotomy "the material" is always expressed negatively. Going back to Long's primitive–civilized dichotomy, we observe that the primitive represents the concrete, material side of the polarity and is expressed negatively in order to illuminate the other side as positive. We cannot stress enough that it is precisely in this context that Long locates the origin of religion. That is, religion presents itself as a problem at the precise moment when the materiality of the primitives is highlighted and then denied.

Conclusion

In this chapter, we stressed the need to raise the question of the origin of religion once again. Why is it necessary to bring it up now? We observed that the search for the origin of religion was the initial mode of inquiry that dominated the modern study of religion. It reflects the positivistic attitude and intellectual energy of the Enlightenment scholars who initiated our discipline. What was common among our predecessors is the feeling that they can positively (and not necessarily favorably) define what religion is without depending on God as its origin. Namely, the question of the origin of religion reflects the shift from theology to epistemology in the human inquiries concerning religion. Prior to the Enlightenment, the origin of religion was not an issue for humans, since it was in the domain of God. In this sense, it was a brand-new question for a brand-new study. "The origin of religion," therefore, must be defined in a larger context. It should not be limited to questions such as in what point of human history "religion" began and in what form. The question of the origin of religion, in other words, has to be addressed in terms of its structural as well as genealogical meanings. Looking at the field of the study of religion from this broad perspective, we can see that scholars such as Hume, Feuerbach, Durkheim, Freud, Otto, and Eliade were all asking the same question of "the origin of religion."

Feuerbach, for example, locates the origin of religion in the separation between God and humans. Eliade, on the other hand, raises the origin of religion question in terms of the archaic–modern dichotomy. One crucial point we need to recognize about the origin of religion is its "problematic" nature. The origin of religion must be addressed and discussed as "a problem" and never as "a fact." When Feuerbach and Eliade are raising the issue of the origin of religion, they are expressing the problem of religion as they see it, rather than making a definitive statement on what religion is. Looking at Feuerbach from this perspective, which is contrary to Wilfred Cantwell Smith's earlier view, we can argue that Feuerbach is not "essentializing" religion, but in fact "problematizing" it. In other words, the origin of religion should be the initial question at the beginning of our inquiry, not the end result of our research. In this sense, we are bound to return to the question of the origin of religion and ask it anew in any age.

Notes

1. F. Max Müller, *Lectures on the Origin and Growth of Religion*, delivered in April, May, and June, 1878 (Varanasi, India: Indological Book House, 1964), 55.

2. Eric J. Sharpe, *Comparative Religion: A History*, 2nd ed. (La Salle, Ill.: Open Court, 1986), 28.

3. Charles H. Long, "Cargo Cults as Cultural Historical Phenomena," first published in *Journal of the American Academy of Religion* 42, no. 3 (September 1974): 403-14, and later reprinted in *Significations* (Philadelphia: Fortress Press, 1986), 114-27.

4. Long, *Significations*, 123.

5. J. Samuel Preus, *Explaining Religion: Criticism and Theory from Bodin to Freud*, (New Haven, Conn.: Yale University Press, 1987), xvii.

6. In this chapter, I do not discuss the methodological feud between the "essential/ theological" and "materialist/scientific" approaches in the study of religion. To mention a few articles on this issue: Donald Wiebe, "The Failure of Nerve in the Academic Study of Religion," *Sciences Religieuses/ Studies in Religion* 13, no. 4 (1984): 401-22; Daniel L. Pals, "Is Religion a *Sui Generis* Phenomenon?" *Journal of the American Academy of Religion,* 55, no. 2 (1987): 259-82; Cristiano Grottanelli and Bruce Lincoln, "A Brief Note on (Future) Research in the History of Religions," *CHS Occasional Papers* 4 (1984).

7. Preus, *Explaining Religion*, 84.

8. Peter Harrison, *"Religion" and the Religions in the English Enlightenment* (Cambridge: Cambridge University Press, 1990), 11.

9. Harrison, *"Religion."*

10. Ludwig Feuerbach, *The Essence of Christianity* (New York: Harper & Brothers, 1957 [1841]), 4.

11. Feuerbach, *Essence of Christianity*, 3.

12. Feuerbach, *Essence of Christianity*, 4-5.

13. Feuerbach, *Essence of Christianity*, 5.

14. Feuerbach, *Essence of Christianity*, 12.

15. Van A. Harvey, *Feuerbach and the Interpretation of Religion* (Cambridge: Cambridge University Press, 1995), 27.

16. Feuerbach, *Essence of Christianity*, 29-30.

17. Feuerbach, *Essence of Christianity*, 33.

18. Wilfred Cantwell Smith, *The Meaning and End of Religion* (Minneapolis: Fortress Press, 1991 [1962]), 47.

19. Smith, *The Meaning and End of Religion*, 51.

20. Smith, *The Meaning and End of* Religion, 43.

21. Tomoko Masuzawa, "Reading in the Wake: Supplementary Remarks on the Dreamtime," *Method & Theory in the Study of Religion* 8, no. 3 (1996): 312.

22. Tomoko Masuzawa, *In Search of Dreamtime: The Quest for the Origin of Religion* (Chicago: University of Chicago Press, 1993), 15.

23. Masuzawa, *In Search of Dreamtime*, 26.

24. Masuzawa, *In Search of Dreamtime*, 28.

25. Masuzawa, *In Search of Dreamtime*, 28.

26. Masuzawa, *In Search of Dreamtime*, 29.

27. Masuzawa, *In Search of Dreamtime*, 15.

28. Masuzawa, *In Search of Dreamtime*, 15.

29. Mircea Eliade, *The Quest: History and Meaning of Religion* (Chicago: University of Chicago Press, 1969), 52.

30. Eliade, *The Quest*, 40.

31. Eliade, *The Quest*, 41.

32. For example, we can argue that the debate between the "creationist" and the "evolutionist" is a feud within this logic of origination. Since they both stand on the same logic, one has to deny the other in order to prove its legitimacy.

33. Charles H. Long, "Mircea Eliade and the Imagination of Matter," *Journal for Cultural and Religious Theory* 1, no. 2 (April 2000), at jcrt.org/-archives/-01.2/long.shtml (accessed January 15, 2001).

34. Mircea Eliade, *Patterns in Comparative Religion*, trans. Rosemary Sheed, (New York: Sheed and Ward, 1958), 39 and 217.

35. Charles H. Long, "Archaism and Hermeneutics" in *Significations* (Philadelphia: Fortress Press, 1986).

36. Long, *Significations*, 50.

37. Paul Ricoeur, *Freud and Philosophy: An Essay on Interpretation*, (New Haven, Conn.: Yale University Press, 1970), 7.

38. Ricoeur, *Freud and Philosophy*, 27.

39. Ricoeur, *Freud and Philosophy*, 38.

40. Ricoeur, *Freud and Philosophy*, 41.

41. Ricoeur, *Freud and Philosophy*. It is interesting to see Ricoeur relating the double meaning with materiality here.

42. Ricoeur, *Freud and Philosophy*, 43.

43. Ricoeur, *Freud and Philosophy*, 45.

44. Ricoeur, *Freud and Philosophy*, 54-55.

45. Charles H. Long, "Primitive Religion," in *A Reader's Guide to the Great Religions*, 2nd ed., ed. Charles J. Adams (New York: Free Press, 1977), 1.

46. Current ongoing debates on various issues concerning postcolonialism indicate that the problem of the civilized and the primitive is not a matter of the past.

47. Long, *Significations*, 91.

48. Henri Baudet, *Paradise on Earth: Some Thoughts on European Images of Non-European Man*, (Middletown, Conn.: Wesleyan University Press, 1988 [1959]).

2

Religion, Globalization, and the University

Kees W. Bolle

Hermeneutics

Under the umbrella of the American Academy of Religion, a group of scholars, modest in number, began a new venture. They felt it was about time to think back to the teachings of Joachim Wach. Wach was a German who had become prominent in the history of religions. He was half Jewish, and the rise of Nazism no doubt facilitated and hastened his acceptance of a job offer at Brown University. When Hitler's Germany was defeated, Wach decided to stay in America, as did other foreign scholars who had been forced to seek refuge there. After the war, Wach moved to Chicago, where he taught until his death in 1955.

These few words I have said about Wach could be said with minor variations about a host of foreigners to whom we are indebted. Not all were compelled by brute political pressure or the threat of persecution or extinction to come here; many came as if "by accident," without the wish to stay, but staying nevertheless. Their total number is not small. And their influence on education in American universities has been significant. How many scholars, in the study of religions alone, would have learned Chinese, Tibetan, Arabic, Turkish, Russian, even Sanskrit (in spite of the great tradition in Sanskrit studies in some Eastern schools) without having been taught by some academic refugee or immigrant who came or was sent packing from a European or Asian country? And some of us, without profiting brilliantly from these variegated immigrants, just gathered general knowledge from their presence. What did these students do with what they learned? They no doubt passed it on as well as they could.

To what extent did we, who learned from the teachings of those learned immigrants, succeed in passing on the traditions of learning we had been exposed to? If we confess that we did not do all that well, we probably understate the case (in spite of great exceptions). To begin with, we ourselves did not have the intellectual background our foreign teachers from Europe or Asia possessed.

Those foreigners, for the most part, did not come here as powerful ambassadors. In fact, they were not powerful at all. The notorious exception is Wernher von Braun, the German missile expert—but I will leave him out of the present discussion. Moreover, we also had Einstein. The point remains that the vast majority came as refugees. Returning to the vignette of Wach: he had reason to feel threatened. Not only was he of Jewish descent; Wach's homosexuality was not high on the list of Nazi preferences.

It is a miracle that for a number of years our education was greatly enhanced by foreigners, and in the field of the history of religions Joachim Wach held a significant place. Wach's scholarly impact on the study of religion in America is no doubt easier to grasp than the contributions, perhaps more esoteric, of other foreigners. Wach's central topic was hermeneutics. It is a big word that connotes the continuous search for consistency in the way we interpret our documents. Who would not want that? In the area of religion, it is absolutely mandatory to apply the same standards and criteria when one moves from Hinduism to Islam to Siberian tribal religions. It is an obvious necessity, yet easier talked about than done. In his masterwork, *Das Verstehen*, Wach presented an extensive discussion of the manners in which Western scholars have been dealing with religion since the eighteenth century, which is to say, the entire period in which our field of study emerged and grew.

The universal appeal of consistency in interpretation makes Wach more attractive than many other immigrant scholars whose focus might be more narrow. Wach was more a philosopher than a philologist. In that capacity, he helped in creating the space in which his students began to look at things in various areas, and, naturally, several of us turned to languages, the most ancient and obvious way toward understanding. Wach did not insist on this. I venture to guess that he took his own background—formed by the great philological and historical achievement in Europe during the nineteenth and twentieth centuries—for granted. Wach's own research into primary documents was no doubt limited, yet his essays on Islam and Mahāyāna Buddhism show him to be quite knowledgeable in the textual foundations which no religio-historical inquiry can ignore.

I would like the first section of my chapter, which mentions an often overlooked part of our own intellectual history in our field of study, to be seen as an introduction to the formidable topic "Religion, Globalization, and the University." Accidentally, because of events no one wanted, Wach came here to expound on an obvious thing that we needed to be told. In my opinion, without such unplanned, accidental beginnings in most of our universities, we could never resist the many misconceptions that the study of religion and religions suffers under today. Hermeneutics is not a commemoration of Wach. It is what good historians of religions do, if they do their job well. It is hard work, and it demands extensive preparation.

The Information Age

A well-known prayer by St. Francis contains the plea: Master, let me not seek so much to be understood as to understand. These simple words may have become mystifying to those who have embraced the information age and set their hopes on the unity of the world created by the global market. We do not need to point out examples in government circles and the World Trade Organization. Our problem for today is that the same mystification occurs among scholars. Some years ago, I became involved in a project sponsored by the United Nations Educational, Scientific, and Cultural Organization (UNESCO), purposely planned for the beginning of the new millennium, surveying the histories of the world's great civilizations. In one of the final meetings, in Paris, I listened in astonishment to the project director, who spoke full of hope about the imminent future, full of confidence in free exchange over the entire globe, serene because of the guiding hand of the United States. We supposedly have entered upon that future. Our wishes with respect to the world as a whole seem to have become fulfilled. As to the wishes of the thus globalized world, we do not seem to bother to raise the question.

There is no doubt something very attractive about such a view of the future. It is reminiscent of the dreams of the more simpleminded rationalists of the eighteenth century, absolutely sure of the conquest by Reason. It suggests that we know the basis on which the future of our world rests: the one free market everywhere.

The governor of Maine in 2001, Angus King, one of the very best governors in the nation, was depicted in the *Portland Press Herald* as the patron saint of our children because he wanted them all to have laptop computers. In spite of his enthusiasm, is there not a little room for the question: Does all knowledge consist in information?

The question may seem feeble in this day and age. All our modern universities are recognizable not by their chapel, as they used to be, but by the gigantic size of their business school. And it is nice to hear the message that our kids should be provided with information, ready for high salaries, ready to embrace the global market.

I will not repeat here warnings that people such as Ralph Nader have conveyed so well. Certainly there are signs that not everything develops as healthily as the trendsetters claim; it just might be, even if globalization came about smoothly, that poverty would simply move from point A to point B. But none of these economic problems concern me for the moment. Where my concern begins is around 1970, when computers began to pervade our universities, and a certain disease began to affect the life of the intellect. In this disease, knowledge *is* information, and information is knowledge. Now it is as if our colleges are swamped with caricatures of prelaw and premed students, lovers of true–false tests characterized by a craving for high grades in order to qualify for the law and medical schools of their choice, yet lacking all inquisitiveness for anything worth knowing. The funny writing mistakes these students make reveal a lack of understanding of the logic and structure of language. Such lack of basics in human speech makes many things, including learning another language, considerably more difficult (splendid spell-check mechanisms in our computers are not human, for they do not "understand," but are themselves based merely on lists of information. They are not capable of distinguishing its and it's, their and there any more than the undereducated keyboard operators). We are not on our way to understanding the world, including its religions.

Some matters concerning our use of language were presented by Jacques Ellul in 1981, in a book entitled *The Humiliation of the Word.*[1]

> Language is a call, an exchange. . . . It is not true that language exists only to communicate information. . . . Obviously, language is *also* information. It communicates information *also*. But if we spoke only to convey information our relationships would be greatly impoverished. . . . Language is uncertain, communicating information but also a whole universe that is fluid, without context or framework, unpretentious, and filled with the rich complexity of things left unexpressed in a relationship. What is not said also plays a role in language. More accurately, what is said sometimes hides what could be said, and on the other hand sometimes it reveals what is not said.[2]

Ellul speaks of the fundamental secret of human communication. The building block of speech is as undeniable as it is invisible. Without it, we could not meaningfully speak with each other, or study philosophy, or anything else that might provide wisdom. Human existence is based on it.

And What of Religion?

As to religion, the idea that was bandied about in the nineteenth century, that religion was disappearing to the extent that true knowledge—one might as well say information—increased, has long ceased to hold water. Religion is not necessarily a nice thing, and the evidence we can see in the daily newspapers makes clear that religion is driving the conflicts and wars that ravish: Hindus and Buddhists on Sri Lanka, Protestants and Catholics in Ireland, the Muslim Chechnians against the Russian state, Muslims and Jews in the Middle East, Christians and Muslims in Indonesia, Sikhs, Hindus, and Muslims in Northwest India, and so on. Who can imagine that religion is dying?

Religion is always wrapped in language. One of the words for *word* is *myth*, the preeminent word that functions in religion.[3] It is always more than information; it precedes information. And no "facts" in history make sense without it.

Following are two examples to show that religion is present even when it is explained away, or when nothing seems to point to what is going on as religious.

(Explaining religion has been tried often, but has been quite characteristic of those whom we might call the information-agers. It can be summed up like this: if religion is not information, we can reduce it to information. "Ritual" is a matter of religious acts, things done. It has puzzled scholars for a long time. Nowadays, we have experts in religion who have solved the matter. Rituals, so they say, came about as the result of a powerful social group suppressing a weak social group. Where is the evidence? you might ask. There isn't any, and they never present any. However, the adherents of such methods of interpreting know the lingo that is "in" in academic circles. And far more respectable in the information age than something called religion are sociology and political science—in which all of us are on our way to a wonderful future in the global market. Hence it is deemed sufficient to assume that a ritual, any ritual, comes about as a result of one group of people suppressing another. Now, that is simple. Who needs evidence? If there is guilt in not noticing religion, the vast majority of us, practicing historians of religion, share in it. In my final illustrations, the central problem is situated right there. I purposely present them without much comment.

The first comes from Japan. Is what is done and spoken here "religious" or not? The very question is not usually asked, yet very much worth asking. *Education about Asia* has an extraordinary article about Japan, called "Voices of the Occupation: Teaching with Haiku," by Edith Roberts.[4] It tells us that when Japan surrendered after the Second World War, and the Japanese people listened to Emperor Hirohito's surrender speech, someone wrote a tiny poem, a haiku. We today in America know about the venerable poet Basho, and haiku is not a strange form anymore. Hence, we also know in some general sense about the "religious" significance of haiku, probably without having thought about "religion" at all. Here is the haiku:

> The flag falls to the ground
> And from a radio box
> Comes the voice of a god
> Hollow, trembling, sorrowful.

And who would hear merely a political statement in the following, written at the time when Japan was occupied by American troops?

> Only the jeeps
> Seem to receive
> The May sunshine.

The second example takes us to a very different issue. It concerns the problem of human situations in which to many observers religion seems to be absent altogether. I am convinced that this problem of understanding should concern all of us. It has been with us for a long time, and in the present day this problem has ceased looking like a problem—for we have learned to explain away religion as a mere by-product of something else we are sure of.

I confess that I constantly become more aware of the importance of *religious documentation that we are not in the habit of recognizing* because—as if instinctively—we look for evidence "out there" that presents itself to us with the label "religious."

Claude Lanzmann's film, *Shoah*, presents the horrors, the flabby self-satisfied human morals, the ruthlessness of the Nazi attempt to exterminate the Jews. The film is deeply moving. But the *Judaism* of the people herded together in camps is never hinted at. It is easy to point out that Lanzmann was close to Jean-Paul Sartre, who felt no urgent need for religion in his presentation of things. But the problem goes far beyond the impact of a once-popular philosopher or a filmmaker. There is something in which that entire ghastly part of history is embedded, something to which *we*—almost as if by nature—have become blind. We do not see prayer shawls and yarmulkes because something in us tells us that none of those things matter. They are things of religion, hence insignificant. They are beside the important point we, scholars, want to make—whatever it is.

Nevertheless, I want to argue, religion is the topic we should study seriously, and our understanding will not fare well if we go on computerizing and globalizing so self-importantly.

The following document was printed by the underground press during Holland's occupation by Germany. It was written by someone with some medical knowledge who assisted the sick in the "holding camp" of Westerbork. This was the principal place from which Dutch Jews were transported to Auschwitz, Dachau, Bergen-Belsen, and other factories of death. The write-up was smuggled out of the camp and appeared in the underground paper *Het Parool*, February 5, 1944.

A TRANSPORT LEAVES
An Eye-Witness Reports on the Sorrows and Strange Joys at Westerbork.

After this night I honestly thought that it would be a sin ever to laugh again. But later it occurred to me that there were some who departed laughing. This time, however, very few laughed. Perhaps, in Poland there may still be occasionally someone who laughs. There won't be many from this transport, I believe.

Early in the morning, after a night in the hospital barrack, I passed by the penal barracks. . . . People stood by, mainly men, ready for the journey, behind barbed wire. Many looked almost stout, and enterprising. One old acquaintance I did not recognize under the shorn scalp that can transform people completely; he laughed and called out to me: "If they don't beat me to death at once, I'll come back!" But those babies, those little piercing cries of the babies that were picked up from their cribs in the middle of the night to be carried off to a distant land—. I must write all this down one thing after the other without stopping. Later I won't be able to do it, because I shall believe that it did not really happen. Even now it is like a mirage that floats away from me. The babies were the worst. And then that lame little girl who did not even want to take a dinner plate with her and who had such trouble with the thought of having to die. And that frightened boy: he had thought he was safe, and unexpectedly he too had to go. And he got into a mad fit and ran away. Fellow Jews had to hunt for him. If he had not been found, dozens of others would have to go on transport for him. They surrounded him soon enough. He was found in a tent, and trotzdem—trotzdem [by which is meant in German: in spite of that] the others had to go on transport too, by way of deterrent, it is called. In this way he dragged several good friends along with him. He caused fifty victims with that moment of mental derangement. Of course, he did not really do it. Our commander, of whom they often say that he is a gentleman, did it.

The previous afternoon, once more, I had walked through the hospital barrack, from bed to bed. Which would be empty tomorrow? Transport lists are not made known until the very last moment, and yet some already know beforehand that they have to leave. A young girl calls me, a girl with thin wrists and a transparent, small face. She is partly paralyzed, and she had just learned to begin walking again, between two nurses, a step at a time. "Did they tell you? I have to leave," she whispers. "What? Do you have to go?" We look at each other without speaking. Her face has disappeared altogether. She has only eyes. At last, she says in a monotonous, grey little voice: "And what a pity, eh, that now whatever you have learned in life—it has all been for nothing." And then she says: "How difficult it is, isn't it, to die, eh?"

In the laundry shed a disheveled little woman has a tray of dripping clothes on her arm. She grips my hand. She pours a stream of words over me. "It can't happen, can it? They are taking me away, and I can't even get my laundry dry before tomorrow. And my child is sick. A fever. Can't you see to it that I won't have to leave? I don't have enough clothes for the child. They sent me these tiny crawlers instead of the large ones—oh, I'm going out of my mind. And on the transport you can't take more than one blanket with you. We''ll freeze to death, won't we?"

Little bottles of milk are prepared for the babies, whose pitiful cries penetrate every crevice of the barrack. A young mother says, almost apologetically: "Normally my child does not cry. It's just as if it knows what is going to happen." She picks up the child, a delightful baby of eight months, from its primitive crib and smiles at it: "If you aren't good, mommy won't take you with her on her travels!" She talks to me about acquaintances: "When the Grüne [the German Grüne Polizei] came to pick them up, the children cried terribly. Then the father said: 'Stop crying, for if you are not good now, you can't come along in the green car, and the green gentleman won't take you with him.' That did the trick, and the children calmed down." She winks courageously. She is a little, olive-dark woman, her face shows her sense of humor. She is dressed in long grey pants and a green woolen sweater. "I am laughing now, but I am not really so plucky," she says.

The woman of the wet laundry is close to insanity. "Can't you hide my child for me? Please, can't you put it away somewhere? He is running a fever—how can I take him with me?" She points to the little heap that is the child, with blond curls and a face of intense red, tossing in its rough wooden bed.

A few beds further, I suddenly see the ashy-pale, freckled face of a colleague at the bed of a dying woman who has taken poison . . . "God Almighty, what's happening, what are you doing?" [While I turn to the patient] the words slip out. She [the patient] is a working-class type from Rotterdam, petite, affectionate. She is in her ninth month. Two nurses are trying to dress her. Now she stands, leaning her misshapen body against the bed of one of her children. Sweat runs over her face. She gazes into a distance where I cannot follow her, and she says in a toneless voice: "Two months ago, I wanted to go with my husband to Poland, and then I was not allowed to, because I always have such heavy labor. And now I have to leave—because this past night someone ran away—." The lament of the babies increases, it fills the nooks and crannies of the half-dark, sepulchral barrack. A name arises in my mind: Herod. On the stretcher, going to the train, labor sets in. That's why they are permitted to carry this woman back to the hospital instead of putting her on the cargo train. This night, this fact may be counted among the unfathomable human deeds.

I pass the lame girl's bed. With the help of others, she is already partly dressed. I have never seen such large eyes in such a small face. "I can't cope," she whispers. She stands before me, her green silken kimono wrapped around her deformed little figure. Her eyes are the eyes of a child, pure yet wise. She looks at me searchingly for a long time without a word, then she cries out passionately: "What I would like—oh, what I would like is to swim away in my tears to a better world!" Then: "And I am so terribly homesick for my good mother." (This good mother died of cancer in the camp, some months before, in the laundry shed near the toilet; in that place she could at least be alone for a moment, in order to die.)

You can tell that the young woman at one time was used to luxury, and that she was beautiful. She has not been long in the camp. She was in hiding, for the sake of her baby. Now she is here, because of betrayal, like so many of those who went into hiding. Her husband is in the penal barracks. She looks pitiful. With a greenish radiance, her own black hair shows here and there through the hair that is bleached. She is wearing several sets of underwear, although one cannot wear everything, especially when accompanied by a little child. As it is, she looks ridiculous. . . . She glances at everyone with her eyes veiled and questioning, like a trapped young animal. Dilapidated now, what will this woman look like when after three days she is unloaded from a cargo wagon pushed full of men, women, children, babies, together with their baggage, and no furniture except in the center one can? Probably, other transition camps will be the next destination, from which other transports will leave. We are being hunted to death across Europe—.

It is six o'clock in the morning now. The train leaves at eleven. A beginning is made with loading the people and backpacks.

Men of the Fliegende Kolonne [the flying column] in brown overalls are bringing baggage on wheelbarrows. Among them I recognize a few of the commandant's court jesters: the comedian Max Ehrlich, and Willy Rosen the song-writer, who looks like a skeleton. A while back he was assigned to a transport, but several nights before he was to leave he was singing his lungs out in front of an audience, among which was the commandant with his entourage. He sang "Ich kann es nicht verstehen dasz die Rosen blühen" [German: "I cannot understand that the roses are blooming"] and other, similar zeitgemässe [in accordance with the time, "relevant"] songs. The commandant, who is so well educated in music, was delighted by the performance, and ordered Willy Rosen gesperrt [exempt from the transport]. There is yet another court jester: Erich Ziegler, the commandant's favorite pianist. Legend has it that Erich Ziegler is such a virtuoso he can jazz up even Beethoven's ninth symphony. And surely, that means something.

From the looks of it, the freight carriages can be called full. That's what you would think. Good heavens, do all those people over there have to go inside as well? . . . Suddenly, a child calls out: "The commandant!" He appears at the beginning of the asphalt road, just like a famous star appearing on stage for the great finale of a revue. Legends are beginning to be woven around this commandant. He has so much charm, and he means so well for the Jews. Considering his position in life, he certainly does hold unusual ideas. Recently he decided we should have nutritional variety, and immediately we were given peas one day instead of cabbage. He is also the so-called father of our artistic life here. Occasionally he invites artists to his home; he talks and drinks with them. And the other evening he accompanied an actress to her barrack, and when saying good-night he shook her hand. Just imagine, shaking hands!

This morning he is sending 50 more Jews on transport, because a boy in blue pajamas hid in a tent. He trots alongside the train, his neatly brushed grey hair showing at the back of his head from under his flat, light-green cap. Many ignorant teenagers here have a crush on that bit of grey hair contrasting so romantically with a rather young face, even though they would not say so publicly.

A number of Jewish big shots in camp life also parade alongside the train. "They try so hard to make themselves 'wichtig' [important] too," someone behind me whispers. And I ask the companion next to me: "Will anybody ever be able to describe what is going on here?" Perhaps the outside world thinks of us only as a homogeneous grey mass of suffering Jews. Outsiders know nothing of the nuances and abysses, the fences between individuals here. They may never be able to understand it.

The light green, rigid commandant, the beige, inmobile secretary, the black bully figure of the Oberdienstleiter [top chief of service] parade the length of the train. Everyone makes room for them; everyone turns their eyes towards them. Heavens, is it true that those doors finally close, completely? The doors are shut against the pile of people in the cargo carriages. Narrow openings near the top reveal heads, and later, when the train begins to move, they will show the waving hands. Once more, the commandant inspects the train, from beginning to end, this time on a bicycle. Then he gestures with his hand, just like a king in an operetta, and a little orderly rushes to him and respectfully receives the bicycle. The whistle makes its piercing sound, and a train with one thousand and twenty Jews leaves Holland; the twenty make up the reserve and serve to cover the risks of transport—.[5]

It is difficult to speak after this. But I am the one who brought it up, and I would like to ask: What are the "religious" dimensions of this report? There are no religious dimensions that we can perceive and trace in order to isolate "religion" as if in a box. This, I would like to suggest, is nothing new—but it is habitually forgotten. Think for a moment of the story of the good Samaritan. Is there anything we can isolate as "religious" about that? No. And so it is with so many important documents we try to interpret.

Religion is but a name. It is not a dogma professed. It is something inseparable from human existence. It is sacrifice. It is martyrdom. It is slaughter. It is also the activity, the vicious ritual of a pseudo-religion that seems to come out on top. We do not have the choice to ignore that part. It cuts into the object we study. It means not ignoring the *racism* of Hitler's racism, and looking anew at E. B. Tylor and Sigmund Freud in that light. In this fragment I have transcribed here, the only ones who could claim to know what was good and holy, to know God (if they had been given a moment to raise their voice) were the sacrificial animals of pseudoreligion. You do not need to be pious to consider the arrival at this conclusion possible. It might be the outcome of a sound, scholarly study, a science.

A philosophical statement that might make my suggestion almost solid comes from Emmanuel Levinas:

> Le réel ne doit pas seulement être déterminé dans son objectivité historique,
> mais aussi à partir du secret qui interrompt la continuité du temps historique, à
> partir des intentions intérieures. Le pluralisme de la société n'est pas possible
> qu'à partir de ce secret. Il atteste ce secret.[6]
> (Reality does not need to be established by its historical objectivity alone, but
> also on the basis of the secret which interrupts the continuity of historical time,
> on the basis of its own inner purposes. Our multifaceted society is not conceiv
> able except for this secret. Our society is a witness to this secret.)

Notes

1. *La parole humiliée* (Paris: Éditions du Seuil, 1981), Joyce Main Hanks, tr. *The Humiliation of the Word* (Grand Rapids, Mich.: Eerdmans, 1985).

2. Ellul, *The Humiliation of the Word*, 16.

3. Bruce Lincoln, whose sense for reality is admirable, suggests that what we normally call religion had better be called ideology. See his *Theorizing Myth: Narrative, Ideology, and Scholarship* (Chicago: University of Chicago Press, 1999). I cannot agree with that. The term *myth* may indeed have been theorized upon abundantly. The term *ideology* however, is not only more limited, but in its use far from clear. Its political connotations do not help a great deal but only add to the abundance of theories, without illuminating our understanding of religion. Could one seriously speak of the ideology of Genesis one?

4. Edith Roberts, "Voices of the Occupation: Teaching with Haiku," *Education about Asia* 5, no. 3 (2001): 37-38.

5. Text in Kees W. Bolle, ed., *Ben's Story* (Carbondale: Southern Illinois University Press, 2001), 115-20.

6. Emmanuel Levinas, *Totalité et infini* (La Haye: Martinus Nijhoff, 1971), 29.

3

Sacred Landscapes and Global Religion: Reflections on the Significance of Indigenous Religions for University Culture

Philip P. Arnold

Mae Bigtree was a world-renowned basket maker from the Mohawk nation of Akwesasne. She was a gifted artist who wove together various natural materials of wood and sweetgrass. Mae recently passed from the world of the living, and while she is greatly missed, she still lives on in her baskets. Mohawk baskets are lessons of how the living landscape comes together. As a tribute to Mae I want to describe something of the meaning of the baskets.

Mohawk baskets are beautiful things. They are used in specific Thanksgiving ceremonies in Longhouses of the Haudenosaunee (or traditional Iroquois).[1] Baskets are used in ceremonies because they are appropriate gifts to various parts of Creation. They are also given as gifts at social events and collected as Indigenous art objects. They are appropriate gifts because baskets articulate a relationship with a living landscape and, therefore, a deeper understanding of inhabiting what we call central New York.

My participation in picking and cleaning sweetgrass has revealed to me some of the depth of the meaning of baskets. For example, when the lightening bugs come out in mid-July we know that the sweetgrass is ready. It must be picked in the morning because after midday the sweetgrass hides. Until recently I wouldn't have believed it if it hadn't been for a group from a local university who came to Mae's home one summer to record her basket making. According to some folklorist, Mohawk basket making is a dying art and needs to be recorded. It is curious to me that while folklorists acknowledge that these arts are dying they seem less interested in asking why. Instead they jump at the chance to record the process as a way of saving it for posterity. Anyway, the film crew came in the afternoon, and Mae took them to her backyard where she had been nurturing a small patch of sweetgrass. She looked and looked, however, and couldn't find the patch in her own yard! When telling us the story she recalled that her mother used to say that the sweetgrass hides, so one must always respect it by giving it tobacco when it is pulled from the earth. After it has been picked, the sweetgrass must be cleaned and then dried in a shed. Mae's sister then braids the sweetgrass. The braids are then woven into the basket and its sweetness can be smelled for years. I was told that it was not good to buy or sell unbraided sweetgrass.

When I first saw one of these baskets I thought that the splints were of some kind of reed, as with many other baskets. They are not reed. The splints are made of black ash, a hard wood. They are not fashioned by a knife or lathe, however, but by pounding the black ash log. Men do the pounding, and now I hear that they are having to go farther and farther north into Canada to find good trees. Akwesasne is the most polluted Iroquois nation because it is downstream from various kinds of car manufacturers, paper mills, and aluminum plants. Not only does this affect the quality of human life but it also affects other lives, including the black ash trees. Today, traditional Longhouse people at Akwesasne are involved in replanting the black ash trees, which take fifty years to grow to maturity.

Pounding the log raises the wood along the year growth rings. These rather thick splints are then given to the basket maker, who continues to wet the wood and pull it apart until it is almost tissue thin. This part takes a lot of time, strength, and skill. The splints and sweetgrass are then woven into a basket around a form. Mae sat at her dining-room table and made the baskets. Important conversations would take place around the dining-room table for there is a steady stream of visitors who could not resist heading right for the smell of fresh-picked sweetgrass.

I wanted to tell you the little I know about Mohawk baskets because this is the sense of religiousness that I want to highlight. Following Charles Long's understanding of religion as "orientation,"[2] I emphasize religion as how people meaningfully inhabit the material world.[3] I refer to this sense of religiousness as Native or Indigenous because of the intimate connections that these communities make with material life. Mohawk baskets are not empty containers but embodiments of a meaningful landscape. Making a basket requires a skill and deep understanding of the land. Knowledge of how to negotiate with trees, grasses, weather, terrain, water, insects, animals, as well as other human beings, comes together as a basket.

A material understanding of religion tends to challenge popular and New Age perceptions of Native American traditions as mystical or mysterious communions with unseen beings. Rather, as several Native American leaders have remarked, Native traditions are focused on appropriate ways in which a community can be involved with the world: Native traditions are negotiations with obvious, commonsense understandings of the world in order to promote the underlying and fundamental elements which sustain life such as food, water, land, trees, and so on. [4] Ceremonies involve people in the processes which sustain life—and not just human life. The basket is, therefore, the embodiment of an Indigenous, or landscape-oriented, way of being in the world.

Throughout American history into the present time Native traditions are under attack. Native and non-Native people are not always interested in addressing what is antagonistic to Native traditions. For example, Native nations along the Eastern seaboard, like the Pequot and Narragansett, who now have great monetary wealth, are trying to buy up the now old baskets that are held by museums. These people have been devastated by contact with Europeans and have gone the route of casinos and other big moneymaking enterprises in an effort to survive. Native people along the Eastern Seaboard were in constant and intense contact with European settlers from the seventeenth century onward. As in the Pequot War of 1637, there was constant warfare over land between colonial and indigenous inhabitants. Trade practices with transAtlantic economic institutions likewise had a debilitating effect on the traditional practices of native people. Disease, conversion to Christianity, and intercultural marriages were fostered between trading groups; and the consequence of these contact situations was that native people in New England were devastated physically and culturally by contact with Europeans. Now some of their group are wealthy and are spending money to reclaim their lost heritage. The Pequot, who own and operate Foxwoods Casino and Resort, have just opened a major research center in Connecticut. But even though they seem to be reclaiming their culture, are they not also complicit in their own cultural destruction? Isn't this New World materiality, in the form of casinos and other big-business opportunities, diametrically opposed to a Native materiality which destroyed their ability to make baskets in the first place? These are tough times for Native American people and what the Iroquois, Pequot, or whomever decide to do is none of my business. But I do think that the various genocides that they have endured do indicate something extremely important about religion in the New World, a New World made by various immigrant communities in opposition to Native communities. My first question, therefore, is to wonder if a religion based on the perpetuation of life is possible in American culture.

To illustrate this I want to contrast the Indigenous world of the Mohawk basket with the willow basket. Willow baskets were very important to the early Syracuse economy. If you go out to the Salt Museum on the shore of Onondaga Lake, you will see pictures of how Syracuse began. It is called the "salt city" because ever since Syracuse's founding late in the eighteenth century, salt was the major export product. In 1829 the Erie Canal opened. It was the most ambitious of the canal projects in the recently incorporated United States. The Erie Canal was financed by major capitalists of New York City to make upstate New York products available to the entire world and also to make it, the traditional landscape of the Iroquois, available to immigrant people. All kinds of people followed the path up the Hudson, across the Mohawk River, and into the canal to Syracuse and points west. In fact, the westward migration was made possible by the Erie Canal. My own family moved from Rhode Island to Michigan in the 1830s by way of the canal.

Immigrants from around the world moved into New York to dig the canal, to move goods along the canal, and to settle. In other words, the Erie Canal was a zone of intense intercultural contact. Numerous languages, traditions, skin colors, and so on, were brought together. But these people, unlike the Haudenosaunee, were committed to a New World landscape. They were part of a new, very aggressive, push toward commodification. It was the economic decisions in New York City based on the comparative value of things pulled out of their native contexts that determined the meanings of their lives. Everything in the world was evaluated in terms of its monetary value, that is, how it was valued on a global economic scale.

Ironically, while people came to the United States for freedom they ended up being enslaved in a mercantile economy over which they had little or no control. While they arrived as Irish, Italian, Russian, African, and so on, the first thing they had to do, in large measure, was to give up their languages and traditions. In their being displaced, therefore, it is no wonder that along the Erie Canal new forms of religion took root. This area has been called the Burned-Over District by historians of American religions. It was a place in the early 1800s of religious intensity that swept through upstate New York like a wildfire. According to Whitney Cross, who coined the term, we could not understand the phenomenon of religion in America without an adequate understanding of the Burned-Over District.[5] Given the lack of control of their lives in a completely new situation it seems quite reasonable that people would turn toward religious experimentation.

What does this have to do with willow baskets? If you go to the Salt Museum you will also see pictures of the willow basket industry. The willow basket was the forerunner of the cardboard box. Its use and function directly connected to the movement of goods along the canal. It was an inexpensive way to pack salt in order to move it through New York City to the rest of the world. In contrast to the Mohawk basket, the meaning of the willow basket, therefore, was in its being an empty container and its value was in its being empty. The legacy of the willow basket is in marked contrast to the Mohawk basket.

The illustration of the baskets, as competing cosmologies for inhabiting the Americas, is an important issue for how the university structures its ways of knowing the world. It is becoming much harder to convince my students of the universal nature of the university's enterprise, as exemplified by the willow basket. More convincing to students and faculty alike are the ways in which knowledge is developed in particular cultural frameworks. At my university, students find much more compelling the different approaches to the meanings of the world, through departments and programs such as Women Studies, African and African American Studies, Latino Studies, Native American Studies, and so on.

The question is, therefore, Can the university contain this universe of interpretations if it has abandoned the rubric of absolute knowledge? This question can also be asked of religion. It is an issue, I argue, that the history of religions has always been well suited to answer.

A few weeks ago I was shoveling out my driveway when a young African American man approached me. I instantly recognized him as an evangelist coming to save me. He first handed me a pamphlet with a painting of a beautiful paradisiacal landscape, and everyone in the picture was smiling and having a wonderful and wholesome time. There are what looks to be an Asian mother and daughter petting a bear near a berry bush, a Latino family petting an African lion, an African man and woman, as well as a white boy carrying food. This is all set in an idyllic landscape with farmlands and mountains in the background. And, of course it is a splendid fall day. Everyone is smiling.

I have seen pictures like this one, and they give me a feeling of intense uneasiness simply because, in my experience, people should stay away from African lions and bears (especially around berry bushes), and people who are deliriously happy for no apparent reason make me nervous. But what really made me mad was the title of the painting, "Life in a Peaceful NEW WORLD." The image that the young man gave me I will label a fantasy of multiculturalism. The reason it made me mad was that it was an image in which the challenge of diversity which has constituted the New World is stripped out of life. It is a very polite, cleaned-up fiction which we in the history of religions might jokingly refer to as the "take a Buddhist to lunch" notion of religious plurality.

The young man asked me if I thought that the world in the painting was possible. Inside I was fervently hoping that it was not possible but instead, thinking of another strategy, I said that I thought it had already been a reality previous to America being labeled "New World." I wanted to throw him off by indicating that language of the New World, as *he* had painted it, was the problem rather than a solution.

He then asked if I believed in God. I said, yes, of course, because I had no tangible knowledge of my creating myself. But I quickly added that I believed in what I could see. I think he was unaccustomed to the pairing of a belief in God *and* a belief in the material world. Then he asked if I believed that the Bible was the inspired word of God. I said yes, but added that I also thought he was an inspired work of God. At this point he opened his Bible.

"Now wait a minute," I protested, "before you start telling me what God says in that book, you have to first explain to me how a text generated in the Ancient Near East, in a language other than the one in which you are reading has anything to do with you and me. Also, you have to demonstrate to me how this book, which has been used to justify the enslavement of your ancestors and the genocide of countless millions of Native Americans, as well as other people around the world, is now a solution to all those violations against humanity. How can your Bible be both?"

I continued to say that he ought to check out other inspired words of God, the Quran and the Talmud, for example. He then looked at me with a tear in his eye, which I think was due to the cold rather than to anything that I had said, and ask if I sincerely believed in all those things. I said of course because I was not an idiot. Then he said that if I believed all of that he couldn't talk to me. I said fine, because I hadn't started the conversation—he had. I was only minding my own business shoveling my driveway.

I wanted to tell you that story, not just as an example of the utility of the academic study of religion in getting rid of Jehovah's Witnesses from your front yard, but to indicate a problematic regarding diversity in the university. From my perspective, which is currently a minority view in the academy, the discipline of the history of religions has always been involved with promoting an understanding of diversity of religious perspectives. But it does this through processes of self-consciousness and self-transformation. Or, put differently, embedded within the seemingly simple task of describing Other traditions in such a way that they are comprehensible, and are enabled to say something about their understandings of the religious dimensions of human existence, one necessarily has to put at risk one's own understandings and orientations. That is to say that the Other, whichever traditions the historian of religions chooses, will always defy being overdetermined by the scholar's language.[6] Or, to put it in Syracusan language, the question of "What is religion?" (or, the cipher of religion) is implied in the historian of religion's work.[7]

The university might be undergoing a radical transformation in the way it is framing the acquisition of knowledge. Recent initiatives of promoting multiculturalism and intellectual diversity had a dramatic effect on the way the university is structured and the academic claim to knowledge. At the very least some sections of the university now claim that all human beings have to rely on their own formation as the basis of their knowledge of the world. These days at least part of our academic work is adjudicating our interpretive positions, or, in other words, in our being involved with our Indigenous makeup in order to be able to say anything about anything. Some find this difficult work, while others see it as an opportunity for self-promotion in an intellectual world that has ignored their voices. What is clear, however, is that the university is now unable to make claims to absolute, universal knowledge as it could only a generation or two ago.

My sense is that this does not come as a surprise to the historian of religions. Getting involved with other religions is often a humbling experience. And yet, at the start of every major symposium on comparative religion, or in the introduction of every big book having to do with religion lately there is an obligatory chastising of Mircea Eliade. He is labeled as a romantic, an essentialist, a cryptotheologian, a Nazi, a monarchist, and so on, and so on. His work is seen by most in my discipline as an impediment to the enhancement of comparative method. My sense is that what drives comparativists nuts about Eliade is his appeal to something he called "the sacred." There is, therefore, something at stake.

My first meeting with Eliade was in 1983 in Boulder, Colorado, when I was working as a research assistant in David Carrasco's Mesoamerican Archive and Research Project. I was an undergraduate at the time and was just beginning my long fascination with Aztec traditions. Eliade was invited by Carrasco to view the photographs of the newly excavated Templo Mayor, the principal temple of the Aztec, which is located in the center of Mexico City. By this time Eliade was a feeble person, a breath of wind. As he sat looking at the slides of the excavated offering boxes he vigorously exclaimed that they were a "sacred language which contained in them the Aztec understanding of religion." Now, you have to understand that these offering boxes that lay at the base of the temple were crammed full of all kinds of ceremonial objects. I think he was looking at the most infamous one, offering number 48, at which lowest level were ocean shells laid out in an east-west direction. Above that was an assortment of animals of both land and sea which were probably sacrificed during the ceremony. Above these were the skeletons of forty-seven children. Then finally, at the top, were about the same number of small figures of Tlaloc, the Mesoamerican god of rain and fertility. In other words, for a young, liberal-minded undergraduate student this offering box was a horror!

In spite of my visceral reaction to the Aztec I thought that Eliade was probably right, and that those offering boxes were in fact a sacred language—one which I didn't like. As I thought about it, the stratigraphies marked out by the archaeologists were also a cosmography. But I also knew that this language of the Aztec had no speakers. They had been silenced in various ways—the most pronounced of which was their conquest by the Spanish in 1521. So how was I to learn a language of the dead, who were not my dead, but nonetheless of a significant dead people? Was I only to appeal to my own imagination or could I appeal to something tangible, something I could see, something obvious, in order to bring this language into appearance? Finally, why should I care about this language? Why would it speak to me, someone reared so far from the Aztec world?

These are urgent questions, or questions that are asked before, during, and after one's research. The history of religions gave me a method for doing this work and that method had to do largely with the cipher of religion, or "the sacred." It culminated in my book *Eating Landscape*. The cipher of religion was the one thing that Eliade insisted on throughout his life. After his major works such as *Patterns*, *The Sacred and the Profane*, and *Myth of the Eternal Return*, he seems to have been moving away from the sacred as a firm reality. Instead the cipher of the sacred became more a necessary methodological feature of the work of the historian of religions in a way analogous to the religious experience itself. In his 1961 article "A New Humanism," which was the first article of the first issue of *History of Religions* (the founding editors of this journal are Eliade, Joseph Kitagawa, and Charles H. Long), he says,

> [I]t is not enough to grasp the meaning of a religious phenomenon in a certain culture and, consequently, to decipher its "message" (for every religious phenomenon constitutes a cipher); it is also necessary to study and understand its "history," that is, to unravel its changes and modifications and, ultimately, to elucidate its contribution to the entire culture. . . . Thus, the historian of religions is in a position to grasp the permanence of what has been called man's specific existential situation of "being in the world," for the experience of the sacred is its correlate. In fact, man's becoming aware of his own mode of being and assuming his *presence* in the world together constitute a "religious" experience. [8]

Paradoxically it is the cipher of religion as an experience of being in the world, or as Long would put it, as an orientation to what is real in an ultimate sense, which allowed me to simultaneously imagine the Aztec language as real—real in the sense that it could reveal something about their world as well as pressure things in mine. If we refuse to acknowledge religion as a cipher then there would be no restraint, no epoché, and the languages of the others, like Aztec, would be already determined and therefore of no consequence.

It is the issue of the relationship of the cipher of religion as a methodological tool and the language of reality, or materiality, with which I want to conclude. As I told the young Jehovah's Witness, I believe in what I can see. But that in no way implies that I know about what I see. In contrast, many or most in the academic study of religion seem to know about exactly what they see. For many comparativists, religion is wholly definable. Ironically, both the Jehovah's Witness and scholars who understand religion to be reducible to some social scientific reality, rely on firm and fixed languages of understanding. My impression, however, is that the Aztec, and Native American religious traditions in general, do not. For example, I could be (and probably will be) shoveling my driveway from now until I die, but I would be extremely surprised if someone came along from the Haudenosaunee (Iroquois) Longhouse tradition to convert me to their religion. I doubt I could even take them to lunch. If we were to reverse the context of the meeting and I were to go to the Onondaga Nation (as anthropologists do every season) and ask them to share with me what they believed, or asked them to tell me about their religion, I would probably be told politely that they didn't know what I was talking about and that they don't have a religion. I suspect they wouldn't talk to me, not simply because they did not understand my questions, but because I would be correctly identified as a colonist, I would reveal myself as less interested in finding out an answer to an urgent question of mine, and more interested in controlling them. That is to say that for many people their sense of religiousness is involved with how they are in the world, and not simply an ideological appendage. On the other hand I would be and have been quite comfortable talking on and on with the Haudenosaunee about the meaning of obvious things in the world such as Mae's baskets. For all scholars' confidence in the languages of the social sciences as explaining religion, therefore, I still think that Eliade was right both in emphasizing the sacred and in locating that cipher in seemingly obvious material phenomena, because it works in both descriptive and contact settings. It marks a respectful distance between the self and the other, which people, both living and dead, deserve. In my case, because I have developed these strange fascinations with and commitments to the horrors of the Aztecs, it more authentically represents the human dimensions of my work.

I have another example. I wrote on behalf of the Onondaga who are trying to stop gravel mining at Tully, which is a sacred site for them for a variety of reasons. To initiate my task I was invited to a meeting in which elders talked about their relationship to Onondaga Creek, which runs from Tully to Onondaga Lakes. They are afraid that the creek will become even more polluted due to the mining runoff from the gravel pits. It was startling to me how profound were the meanings of the creek, because as they talked it was clearly the site of their identity, a site of ritual events, childhood, and so on. Talking about the meaning of the creek, therefore, was much more profound than a conversation about religion. There is, therefore, a gap between Onondaga understandings of their creek and the Erie Canal.

Below are the lyrics to the tune "Esperanto" by Kurt Elling. This was released on his fourth album, *Live In Chicago*, for which he received his fourth Grammy nomination. Kurt was a graduate-student colleague of mine at the University of Chicago Divinity School. In "Esperanto" he captures the ambiguity intrinsic to the study and the phenomena of religion.

Esperanto

There's a secret that never dies—
like a dance of hidden meanings that we never apprehend.
There are questions just as old as time
and the answers that come never quite make amends.
Even so when you look at time you can get a subtle feeling of the way it
   oughta be.
Take a good look at your own real life,
and you will see if you want what you've gotten to be.
It's a hope, a sign, a measure of quiet rapture—
of love and what might come after.
It's letting go and letting no answer be an answer.

How did smoke learn how to fly?—Where do birds go off to die?
Why does coal sleep in darkness?— Do dreams live in apartness?
Is a number forever?—Where's the soul of the water?
How old is "Old November?"—No one here can remember.

If I die where does time go?—Do the bees feel vertigo?
To get love is there potion?—Or is love only motion?

Holy lift, holy reading—holy gift, holy needing.
Holy sound, holy waiting—holy spark animating.
Holy food, holy breathing—holy light interweaving.
Holy night, holy handwrite—holy flight, holy insight.
Holy sun, holy brother—holy moon, holy mother.
Holy dream, holy vision—holy scheme, holy mission.
Holy one to another—holy me, holy other.
Holy lives, holy blending—holy start, holy ending. [9]

Kurt plays off the notion that there is a universal language, but that language can only indicate meanings with regard to the cipher of the human condition. Also, it is the nature of the cipher which generates creativity, imaginative recreations of reality. It is that play with our material condition, or with the other, which keeps me going. Like Kurt I feel that maintaining our understanding of religion as a cipher, or maintaining the category of the "sacred," is essential to my work with Native traditions of the Americas. It orients the history of religions to the human sciences as an essentially creative activity. It also maintains a respectful distance between those things that constitute one's self and other. This difference is essential for genuine learning to take place. Unlike other programs of religion I think Syracuse welcomes that creativity out of diversity because it insists on the cipher of religion.

If the university is admitting to the particularity of knowledge by promoting diversity it seems also to be promoting the reality of the cipher as the center of knowledge. The extent to which we value the Indigenous nature of our understandings of the world is the extent to which we will value other perspectives. Or does multiculturalism mean that we can all be part of the same universal structure of the world—as with the willow baskets of the Erie Canal? We at the university have a choice. As with Elling's refrain, however, promoting the cipher at the center of our deliberations on the significance of the world makes the work of the university much less universal and, therefore, much more important.

Notes

1. The Haudenosaunee (which means "People of the Long House") is a confederation of autonomous Indigenous communities which include the Mohawk, Oneida, Onondaga, Cayuga, Tuscarora, and Seneca. They are often referred to as the Iroquois.

2. Charles H. Long, *Significations: Signs, Symbols, and Images in the Interpretation of Religion* (Aurora, Colo.: Davies Group, 1999), 7.

3. Philip P. Arnold, *Eating Landscape: Aztec and European Occupation of Tlalocan* (Boulder, Colo.: University Press of Colorado, 1999).

4. Oren Lyons was visited by Steve Wall and Harvey Arden and became suspicious when asked about his religion. "He gives us a long, hard look and shakes his head. 'Why come to us? We're the toughest nut to crack. You think we turn our Elders over to anyone who walks in the door?' He leans forward, elbows planted on the table. His eyes probe us. 'We guard them like pure spring water. So what is it you guys want from the Elders?' Oren asks. 'Secrets? Mystery?' We explain that we want only to meet them and hear whatever they care to share with us, that we're not looking for secrets. 'That's good,' Oren says, 'because *I can tell you right now, there are no secrets. There's no mystery. There's only common sense.*'" In *Wisdom Keepers: Meetings with Native American Spiritual Elders*, by Steve Wall and Harvey Arden (Hillsboro, Oreg: Beyond Words Publishing, 1990), p. 64.

5. Whitney Cross, *The Burned-Over District: The Social and Intellectual History of Enthusiastic Religion in Western New York, 1800-1850* (Ithaca, N.Y.: Cornell University Press, 1950).

6. In *Imagining Religion: From Babylon to Jonestown* (Chicago: University of Chicago Press, 1982) Jonathan Z. Smith says that religion is solely the creation of the scholar's imagination and that the historian of religion's primary skill is in self-consciously articulating his or her choice of subject. See his "Introduction," xi-xiii.

7. See Philip P. Arnold, "Diversity in the History of Religions." *Journal of Cultural and Religious Theory* http://www.jcrt.org, 2001, and "History of Religions," entry for *Encyclopedia of Postmodernism*, ed. Victor E. Taylor and Charles E. Winquist (New York: Routledge, 2001), 333-38.

8. In Mircea Eliade, *The Quest: History and Meaning in Religion* (Chicago: University of Chicago Press, 1969), 8.

9. By Vince Mendoza and Kurt Elling. Lyrics inspired by the poems of Pablo Neruda. From Kurt Elling, *Live in Chicago* (Blue Note, 2000). Poem is from the Kurt Elling lyrics project, at www.kurtelling.com/ (accessed November 11, 2001).

4

"Faire Place à une Race Métisse": Colonial Crisis and the Vision of Louis Riel

Jennifer I. M. Reid

Louis "David" Riel was born in the Red River settlement of St. Boniface, Manitoba, in 1844.[1] He was Métis[2]—a member of a community of predominantly French and aboriginal ancestry—by virtue of the fact that his grandfather, Jean-Baptiste Riel, had married Marguerite Boucher, whose parents were French and Chipewayan.[3] His astute mind caught the attention of Alexandre Taché (who would become the first Roman Catholic archbishop of St. Boniface),[4] and at fourteen years old, Riel was sent to the Sulpician College at Montreal, where he studied for the priesthood. He did not, however, receive ordination (a decision precipitated by marriage plans that later collapsed),[5] and returned to Red River in 1868 where he quickly emerged as a leader of the frustrated Métis population in the region. He would ultimately lead the Métis in two uprisings against the Canadian government in 1869 and 1885.[6]

In the years between these uprisings, Riel was exiled to the United States; he was three times elected to the Federal House of Commons (although never able to take his seat); he was twice committed to asylums at Longue Point and Beauport, Quebec; and, during this confinement, he began having religious visions calling him to lead the Métis in the creation of a sovereign nation in the Canadian Northwest. In the wake of the rebellion of 1885, Riel was tried for treason, found guilty of the crime, and hanged.

Discussion of the religious significance of Louis Riel has in recent years undergone an interpretive shift away from more traditional interpretations that seized upon his visions and discourses as evidence of insanity.[7] Focusing instead on his psychological development, some scholars of the past two decades have attempted to account for Riel's religion by locating it within a context of third world millenarian movements. There is no doubt that this work represents a refreshing shift in focus; as Thomas Flanagan noted, the problem of Riel's sanity

51

has generally diverted discussion away from the more salient question of why the man led Métis rebellions in 1869 and 1885. Flanagan suggested that the question of Riel's sanity during his trial diverted critical focus away from the issues of what actually transpired in 1885, and why it occured.[8] However, in more recent scholarship such as Flanagan's, Riel's religion remains problematic, since, by these accounts, psychological processes (e.g., role playing and sublimation) led him to what is ultimately aberrant religious behavior. Despite the fact that in this literature he has been categorized with other "messianic" figures in the colonial period, he remains situated with these other figures outside what is considered religiously normative and, perhaps more importantly, authentic; since this category is presented as one in which religious experiences and articulations are products of social, political, or psychological forces, and messianism is regarded as self-stylization and imitation: "Riel slipped into the messianic role at times, as when he styled himself the redeemer of the Jews or when he speculated on his own resurrection. But whether as prophet or messiah, he was imitating models of biblical tradition and acting in a way typical of millenarian leaders."[9]

These more recent discussions of Riel's religion as an instance of a marginal and imitative enterprise that is reducible to social or psychological factors raise a significant issue relating to the study of religion in modernity: these arguments ensure that the religious content of his visions, poetry, and the movement that spiraled around him remains significant in an ultimate (rather than purely historical) sense for only a circumscribed group of nineteenth-century people. Hence, while the uprisings and Riel's final execution cannot be extricated from the meaning—and study—of Canadian history, his visions, poetry, and the insurrections remain removed from the meaning—and study—of religion.

This failure to take serious account of the implications, for the study of religion, of both Riel and the Métis insurrections, is problematic. The content of Riel's visions and the movement that emerged around him mapped out a *total cultural and material situation*. A short digression might be useful at this point. I have loosely paraphrased here from Charles Long's discussion of cargo cults, a religious phenomenon that emerged in Melanesia following colonial contact in the late nineteenth century. The cults derived their collective name by virtue of the fact that the acquisition of European commodities featured predominantly in their mythic and ritualistic configurations, alongside a redefinition of time, and communal, ancestral, and colonial power relations. Within their mythic frameworks, the ancestral and mythic pasts were redefined in relation to the historical experience of colonization, ultimately pointing to an entirely new mode of human definition. Long suggests that the mythic structures of cargo cults constitute an attempt to

> synthesize the fragmentary forms of experience and point to a mode of conduct and behavior that will approximate not only the renewal of New Guinea culture but also the total situation of the cultural contact between New Guinea and the

Westerners—in short, through the cargo cult, the possibility of creating new human beings, neither New Guineas nor Westerners.[10]

Resonances between cargo movements and the Métis resistances are unmistakable, and will become clearer as we proceed. Viewed in concert, however, their correspondences provide persuasive evidence of a generalized interpetation of modernity emerging from colonized peoples that must be accounted for within a responsible study of religion.

Riel and the Métis were the offspring of the Canadian fur trade, the descendants predominantly of European men and aboriginal women brought together by the modern world system. Riel's visions were mystical and blatantly theological; but under-girding these features—and the uprisings themselves—were affirmations of the fundamental character of the world in which the Métis were located: a world of mercantilism and colonialism, with attendant disparities of power relations, and large-scale cultural contact and exchanges of commodities, people, languages, and ideas. It was in relation to the material structures of modernity that Riel's religion took form. I shall suggest that, for reason of this relationship, it is a serious error in respect of our understanding of both Riel and religion, to define his religion as marginal.

Riel's prophetic nature has traditionally been a troublesome issue for both historians and scholars of religion. Historical accounts of the events and meaning of the Métis uprisings of 1869 and 1885 have tended to parenthesize Riel's religious experiences, at times mentioning them only briefly, but often times ignoring them altogether.[11] When Riel's prophetic claims have received attention, he has too often been relegated to the realm of the religiously deranged;[12] and, as alluded to above, even legitimate attempts to take Riel's religion seriously have succumbed to a similar pitfall. He has emerged from this research a victim of eccentricity—a man whose "vainglorious belief in his own inspiration" disposed him to "play the role of prophet"; or who delved into things mystical as a kind of compensation and spiritual sublimation of years of failure and frustration.[13]

It is in Thomas Flanagan's *Louis "David" Riel: "Prophet of the New World"* (first published in 1979 and reprinted as a revised edition in 1996) that Riel's propheticism received the most comprehensive and charitable consideration. Due to its focused treatment of Riel's recorded visions and religious poetry, the book has been recognized by historians of the subject as "the most important recent book" on Riel.[14] According to its author, Riel could be fully understood only if he was regarded as "a spiritual figure, a would-be religious founder and millenarian prophet."[15] The book was undoubtedly a welcome addition to historical studies; however, it ultimately buttressed an established—and, I suggest, flawed—discourse about religion that obscures the significance of figures such as Riel.

On Flanagan's account, Riel's visions were a product of first, preexisting theological ideas; and second, cultural dislocation and domination. His religion provided the promise of ultimate escape from domination,[16] and was expressed as an ideational exaggeration of French Canadian Catholic theology. Catholic clergy of the period had wedded ultramontanism (recognition of the authority of the pope over that of the state) with French Canadian nationalism, maintaining a providential theory of history in which French Canada bore the responsibility of extending the Kingdom of God in North America. The notion was given coherent expression in 1866 by a book entitled *Quelques Considérations surs les rapports de la société civile avec la religion et la famille*, written by Mgr. Laflèche. Laflèche, as Flanagan pointed out, worked for a time as a missionary in the Northwest and had been one of Riel's first teachers.[17] Based upon its political promises and its theological structure, Flanagan blieved that Riel's religion could consequently be categorized with other nativistic resistance movements the world over.[18] Flanagan unfortunately ran into a problem here. Although there is no doubt that the experience of colonial domination and the presence of pre-existing theological ideas came together in Riel's vision, the man and the resistance he led did not fit neatly into the category of millenarian resistance movements, since, as Flanagan pointed out, they lacked certain key components generally associated with these movements.[19]

Still, it seems, a close fit was sufficient. Riel's religion could now be accounted for, not by insanity, but by its admittedly restricted affinity with other nativistic responses to colonial domination. His propheticism was consequently characterized as a marginal instance of a category of religion specific to what are equally, from this standpoint, ultimately marginal groups of human beings. From this perspective, a serious consideration of Riel's religion had the dual effect of, first, overlooking the specificity of the historical context of the nineteenth-century Canadian Northwest; and, second, by having located Riel's experience within an extra-normative religious category, ensuring that this experience remained peripheral to the meaning of religion.

There is much yet to be said about the religion of Louis Riel, but to do so, I submit, requires a shift in focus. Flanagan's Riel was, in the first instance, possessed of theological ideas learned from French Canadian Catholic clergy— ideas that took on an extreme disposition in a characteristically colonial context. His religion, from this perspective, was overwhelmingly a configuration of beliefs resembling those of other nativistic prophetic figures; and the nineteenth-century Northwest was, at least to some degree, reduced to a backdrop for the development of these ideas.

A significantly different interpretation can present itself if the emphasis is reversed: that is, if the material—as opposed to the ideational—structure of religion is assumed as a starting point. In the scenario this reversal presents, the specificity of the nineteenth-century Northwest becomes crucial, as the tangible arena in relation to which a religious vision is experienced and articulated. More important, perhaps, this interpretation cannot allow for the situation of Riel within marginal categories of religious normativity. Rather, there is a potential for an amplification of meaning from his particular experience that can contribute to a broader understanding of what constitutes both religious normativity and the relationship between religion and history in the colonial period.

It has been said that the strength of Thomas Flanagan's work resides in its focused exploration of the theological and philosophical ideas that informed Riel's religious experience.[20] I wish to suggest that to understand this experience more fully it may be profitable to divert our attention from the ideas Riel learned from French Catholic clergy and focus, rather, on the various material confrontations that were insinuated in his experience. Ideas can well be religious, but religion is not primarily a system of ideas. It is, in the first instance, a relational phenomenon through which human beings come to know who they are in an ultimate sense; or, as Charles Long has said, it is a "turning of the soul toward an*other* defining reality."[21] The material structure of religion rests in its relational character, and this can be discerned in both the individual and social spheres.

In his pioneering work, *Patterns in Comparative Religion*, Mircea Eliade exhaustively sought to demonstrate the way in which human consciousness evolves within an ongoing process of confrontation and negotiation with things other than the self; so that the religious imagination expresses itself in relation to the world. At root, religious consciousness is necessarily *intentional*: it is consciousness *of* something; and the religious object—or the matter—of the religious imagination can consist in virtually anything that is set apart from consciousness itself. In his foreword to the volume, Eliade suggests that although the sky, sun, moon, water, stones, and the earth all constitute primordial matter that relate directly to the beginning of awareness and consciousness, "we cannot be sure that there is anything—object, movement, psychological function, being, or even game—that has not at some time in human history" fulfilled this role.[22]

The religious significance of materiality, however, extends beyond the individual and into the social body, as Marcel Mauss's still-brilliant little book, *The Gift*, pointed out decades ago. Mauss regarded matter as the instrument of exchange; and exchange as a fundamentally defining human activity. He located the values of both exchange and matter in their capacity to facilitate human definition, since things exchanged, he wrote, exert "a magical and religious hold over the recipient."[23] Exchanges occur at boundaries, and what is conveyed across a boundary negotiates an initial incompatibility. Refusal to enter into this reciprocal process with another human being is, in essence, a refusal to acknowledge the boundary and, consequently, to recognize the meaningful presence of that person.

It is through the experience and the exchange of matter that individuals and communities come to understand—and sustain a sense of—their fundamental meaning. The idea that the structure of the world and the structure of consciousness are enmeshed in one another—that there is, in Charles Long's words again, a "religious imagination of matter" in consciousness[24]—has unfortunately been afforded too little attention in our discourses about religion. In order to explore the possibility, scholars like Eliade and Mauss had to look to the realm of the archaic, but in so doing, they allowed for the discussion to remain comfortably distant from our scholarly conversations about religion and the West. These conversations have generally owed their form to the Enlightenment, an arena in which—from Descartes's *cogito* to Kant's *a priori* mathematical judgments[25]— the world in extension was prevented from entering into constructions of the self. This negation of the material structure of the self—which curiously occurred at a historical juncture at which European mercantilism was leading the world into a period of unmatched exchanges of matter—definitively shaped the modern study of religion. The enlightenment effectively disenchanted the world; and those human beings who retained an intimate relationship with the world have been generally relegated by scholars to the realm of the *primitive*. From this vantage point, the Western human being and our intellectual discourses have been free to reside in a period marked by unprecedented exchanges between cultures, without acknowledging an impact of matter, or its exchange, on the construction of the self.

As a consequence of this Teflon conception of the self in relation to the world, there has been a general failure to take serious account of the religious significance of colonialism and, as a result, figures like Riel have remained problematic. For scholars who have sought to understand the historical significance of the Red River rebellions, Riel's propheticism has generally been afforded little attention; and, again, those who have sought to understand Riel himself have been compelled to place him in a category of, at best, the religiously marginal, and at worst, the misguided, the deranged, or to quote the historian of religion Joachim Wach, the "sick-minded."[26] Clearly, however, the historical significance of the Riel rebellions and the man himself are inseparable and, further, a clearer understanding of this significance requires an interpretation of Riel that courts the possibility that his experience was religiously normative. Riel should be considered within a discourse about human constitution that is situated firmly within the colonial period. The discussion of religion must begin with the materiality of the colonial period—considering the possibility that commodities (the most intense form of matter in the world since the sixteenth century), colonized bodies, and the exchanges that have defined the period are related to religious consciousness.

The issues of Métis land loss and dislocation in the nineteenth century were neither simply economic nor political problems. Neither was Riel an anomalous madman nor a pseudoprophet who, by coincidence, crossed paths with a politically disenchanted community. Rather, the conjuncture of this figure and a revolutionary movement points to an exfoliation of meaning that transformed the uprisings from a purely political and economic problem to one that was religious. Eastern Canadian movement westward, mapping of the Northwest, the disappearance of the buffalo, the emergence of an agriculturally based economy, and rebellion itself were political and economic events that impacted overwhelmingly on the meaning of the Métis. They signaled a breakdown in exchange, a negation by Upper Canadians of the significance of the Métis community, and, consequently, a reimagining of meaning that both Riel and rebellion signified. In the end, Western expansion created a religious crisis within which politics and economics figured.

The nineteenth-century Northwest underwent a relatively rapid transformation through which the Métis were stripped of their central position in the fur trade and relegated to the peripheries of an agricultural economy. The Hudson's Bay Company had founded the Red River settlement early in the century to supply its expanding network of posts with provisions. The settlers, however, were unable to provide even for their own needs and came to rely substantially on provisions supplied by the Métis buffalo hunt.[27] As exploiting the West, and creating a nation that spanned from sea to sea, became viable options for eastern Canada, the area was purchased by the Dominion from the Hudson's Bay Company. A petition written to U. S. President Ulysses S. Grant by Riel shortly after the sale expressed the rage of the Métis:

> [We learned] through the public press, our only medium, that we had been sold by a company of adventurers residing in London, England, with our lands, rights and liberties as so much merchandise to a foreign government; and further [learned] through the same medium, the press, that the Parliament of the Dominion of Canada had organized a Government for Our country, as if it had jurisdiction over us, and that we were to have no voice in the Government, and that a Governor appointed to rule over us, clothed with almost despotic power had started from Canada en route to our country, accompanied by a band of unscrupulous and irresponsible followers, who were to form his Council . . . and thus plunder and eat out our subsistence.[28]

In the end, the sale did indeed have much of the effect that Riel had anticipated. The significance of the Métis buffalo hunt faded briskly after the transfer of title in 1869. Métis land holdings were disregarded by initial government mapping, and although the Dominion afforded the Métis some legal protection following the uprising of 1869, it proved inadequate as settlers inundated the region, encouraged by the Canadian government and groups such as the North-West Emigration Aid Society (which had urged settlers of British descent to colonize the region in 1870, in order to undermine Riel and his provisional government). The Métis were forced westward in search of land and buffalo, restrictions were placed on the hunt in 1877, and American hunters subsequently decimated the herds. Any remaining buffalo roamed southward as increasing numbers of settlers followed an expanding infrastructure of telegraph and railroad lines.[29]

What occurred at Red River during this period was a complete disruption of exchange between the Métis and colonial Canada. During the fur trade period, the Métis were regarded as critical participants in a tenuous economy, but as the period ended they were not only stripped of this status but were essentially rendered invisible. Their presence was disregarded as the land was mapped, as though they did not exist; and when they petitioned the Canadian Government for recognition of land claims they were ignored. In order to enter an altered economic structure, they then requested that the Dominion proffer initial assistance to Métis who wished to engage in agriculture and commerce: "We ask the government to set apart a portion of land," wrote Louis Riel, "as a special reservation in this territory for the [Métis], as, scattered amongst other settlers, it becomes a very difficult matter for us to make a living and owing to our present limited means and want of experience in economy, we cannot compete with the majority of our fellow countrymen."[30]

Requests like these were also ignored.[31] The Canadian government and the colonial population refused to acknowledge the presence of Métis bodies on prairie land and, by rendering it virtually impossible for the Métis to take part in the exchange of commodities in the region, ensured that no form of reciprocal relationship could emerge. The refusal to enter into any form of exchange with the Métis constituted an unwillingness to acknowledge their significance as human beings.

The religious task for the Métis was to forge, within a historical context of oppression, a new meaning of the human that could negate those meanings explicit in the experience of being rendered invisible. New humans, in some manner, needed to come into existence. In other words, the structure of the world had altered sufficiently to cause an alteration in the structure of human constitution.

The visions of Louis Riel and the uprisings he led were arenas in which this religious transformation was articulated. As Riel recalled in his correspondences, he was visited by the Holy Spirit and informed that he was, "le David des temps chrétiens," [32] an embodiment of the biblical King David chosen by God to bring about an extensive reconstruction of the Church and of Canadian society (in his diaries written during the rebellion of 1885, Riel referred to the Northwest Mounted Police as "Goliath").[33] The result of this reconstruction was to have both practical and cosmic implications, altering the basic structures of Canadian society and global power, as well as bringing to fruition the prophesies of the four kingdoms Riel had discovered in his reading of the Book of Daniel. In the biblical text, Daniel predicts the successive emergence and disintegration of four worldly empires, to be followed ultimately by one that is divinely instituted and interminable. Riel was afforded a vision of four kingdoms, the last of which (the British colonial empire) was to fall immediately prior to the emergence of a fifth; Riel was divinely charged to bring this last kingdom into being. "The four great empires," wrote Riel, "of Mahomet, of Photius, of Luther, and of the English colossus have appeared before my eyes like the four sparks of light you might see from four fireflies lost in the night."[34] Unlike Daniel, who identified the four earthly kingdoms as beginning with that of Nebuchadnezzar,

Riel reported a vision that specified Mohammed's Islamic empire as the first, Byzantine Christian Europe as the second (Photius, c. 820-891, was principally responsible for the expansion of medieval Byzantine Christianity, and the schism that occurred between the Eastern and Western churches), Europe of the Protestant Reformation as the third, and colonial England as the last.

The earthly society envisioned by God was to take account of the irreversibility of the colonial experience; rather than promoting a return to a previous period, a new kind of human being and community were to come into being. Riel expressed this new creation in personal terms in a poem written while he was a patient at Beauport Asylum, in which he claimed to have already received "a second birth," through which he "took the great cross, the yoke of obedience."[35] This second birth, however, had much wider repercussions. In respect to the church, Riel foresaw the emergence of what he called a new "religious order" to which all New World Catholics who recognized his revelation as authentic (Riel called these the "Catholics of Mount Royal), "the Episcopalian Catholics," he said, "the Methodist Catholics, the Lutheran Catholics, the Universalist Catholics, etc.—all according to their own faith will belong."[36] In respect of the ethnic composition of the New World, Riel anticipated an even more dramatic alteration: "Ainsi toute la sauvage de l'Amérique du Nord ferait place à une race Métisse, qui varierait selon les pays,"[37] wrote Riel [Thus all Native North Americans will make a place for the Métis race, which will vary in all parts of the country]. In Riel's visions, aboriginal people, Métis, French Canadians, and European immigrants were to ethnically merge, creating an absolutely "new race" of human beings. In his diaries, Riel ascribed moral and religious superlatives to these various ethnic groups: "the religious Irish, the pious Bavarians, the faithful Poles, the wise Italians, the sincere Belgians, the intelligent *Canadiens*, the intrepid and good French and the hardworking and docile Scandinavians . . . ." while English Canadians were left noticeably absent from both moral description and the ethnic formation of this new being.[38] The border created by English Canadians between Canada and the United States was to disappear,[39] and God was planning to travel the length of the Mississippi in order to strike down any whites who had failed to do penance for holding slaves. Christ's spirit was to "shatter all British possessions"; and Edinburgh, London, and Liverpool were to "plunge into the ocean and disappear . . . sink to the bottom of the water."[40] Along with all these changes—the creation of a new church, the dissolution of ethnic delineations, the end of the British colonial empire, and the negation of the Dominion's boundaries—Riel was informed that hell itself would also disappear.[41] In the meantime, Riel would pray: "O Virgin Mary, Tower of Ivory . . . plead with Jesus Christ that it may please Him to strike fear, dread, and terror into the heart[s] . . . of all French Canadian Bishops, of the whole Roman curia, and of the entire British royal court."[42]

Riel was told that he was to "introduce necessary changes into religion, science, politics, and letters,"[43] and for this charge, God had given him "a genius much greater than that of Mahomet" so that he could "found a religion and empires more famous than his."[44] He was to be the prophet of the New World, a vehicle through which God's voice would be heard in America for the first time,[45] revealing "more to the New World than he had judged appropriate to reveal to the Old."[46] Employing a very new metaphor, Riel described his role in transmitting God's voice in the following manner:

> When I speak to you it is the voice of God who is ringing
> And everything that I say to you is essential.
> I am the joyous telephone
> Who transmits to you the songs and discourses of heaven. [47]

The rebellions that Riel led were means by which to force the Canadian government to acknowledge the material and consequential presence of the Métis within the colonial landscape; and they were motivated by a religious understanding of who the Métis were in relation to a power (God) that transcended colonial power in the New World. As Riel pointed out in his closing remarks at his trial: "God cannot create a tribe without locating it. We are not birds. We have to walk on the ground."[48]

Riel and his compatriots shared an unfailing certainty about the veracity of this transcendent relationship. Flanagan noted that Riel apparently firmly believed that God would ultimately ensure Métis victory in all the battles that were fought during the rebellion; and he consequently spent his time in prayer rather than taking up arms himself at the battles of Duck Lake, Fish Creek, and Batouche. This was most striking at the battle of Batouche in particular, where the Métis were decisively defeated in 1885, and where Riel prayed continually and led the women in reciting the rosary. He believed throughout the battle that a miracle would occur, as did the soldiers fighting around him. A man by the name of Patrice Tourond is recorded as having called out to Riel toward the end of the battle, "Work your miracle now, it's time." Arms lifted in the sign of the cross, Riel fell to his knees and directed those around him: "All together, let us say three times, very loudly, 'My God, have pity on us.'" The others knelt and did as he'd instructed while Riel, arms held up by two Métis soldiers, cried out, "My God, stop those people, crush them."[49]

Both Riel's visions and the act of rebellion can be regarded as forms of discourse about relationships and mutual recognition. The particular ethnic diversity of the New World, the need for reciprocal relationships, and the knowledge that identity had been altered by colonialism were inescapable for Riel. English Canada seemed incapable of recognizing these facts; and so Riel and the Métis attempted, through political discourse initially and subsequently through rebellion, to bring this knowledge to the Dominion's attention. The shift from discourse to physical violence was precipitated by Riel's directive to execute a Canadian prisoner, Thomas Scott, on March 4, 1870; and Riel clearly regarded the move as a necessary act intended to secure Canadian recognition of the Métis. A number of Riel's colleagues, among them Donald Smith, advised against carrying out the execution of Scott (a man described by contemporaries as so "violent and boisterous" that his fellow prisoners had requested to be removed from his company). Smith believed that bloodless negotiations with the Canadian government should be sustained, but Riel refused to rescind the execution order, apparently believing that a flagrant act of sovereignty on the part of his regime would compel the Canadian government into authentic negotiations with the Métis. Despite the fact that Riel is generally considered to have been militarily inept due to his aversion to violent confrontation,[50] he nonetheless believed that a dramatic expression of autonomous authority would force the Dominion to take serious note of the Métis—that the government held regard for those capable of violence: "we *must* make Canada respect us," he reportedly told Smith.[51]

The reality of colonial contact was that an unprecedented number of different kinds of people had gathered in the Northwest, and that dominant Upper Canadian whites appeared intent upon rendering others invisible. Transcendence of ethnic lines figured substantially in Riel's visions; and, not incidentally, support for his leadership did the same. In 1884, Riel was persuaded to leave Montana (where he was teaching native children at a Jesuit mission) and return to the Northwest in order to rally the support of the Métis in joining a settler's union formed at Prince Albert to press for government reform. The four-man delegation that succeeded in securing Riel's return represented not only Métis, but also English mixed-blood peoples and disgruntled white settlers.[52] Louis Riel could not ignore this reality, and was he compelled through his visions to imagine a new meaning of the colonial human that was situated within historical experience while being capable of negating the human devaluation the Métis (as well as other members of his community) were forced to undergo. Ultimately, he demonstrated a religious imagination of matter in consciousness, as he testified to the way in which bodies, land, commodities, and knowledge were specifically tied to conceptions of human meaning and the experience of God.

Conclusion

The material structure of Riel's religious vision points to the need, within the study of religion in modernity, to afford serious consideration to the relationships (both conflicted and cooperative) of the colonial period. It is not sufficient to locate existing categories (e.g., third world millenarian movements) within established discourses in which to situate figures like Riel if, repeatedly, the categories do not contain them. We must finally consider the possibility that this limitation points to a problem with the way in which religion has been understood, rather than with the figures themselves.

The matter that underlays Riel's visions (land, bodies, commodities) raises the problems of exchange, of reciprocity, and of identity in an ultimate sense;

and the resolution of these problems, according to Riel, was a "sacred cause."[53] "The spirit of God showed me the upper road," wrote Riel in his diaries. "It is open, it is clear, it is wide. . . . It is also the heavenly route which leads the souls of those whom the Lord has chosen on the battlefield to Paradise."[54] The sacred character of violent resistance was made clear when, on the eve of the Northwest Rebellion, Riel and ten of his closest associates drafted and signed the following oath:

> We, the undersigned, pledge ourselves deliberately and voluntarily to do everything we can to:
> 1 save our souls by trying day and night to live a holy life everywhere and in all respects.
> 2 save our country from a wicked government by taking up arms if necessary.[55]

The issues of exchange, of reciprocity, and of ultimate notions of identity are not unique to the Red River Métis. The colonial and postcolonial periods are defined by unprecedented global exchanges of matter, and these have impacted indelibly on the ways in which communities have sought to sustain a sense of their most basic meaning. This has undoubtedly been an era of religious crisis. A study of religion that is located within this period, but does not take seriously the religious significance of matter and reciprocity, courts not only the possibility of undermining its own efficacy, but of contributing discursively to the propagation of the sort of cultural imbalances out of which this crisis initially emerged. In the end, those who trade in knowledge must confront the limitations of a postcolonial discourse that disregards the impact of land, commodities, colonial bodies, and their exchange on human meaning since 1492. In a sense, the conversation about religion—in order to accurately reflect the reality and absorb the meaning of the crisis out of which it was born—might be well served to regard the knowledge in which it trades as matter and its language as a form of exchange. The alternative is to continue, like the Dominion government, to map territory as though the human beings who inhabit it simply are not there.

Notes

I wish to thank Kristin McLaren for her assistance in the preparation of this chapter; and David Carrasco, for his insightful critique of the initial presentation on which the chapter is based.

    1. The site of present-day Winnipeg.

    2. According to the *Encyclopedia Canadiana*, vol. 7 (Toronto: Grolier, 1968), 53, the term derives of the same Latin root (*miscere*) as the Spanish word *mestizo*, meaning "to

mix." Its original form was *matives*, and was altered to *métifs* before assuming its final form. Riel himself employed *métisse*.

3. Thomas Flanagan, *The Diaries of Louis Riel* (Edmonton, Alberta: Hurtig Publishers, 1976), 3.

4. Taché was appointed archbishop of St. Boniface in 1871.

5. Flanagan, *Louis "David" Riel: "Prophet of the New World,"* revised edition (Toronto: University of Toronto Press, 1996), 9.

6. These are generally referred to as the Red River Insurrection of 1869, and the Northwest Rebellion of 1885.

7. Flanagan, *The Diaries of Louis Riel*; Manfred Mossman, "The Charismatic Pattern: Canada's Riel Rebellion of 1885 as a Millenarian Protest Movement," *Prairie Forum* 10 (1985): 307-25; and Gilles Martel, *Le Messianisme de Louis Riel* (Waterloo, Ontario: Wilfred Laurier University Press, 1984); Gilles Martel, "L'idéologie messianique de Louis Riel et ses determinants sociaux," *Transactions of the Royal Society of Canada,* series 5, no. 1 (1986): 229-38.

8. Flanagan added: "To focus on those questions requires moral judgment. . . . The issues remain the same today. Those who ask whether Riel was 'really crazy' are in effect looking for a way out of this moral dilemma." Thomas Flanagan, "Louis Riel: Was He Really Crazy?" in *1885 and After: Native Society in Transition,* ed. Laurie Barron and James B. Waldram (Regina, Saskatchewan: University of Regina, 1986), 115.

9. In respect of the reductionist approach, Flanagan, *Louis "David" Riel*, 201, offers the following explanation for millenarian resistance movements: "This general setting [the nineteenth-century Canadian Northwest] is identical to the situation in which millenarian movements have arisen among colonized peoples around the globe. The pursuit of the millennium is activated by the threat of destruction to a people's way of life by forces over which they have no control. When the natives see the collapse of the world they have always known, they become susceptible to promises of a new world to come. . . . The movements themselves are often triggered by immediate events that bring matters to a head. Common causes have been war, famine, drought, plague, or other natural calamities." The latter issue of the authenticity of religious experience in this context is raised on page 203.

10. Charles H. Long, *Significations: Signs, Symbols, and Images in the Interpretation of Religion* (Aurora, Colo.: Davies Group, 1999), 135.

11. See, for instance, Olive Dickason, *Canada's First Nations: A History of Founding Peoples from Earliest Times* (Toronto: McClelland and Stewart, 1992), 306, 309. Dickason deals extensively with the rebellions, but refers only twice to Riel's religious significance: "In 1869-70, Riel and the Catholic Church worked closely together; in 1885 there was estrangement, particularly when Riel proposed reforming the Church and creating Ignace Bourget, Bishop of Montreal, 1840-76, as 'Pope of the World'"; and "Riel's relations with Father Alexis André were already strained, and he was beginning to set himself up as a prophet." See also Eric R. Wolf, *Europe and People Without History* (Berkeley: University of California Press, 1982), 182; Frits Pannekoek, *A Snug Little Flock: The Social Origins of the Riel Resistance, 1869-1870* (Winnipeg: Watson and Dwyer, 1991); David Boisvert and Keith Turnbull, "Who Are the Métis?" *Studies in Political Economy* 18 (Autumn 1985): 107-48.

12. See, for instance, H. Bowsfield, ed., *Louis Riel: Rebel of the Western Frontier or Victim of Politics and Prejudice?* (Toronto: Copp Clark Publishing, 1969), 131; and J. R.

Miller, *Skyscrapers Hide the Heavens: A History of Indian-White Relations in Canada* (Toronto: University of Toronto Press, 1989), 178, 186.

13. Flanagan, *The Diaries of Louis Riel*, 18, for instance, writes: "Riel's charisma flowed from the sublimation of his personal ambition into his chosen role as the selfless incarnation of Métis nationalism and the humble instrument of God's will." See also Flanagan, "Louis Riel: Was He Really Crazy?" 116-17; and Martel, *Le Messianisme*.

14. Desmond Morton, "Reflections on the Image of Louis Riel a Century After," in *Images of Louis Riel in Canadian Culture*, ed. Ramon Hathorn and Patrick Holland (Lewiston, N.Y.: The Edwin Mellen Press, 1992), 47-92, 56.

15. Flanagan, *Louis "David" Riel*, xi.

16. Flanagan, *Louis "David" Riel*, 201.

17. See Flanagan, *Louis "David" Riel*, 45-47, 89. Flanagan, 198, also suggested that contemporary Protestant millenarian movements in the United States, such as the Millerites, Seventh-Day Adventists, and Mormons, may have influenced Riel.

18. Flanagan, *Louis "David" Riel*, 197-98, 204, referred for comparative purposes to Vittorio Lanternari's now classic *Religions of the Oppressed: A Study of Modern Messianic Cults*, trans. Lisa Sergio (New York: Alfred A. Knopf, 1963), which is a compendium of hundreds of nativistic movements recorded from the sixteenth century onward; and Michael Ada's *Prophets of Rebellion* (Chapel Hill: University of North Carolina Press, 1979), which explored the presence of such movements in Burma and New Zealand. A discussion of the similarity between Riel and the cases reported by Ada appears in Mossman, "The Charismatic Pattern; and Flanagan, *Louis 'David' Riel*, 229, n. 6.

19. Riel's visions lacked, for instance, a visibly 'syncretic' component that Flanagan deemed significant in discussion of these movements, as well as the tendency for nativistic movements to engage in a glorification of the past. Flanagan, *Louis "David" Riel*, 198, 203-04.

20. Morton, "Reflections on the Image of Louis Riel," 56, contends that Flanagan's work is "the most important recent book about [Riel] . . . combin[ing] the best of Catholic theological and philosophical training with an outsider's objectivity to treat seriously the religious writings and reflections which plainly were Riel's prime concern in the second half of his life. Religion, not politics, had become Riel's central passion."

21. Charles H. Long, "Passage and Prayer: The Origin of Religion in the Atlantic World," in *The Courage to Hope: From Black Suffering to Human Redemption*, ed. Quinton Hosford Dixie and Cornel West (Boston: Beacon, 1999), 14 (my italics). For other similar discussions of the meaning of religion, see Charles H. Long, "Silence and Signification: A Note on Religion and Modernity," in *Myth and Symbol: Studies in Honor of Mircea Eliade*, ed. Joseph M. Kitagawa and Charles H. Long (Chicago: University of Chicago Press), 1969, 141-50; Catherine Albenese, *America: Religions and Religion* (Belmont, Calif.: Wadsworth), 1981, 3-9; Jonathan Z. Smith, *Map Is Not Territory: Studies in the History of Religions* (Leiden: E. J. Brill, 1978), 291; and Sam Gill, *Native American Religious Action* (Columbia: University of South Carolina Press, 1987), 153.

22. Mircea Eliade, *Patterns in Comparative Religion*, trans. Rosemary Sheed (Lincoln: University of Nebraska Press, 1999).

23. Marcel Mauss, *The Gift: Forms and Functions of Exchange in Archaic Societies* (New York: W. W. Norton, 1967), 10.

24. The phrase "religious imagination of matter" is a phrase that Charles H. Long has used extensively. I find it a most succinct way of articulating this relationship.

25. Both primary and secondary qualities such as height, weight, and color were excluded from the construction of the self by Descartes's reflection on the cogito; and with Kant, even a priori mathematical judgments no longer directly correlated with the world prior to experience.

26. Joachim Wach, *Essays in the History of Religions*, ed. Joseph P. Kitagawa and Gregory D. Alles (New York: Macmillan, 1988), 166.

27. See George Herman Sprenger, "The Métis Nation: Buffalo Hunting Versus Agriculture in the Red River Settlement, 1810-1870," in *Native People, Native Lands: Canadian Indians, Inuit, and Métis*, ed. Bruce Alden Cox (Ottawa: Carleton University Press, 1988), 122ff.

28. Louis Riel, *The Collected Writings of Louis Riel/Les ecrits complets de Louis Riel*, 5 volumes, ed. George F. G. Stanley, Raymond Huel, Gilles Martel, Thomas Flanagan, Glen Campbell, and Claude Rocan (Edmonton: University of Alberta Press, 1985), vol. 3, 12. See also Maggie Siggins, *Riel: A Life of Revolution* (Toronto: Harper-Collins, 1994), 101.

29. See Jennifer S. H. Brown, "The Métis: Genesis and Rebirth," in *Native People, Native Lands: Canadian Indians, Inuit, and Métis*, ed. Bruce Alden Cox (Ottawa: Carleton University Press, 1988), 141; Thomas Flanagan, "The Political Thought of Louis Riel," in *Riel and the Métis: Riel Mini-Conference Papers*, ed. A. S. Lussier (Winnipeg: Manitoba Métis Federation Press, 1979), 122; Mossman, "The Charismatic Pattern," 309; and Mason Wade, "A Sequel to 1869," in Bowsfield, *Louis Riel*, 123.

30. From Riel, *Collected Writings*, vol. 4; cited in Pannekoek, *A Snug Little Flock*, 4.

31. Wade, "A Sequel to 1869," 123.

32. "Tu es le David des temps chrétiens dont l'ancien David n'était que la figure." Lettre à Ignace Bourget, May 1, 1876 in Riel, *Collected Writings*, vol. 2, 44.

33. Flanagan, *The Diaries of Louis Riel*, 68.

34. Riel, *Collected Writings*, vol. 2, 41, 1876-1877.

35. "Une seconde naissance,/J'ai pris la grande croix, le joug d'obéissance." Riel, *Collected Writings*, vol. 4, 66.

36. Riel, *Collected Writings*, vol. 2, 77. See also Thomas Flanagan, "On the Trail of the Massinahican: Riel's Encounter with Theosophy," *Journal of the Canadian Church Historical Society* 37 (1995), 89-98, 90.

37. Martel, *Le Messianisme*, 195; and "L'idéologie messianique," 236.

38. Flanagan, "The Political Thought of Louis Riel," 143-44; *The Diaries of Louis Riel*, 52.

39. Bowsfield, *Louis Riel*, 179.

40. Riel, *Collected Writings*, vol. 2, 41; Flanagan, *Louis "David" Riel*," 100-01.

41. Bowsfield, *Louis Riel*, 179.

42. Riel, *Collected Writings*, vol. 2, 40. See also Flanagan, "On the Trail of the Massinahican," 89.

43. Riel, *Collected Writings*, vol. 2, 176, 178. See also Flanagan, "On the Trail of the Massinahican," 90.

44. Riel, *Collected Writings*, vol. 2, 176. See also Flanagan, *Louis Louis "David" Riel*," 126.

45. Riel, *Collected Writings*, vol. 2, 984. See also Flanagan, *Louis "David" Riel*, 85.

46. Flanagan, *Louis "David" Riel*, 173. The quote is taken from Louis Schmidt, "Notes," Archives of the Archdiocese of St. Boniface.

47. Quand je vous parle, c'est la voix de Dieu qui sonne/Et tout ce que je dis vous est essentiel./Je suis le joyeux telephone/Qui vous transmet les chants et les discours du ciel. Riel, *Collected Writings*, vol. 4, 65. See also Flanagan, *Louis "David" Riel*, 84-5.

48. Riel, *Collected Writings*, vol. 3, 547 (n.13). See also Siggins, *Riel*, 433.

49. Statement of Elie Dumont, Cloutier Notebooks, Archive of the Archdiocese of St. Boniface. Cited in Flanagan, *Louis "David" Riel*, 157, 204.

50. Flanagan, *The Diaries of Louis Riel*, 15. During the Northwest Rebellion, for instance, Riel wrote in his diaries: "Oh, how hard it is to wage war. O my God! Guide me, help me in war that I may have the good fortune to conclude a peace in accord with your intentions, and honourable peace before God and men." See Flanagan, *The Diaries of Louis Riel*, 77.

51. Flanagan, *Louis "David" Riel*, 33; and J. M. Bumsted, "Crisis at Red River," *The Beaver* 75, no. 3 (June/July 1995): 23-34, 25 (my italics).

52. Flanagan, *The Diaries of Louis Riel*, 13; *Louis "David" Riel*, 136; and J. M. Bumsted, "Louis Riel and the United States," *The American Review of Canadian Studies* (Spring, 1999): 31.

53. From Riel's statement on the subject of his sanity, made to a Quebec doctor at the time of his discharge from Beauport Asylum, January 23, 1878. Cited in Flanagan, *Louis "David" Riel*, 78.

54. Flanagan, *The Diaries of Louis Riel*, 71.

55. Riel, *Collected Writings*, vol. 3, 194. See also Flanagan, *The Diaries of Louis Riel*, 54.

5

Mthunzini (A Place in the Shade): Religion and the Heat of Globalization

Chirevo V. Kwenda

This chapter explores meanings of religion by examining two uncanny coincidences. First, there is the coincidence of the metaphor "a place in the sun" with the reality of a planet that is literally and materially in the sun in a very special way. The second coincidence is that of the perennial human fascination with the sun, which spawned the place-in-the-sun metaphor in the first place with the equally human quest for mystical union with the divine. These two sets of coincidences may be said to constitute one orientation in the world—that of uninhibited desire to penetrate and consume the inner mysteries of all things. In the course of this study an alternative orientation is explored and juxtaposed to the first. Issuing forth as it does from the symbolic world of the heat-coolness dichotomy that imbues many African thought systems, it can be captured in the metaphoric formula "a place in the shade." This chapter suggests that adoption of this latter metaphor affirms an alternative human orientation in the world and inaugurates an alternative meaning of religion.

Sites of Coincidence

In 1999 Ali Mazrui published an essay titled "From Slave Ship to Space Ship: Africa between Marginalization and Globalization." Later, I take a look at what he has to say about globalization. Presently my interest is in his use of coincidence to frame his discussion of the topic. When early in the essay he describes as a coincidence the link between the essay's title and Senator John Glenn's 1998 return excursion into space, he is neither treating the coincidence as a matter of indifference nor dismissing it as meaningless. In fact this coincidence may very well be the cornerstone of his argument. Mazrui himself underscores this conclusion by drawing our attention to yet another coincidence—that of Walter Rodney's stay in Tanzania with the "promulgation and aftermath of the 'Arusha Declaration on Socialism and Self-Reliance.'" Coincidences have meanings; they invite interpretation. And Mazrui does interpret the coincidences he cites in his essay, though without formally stating his method.

In case one lone example is not sufficient to establish a methodological approach, let me give a second example. If the first example comes from academe, the second is of a popular pedigree. My late father once told me that the visit of King George VI to Zimbabwe (then Southern Rhodesia) in 1947 became the occasion for an interesting revelation. Rev. Matthew Zvimba, a creative individual with a sharp wit, founder of the Church of the Original White Bird—a breakaway from the Wesleyan Methodist Church—and generally a pain in the neck for the colonial settler administration, insisted on being included in the welcoming motorcade, representing his father, Chief Zvimba.[1] The Chief Native Commissioner (CNC) retorted that Zvimba's old truck, with its torn canvas flapping in the wind and a backfiring engine to match, was to be seen nowhere near the royal motorcade. Zvimba went out, then came back with a sparkle in his eye. He pointed out to the CNC that the visiting king was George VI, just as the incumbent Chief Zvimba was Zvimba VI. Exhorting the CNC to work out the significance of the coincidence, he trudged out triumphantly. The CNC must have worked it out without delay, for within days Zvimba received an invitation to join the motorcade, in his old truck—torn canvas, backfiring engine and all.[2] If to the CNC the chief's argument was based on *mere coincidence*, it was not so to Rev. Zvimba. For the cleric the apparent coincidence was fraught with meaning; it was something to be interpreted. At any rate, it was a site or an occasion for the work of interpretation.

I have taken a methodological cue both from Rev. Zvimba and Professor Mazrui. Instead of trying to establish causal linkages between the metaphor "a place in the sun" and certain materialities, such as the threat the sun in this age poses to the planet earth and its denizens, which is a significant feature of globalization, I shall only point to the coincidence of the two, leaving the declaration of a causal link either to a moment of greater confidence or to disciplines with bolder methodologies.

Metaphor as Product (and Producer?) of Consciousness

It should not be too hard to see that metaphor is a product of consciousness. Put more succinctly, as producers of consciousness, historical processes create the metaphors by which we think and with which we apprehend reality.[3] What may not be as obvious is whether the reverse is also true. That is whether our metaphors produce wholly or in part certain types of consciousness in us. In other words, are certain of our habits of thought and, consequently action, products of certain metaphors that pervade and color our cultures? It is this very probability that is behind the age-old animosity toward rhetoric among some thinkers. For our more limited purpose the question might be: While we could trace the historical genesis of the metaphor "a place in the sun" to a cultural locus, could we likewise attribute certain contemporary cultural phenomena to the mass internalization and cultural exfoliation of this metaphor?

It is tempting to declare discovery of causal links in this regard. But in order to avoid the detraction such a move inevitably entails we shall take the safer route of coincidence. This is chosen in preference to analogy or homology, both of which already state too much in terms of correspondences. Such strictures would no doubt diminish our interpretive leverage. Coincidence allows us to juxtapose situations, statements or events and discuss them in a manner that creates a certain flexible ambience or atmosphere of understanding. We do not need to (in fact we should not) draw lines of correspondence between the points of discussion. We may, and indeed should, draw lines from such situations to a common meeting point, which may be a text that needs to be interpreted, or a problem that needs to be solved.

In this case I shall make certain statements and conduct some discussions about the place-in-the-sun metaphor, the spirituality of union with the sacred, the spirituality of distance from the sacred, and other issues, and then bring these over to the point where religion and globalization intersect. This will allow us to ask questions about significance and meaning of both religion and globalization in themselves, in juxtaposition, and in intersection.

Place in the Sun

Theo Witvliet, writing an introduction to Third World theologies in the 1980s, titled his book *A Place in the Sun.* He was invoking what in the English-speaking world has evolved into a popular metaphor for the quest of the good life. Not just any good life, of course, but the good life according to Wall Street, Madison Avenue, and Hollywood. The message of the book is that liberation theologies in the Third World are theological articulations of Third World peoples' aspirations to have their share of the world's economic pie. In Africa today this quest is being given voice and content by the contemporary prosperity gospel of the new Pentecostalism that is sweeping the continent like a tidal wave.[4] According to this gospel, material wealth is a sign of God's blessing on the person who possesses it. At the same time it is this quest that drives the policies and programs of governments as well as the strategies of the business sector and the visions of nongovernmental organizations and civil society. In this, Africa is only trying to be like the rest of the world. It is pursuing a global quest.

While the extratropical preoccupation with heating and staying warm localizes the metaphor's genesis in a specific physical geography and cultural history, there can be no disputing the near universality of the bliss of basking in the sun. Even those from the tropics know of this fundamental joy, and have vernacular expressions of it. The Shona people of Zimbabwe call this mode of the sun *mushana*, and basking in the sun is to be *pamushana*. In this mode neither is the sun hot nor the air cold. It is pleasantly warm, or even slightly cool. Although mushana and pamushana would make fine names for children, male or female, I know of no one who bears such a name. There is a school, though, in the rural southeast of the country, called Mushana Mission.

The story is quite different with the opposite of pamushana. *Pazuva* or *Muzuva*, which means in the sun (as in, in the year of the sun, i.e., drought), are common names. But only for boys, and never for girls. I don't know why this is so. No one runs workshops on what names are appropriate for what sex. Neither are there sourcebooks of names from which to draw. People just know. It is coded in the culture and taken up by one generation from another. Maybe it is one of those coincidences that most Africans would see as bearing religious significance, and may invite interpretation. On the one hand the giving of historically significant names to males may be seen as just one more indication of male dominance of history. A purely religious explanation, on the other hand, could readily show how easy it is, in sunbathed Africa, to be ambivalent about the sun. In one complex moment its life-giving attributes are celebrated, while at the same time there is decrying of its association with dryness, bones, and drought, all symbolic markers of masculinity, virility, and death. Thus it would be a contradiction, if not contravention of cosmic order, to associate a female of childbearing potential with dryness and the forces of death. In fact, it would be a bad omen. It would be tantamount to casting a curse on the girl.

Thus apart from it being a misplaced metaphor in the tropics, "a place in the sun" can have ominous connotations when viewed from an indigenous southern African religious perspective. It must be emphasized again, though, that this is a one-sided and oversimplified view of the sun. We must not forget that for millennia the sun in its dazzling splendor was truly *mysterium tremendum et fascinosum* and widely compelled worship among humans.[5] Indeed the preeminence accorded sky gods everywhere may, in part at least, stem from association in one form or another with the sun, or the sky as the abode of the sun. In secular matters, the importance of the sun in the generation and sustenance of life is not lost on Africans. They know that seeds need the sun to germinate, and plants need the sun to grow. However, as we saw among the Shona, mushana is the best mode of the sun for humans.

Place in the Sun as Cultural and Religious Orientation

Were it universally known and applied as such, the metaphor "a place in the sun" would have meant different things to different people in a plethora of contexts and at different times in history. It would have conjured up different things to roving hunter-gatherers than to sedentary agrarians or nomadic pastoral hordes. It certainly would have meant one thing to denizens of citied agricultural civilizations and quite another to the different social strata of hegemonic imperial regimes. However, it is in the industrial capitalist civilization of modernity that this metaphor truly fits, and probably had its origin. Its very emergence suggests its opposite—a place in the cold that, in extra-tropical regions, must strike terror in the hearts of the poor who cannot afford heating. It is a function of the exclusionary manner in which the sacred space of the modern "place in the sun" is occupied that racial, ethnic, class, and gendered voices ceaselessly clamor to be heard.

This is not exactly a cordial, much less a familial, metaphor, it seems. In fact there is a definite air of belligerence about it, something suggestive of force and violence as means in the pursuit of this goal. A 1951 movie starring Elizabeth Taylor and titled "A Place in the Sun" is tellingly billed as being about "love, murder, and class distinctions." The message is clear: a place in the sun is not something that is handed to new aspirants on a silver platter by those already occupying it. The latter must fight for it.

And fight, indeed, they do. Wars of liberation across the colonized world have been as much about politics as economics. Similarly, civil rights and human rights movements are as much about getting a share of the good life as defense of a hallowed principle. There is a religious dimension to this, the idea of election. It seems that for some inscrutable reason salvation, in the reckoning of some faiths, is only for the few. By an uncanny coincidence the global capitalist system, for its part, thrives on the doctrine of scarcity, one of its founding and sustaining myths being that there is not enough of the good life for everyone. Not everyone is guaranteed a place in the sun. There is not enough room. Little wonder, then, there is strife. Thus is born or reinforced the cultural and religious orientation of craving what is forever elusive.

Divine Presence as Place in the Sun

A question that is at once fascinating and troubling in the history of religion is that of radical transcendence. Simply stated, the divine is unapproachable. This is the testimony of sacred scriptures, ancient creeds, and solemn hymns. Listen to this one:

> Immortal, invisible God only wise,
> In light *inaccessible*. . . . (emphasis added)

And these sentiments go back to the earliest epochs of recorded religious history. When Isaiah had his vision in the temple (Is 6:1) he noted that the seraphim that surrounded the divine throne used their hands to shield their faces from the splendor of the divine light. When Moses came down from a forty-day leadership workshop on Mt. Sinai (Ex 34:29-30), it is reported that his face shone like the sun, just for having been exposed to the divine presence. Later, in the days of Solomon's temple, the high priest was the only mortal who was permitted to make cautious entry into the Holy of Holies once a year to make atonement for the sins of the nation. The history of religion is littered with instances of transcendence that occur across cultures and religious traditions. In all these cited cases, provision was made to mediate radical transcendence to humans. And the practice continues in various ways in different traditions around the world. As far as response is concerned, we see at least three directions. On the one side is a flinching, a drawing back and turning away in fear on the part of humans. In this response, the divine is kept at arm's length. All contact is not terminated, though, as the next response shows. In a second response, mechanisms of mediation are devised to allow a controlled mode of trafficking between the two sides. Some traditional religions are happy to keep things this way. Others are not. In the case of Christianity, we see radical impatience with this arrangement.

Christianity asserts that the partition that used to keep ordinary people out of the Holy of Holies in the temple of Israel (symbolizing the inaccessibility of Yahweh) was ripped open when the Christ rose from the dead. As a result worshippers can approach the divine presence directly. Yet we know that even in Christianity, the issue of transcendence has never been solved. Thus, as Robert Hinde, following Smart, aptly points out, "the Christian God, though having some human attributes, is seen as absolutely Other than humans, so that claims to have contact with Him have been seen as blasphemous."[6] And the issue's persistence in different religious traditions has, among other outcomes, led to the emergence and development of various forms of mysticism. In the latter the question of transcendence is crucial to a determination of the nature of the mystic's relationship to the divine. Is it union of substance or is it communion of separate entities?[7] Even some African religious expressions, we are told, have their own version of this dilemma and offer ways of resolving it.[8]

Our interest is in spiritualities of questing after the divine. We meet this in the Abrahamic religions as well as in some eastern faiths. This is precisely the point where eastern religions, though largely agreeing with the African assumption that inactivity is the proper condition of the divine, differ from traditional African thought. For, while in the eastern faiths union with the divine is not only possible but desirable, African religions neither see the desirability of uniting with divinity, nor accept the possibility of that actually happening. In the spirituality of union the soul longs and pines for the divine. And this is not limited to the mystical fringe of these traditions, either; it colors mainstream theology and practice as well. The following line from a Christian hymn that is in the public domain of mainline hymnody captures the essence of this type of spirituality: "As pants the heart for cooling streams/When heated in the chase,/So longs my soul, oh God, for Thee/And thy refreshing grace." And verse 2 goes on to say how the worshipper's thirsty soul pines for the living God.

This is the language of love that, by the way, is no rarity in the Bible. In the case of Israel, it is true that the first of the Ten Commandments enjoins Israel to "love the Lord thy God with all thine heart, and all thy soul, and all thy might" (Dt 6:5, King James Version). But what did love then mean? Did it mean longing for, pining after, and missing the divine? Or would this constitute an illegitimate reading back into this text of modern Western notions of romantic love that do not apply even to premodern European views of love?

Of course, an appeal could be made to such biblical pieces as the Song of Songs, that beautiful love song that is the mystic's spiritual charter. But the history of this text's inclusion into the canons of both the Jewish and Christian scriptures may be indicative of its peripheral status in the biblical spiritual corpus. Although classical Jewish mysticism can be traced to the period of the Second Temple (about 536 B.C.E. to C.A. 70), the *Zohar*, which is the "central text of Jewish mysticism"[9] appears only in the thirteenth century. More sexually explicit in tone and strategy in its depiction of the divine than the Song of Songs, the *Zohar* is, for all this, careful to highlight the problem of transcendence. In somewhat gnostic fashion, the *Zohar*, anxious to underline the importance of transcendence and the theological problems it presents, puts forward ten divine emanations as the mechanism by which ultimate divinity is linked to the created world.[10]

Against this background of an unapproachable divinity we are tempted to ask if it isn't this distancing and sanitization that create the response of hungering and thirsting after the divine. Christianity complicates the matter further still by holding that the divine comes to dwell in the heart of the believer permanently. Even when this is understood metaphorically, it still begs the question of human capacity to contain the divine. With further alienation of a different kind in the processes of the Protestant Reformation and the Enlightenment, the longing for the divine must have grown sharper and more urgent. Jewish and Christian trajectories in mysticism are both different and similar. They are different in that in Jewish mysticism the starting point is radical transcendence, while in Christianity it is immanence, although historical alienation reintroduces distancing between humans and the Christian God and again forces the issue of transcendence. They are similar in that both traditions hold that union with the divine is both desirable and achievable. As I show below, this is quite different from the point of view of African religion in many parts of the continent. The latter starts with an oversaturation of sacrality. And, although in general agreement with Jewish mysticism on the need of mediation between divinity and humanity, African spirituality staunchly holds that permanent union of the two is neither desirable nor possible.

To the extent that the quest for mystical union with the divine succumbs to an otherworldly spirituality, which is detached from the problems of this world, it loses its relevance to this life. It comes to fit the imagery of what liberation theologians used to derisively caricature as "pie in the sky by and by when I die." On the other hand, to the extent that the quest for a place in the sun of modern capitalist acquisitiveness, graft, and consumerism creates the conditions that literally expose the earth and all life on it to the sun's harmful side, it debases its meaning. And it mocks and curses those who embrace it.

Despite all this, though, there is a silver lining even in these orientations. The possession and cultivation of strong inner worlds could not but leave a mark on the external world. And there can be no denying the positive transformations in quality of life that have come with the material development that science and technology and the information revolution have made possible, and continue to foster.[11]

But doubts abound still about the direction these developments have taken. Feelings of betrayal and apprehension deepen in the wake of the global environmental crisis, organized crime, intractable diseases in both humans and animals, whether domestic or wild, that defy scientific and technological advances, poverty, massive unemployment, and wars of varied intensity. In religious terms, one of the ways in which this disaffection and disenchantment expresses itself is in the rise and mushrooming of alternative forms of spirituality, such as New Age, Paganism, and others. Though marked by significant differences in certain respects, the main features and commitments of these spiritualities echo those of African spirituality.

Place in the Shade as Cultural and Religious Orientation

In warmer climates, the sun can be merciless, just as in colder climates the cold weather can be life-threatening. In much of sunbathed Africa a preoccupation with the shade and staying cool is understandable. It is not surprising, either, that this overriding concern has woven its way into the religious thinking of the people. There is a small village on the coast of Kwazulu Natal in South Africa, called *Mthunzini*, which means "a place in the shade." How the place got its name is not clear. It is a village of a few hundred people bounded on the one side by the Indian Ocean and miles of the most crystalline beaches and on the other by thick coastal forest. It is a meeting place for old and new, as a modern motel on stilts overlooks a game park, home to animal species that play a central role in Zulu cosmology and religion. Whether the place in the shade has any connection with the ancestors (shades) or refers simply to the shade provided by the huge driftwood trees, we do not know. It is possible that both meanings may be implied.

The point to note is that a place in the shade is a place with a shield, something that comes between the sun and the person or earth. It is a complicated place in which knowing how to approach the shade is as critical as staying out of the sun. Respect for mystery and appreciation of otherness is its trademark. In this place the principle of mediation, which pervades all aspects of African thought and practice, is upheld. By no means unique to Africa, the principle of mediation is recognized and employed in European and other societies around the world. What sets the African version apart is how it has been elevated to a cornerstone of all human interaction and exchange, as well as human exchanges with the domain of spirit. Marriage negotiations, politics, diplomacy, social life—all these are arenas in which the principle of mediation is central. But it is in religion that the principle reaches the zenith of its elevation and complexity. However, before we explore its ramifications in this area, let us first examine another system, the understanding of which will throw much-needed light on the analysis of mediation. It is the complex symbolic system of heat and coolness.

Anthropologists have amply pointed out and analyzed the centrality of the heat-coolness dichotomy (sometimes complementarity)[12] in African philosophies of sickness and wellness, safety and danger, witchcraft and healing.[13] According to Anita Jacobson-Widding, writing about the Manyika of eastern Zimbabwe, "Heat is connected with disease, excitement and anger, while coolness is connected with health, peace and order." She lists things, places, as well as moments in time and persons that may be classified as hot. In general these may be summarized as involving "mixtures, encounters, boundary crossings or some special characteristic that makes them suitable as devices for the kind of fusion whereby it is no longer possible to distinguish one thing from the other." [14]

One state that Jacobson-Widding lists as being hot and therefore dangerous is "when you are standing in the shade of a tree and feel that the air is cool although the weather is hot."[15] This seeming paradox is really not as self-contradictory as it seems. It is true, as we saw above, that coolness is the ideal auspicious condition. It is also the condition of divinity. And this is exactly why being in the shade in the midst of heat can be quite dangerous. The assumption is that divinity is present in and saturates the shade of a tree. It could be argued that there is nothing unusual about feeling cool while standing in the shade of a tree, as this is to be expected. But I believe we must sense here a coolness that goes beyond the usual contrast between being in the shade and standing out of the shade, something of an uncanny quality. This is hot and dangerous. Where the tree is not an ordinary tree, but one of the "trees of the spirit,"[16] or trees that serve as "living shrines,"[17] we could safely envision an increase in the heat and level of danger.

In most parts of Africa, religious activity is preoccupied with keeping divinity at a safe distance. Of Nuer sacrifice, Evans-Pritchard reports that its aim is the separation of God and humans and "not to unite them."[18] Too close a brush with divinity, so hold many African peoples, is sure to result in madness.[19] Richard Werbner adds his experience among the Kalanga of Botswana. He speaks of the keeping of an "appropriate distance between the living and the dead as divinities. Ideally it involves a good measure of separation. . . . Once awakened, the dead as divinities come too close; they have to be driven away if the living are to rest easy."[20] I shall not belabor the point. There is ample evidence of an African religious orientation in which separation rather than union characterizes the relationship between the human and the divine.

From this I want to make three theoretical and methodological points. The first is that blanket imposition of a spirituality of closeness on African religious data, as is often the norm in the study of African religions, only serves to conceal important aspects of African religious thought, practice, and experience on the one hand, and distorts the rest on the other hand. Second, theoretically, in a spirituality of distance from divinity, a distant God is the norm, rather than a problematic exception. Third, the spirituality of distance has its own ways of articulating and achieving closeness through a complex series of mediations. At this point, the notion of mediation becomes primary and everything else takes a secondary place. Indeed, the debate about whether a God in the sky is superior to a deity in the ground is rendered irrelevant.[21] To this class of secondary importance also falls such questions as whether one God or the other is to be seen as a sky divinity or a water divinity.[22] As all deities, including those responsible for rain and fertility,[23] require mediation in their relations with humans, the centrality of mediation is all but sealed.

All this has implications for the old debate about the high God in Africa, which we cannot go into here. It has much to say also about human-animal relations and human representations of animals, as I detail below. Let us briefly look at two forms of mediation that are widespread in central and southern Africa, namely spirit possession and mediation through the intervention of animals, mostly wild animals but also domestic animals to a lesser extent.

In spirit possession, whether of the strong type in which the votary's ego is fragmented and eclipsed, or the light kind that allows the ego to remain intact and centered, divinity is transformed into a mode that is safe for human contact. In other words, the heat of divine closeness, which might otherwise bring sudden madness or death, is toned down to tolerable and manageable levels. Where direct unmediated possession takes place, the experience is for a relatively short duration, apparently to prevent possible harm to the possessed individual. In Haitian Vodun, the handler or facilitator in a possession session goes to much trouble to ensure that the "horse" or "mount" is of the correct spiritual "weight" to bear a specific load. Once again, the point this reiterates is that closeness of divinity, especially in an agitated mode, is hot and dangerous. It is therefore to be avoided at all costs or, where this is not possible, the greatest care must be taken, through regulation and mediation, to minimize the potential harm to humans that contact entails.

Another form of mediation involves the intervention of wild animals as a kind of step-down transformer to enable divinity safely to flow through to humans. Among the Shona the spirits of deceased great chiefs take the form of a lion before possessing the body of a medium. While this has been interpreted in many ways by scholars, I am arguing here that this is a mechanism of mediating the otherwise dangerous transcendence of divinity and making it safe for humans. Other animal forms associated with the appearance of royal ancestors are snakes, such as the python throughout much of Africa, and the mamba among the Zulu. Brian Morris discusses this phenomenon in relation to the possession of rainmaking mediums with the rain deity, *chisumphi*, in central Malawi.[24] He argues persuasively that the agent of possession is not an animal spirit, as some scholars allege, but the rain deity in the form of an animal, often a python. The possessed person is thus not possessed by the python, or even by the "spirit" of the python (as Yoshida suggests)[25] but by the chisumphi spirit, which is identified with the python, with the wind, and with the power of rain.

It is clear that living animals, as distinct from the dead animals offered in sacrifice, serve to bridge the gap between a distant God and humans in indigenous African spirituality. They transform the heat of closeness to the coolness of the sacred into positive power for the bringing of rain, healing, and other socially beneficial services. There are many other ways in which animals are thought to be intimate to human beings by nonmodern thought. Totemism, for instance, reveals a whole range of assumptions about the kinship relationship that exists between humans and animals. Implicit in this is a belief that animals, especially those in the wild, are closer to the sacred than humans. This makes them more compatible with divinity than humans. They are more at home with deity generally, and not just the "gods of game."[26] These are radical notions. To concede animals' superiority to humans in an area that, in modern terms, is supposed to distinguish the essentially human from the strictly beastly, calls for a radically different meaning of the human wherein rationality and will are rendered insufficient descriptors.

It is interesting to note how almost suddenly science is discovering that animals have consciousness. More and more it is conceded that they grieve, think, and possess many of the qualities that modern humans once reserved only for their species.[27] Even more intriguing is the coincidence of this fascination with the animal form of being and renewed questioning about what is the human at the turn of the millennium. What, if anything, can we learn from those who have

always had a different meaning of animal being? Is it a legitimate, let alone sufficient response, in the name of science, to dismiss their knowledge as sentimen-
tality? Maybe a day will come when science will concede this truism too. But let
me now, using the method of juxtaposing coincidences, proceed to a consideration of the heat of globalization.

The Heat of Globalization

What is the heat of globalization? In other words, since heat here is a religious
concept, what in globalization is coincident with states that generate heat?
Jacobson-Widding sees the production of mixtures that eradicate all traces of
identity as a source of heat. Mere mixing of different elements does not seem to
be the problem. Loss of identity does. Hence, it will not come as a surprise that
recovery and assertion of ethnic identities are constituent features of the cultural
mixtures that characterize globalization today.

   Mazrui's analysis of globalization adds some useful insights here. I find three
of them to be particularly pertinent to this discussion. He says that globalization
involves processes aimed at homogenization, that is, reducing things, people,
and cultures to common denominators. This has been called the melting-pot theory of cultural assimilation. A better metaphor for the implied symbolic heat of
globalization is hard to imagine. Incidentally, there is a sense in which this intention is echoed in the religious quest of the spirituality of closeness generally, and
of the mystic in particular. The sentiment is also present in all spiritualities that
seek and promote the interrelatedness of all things. But there is a marked difference between this religious quest and the mission of globalization. In the latter
another intention is at work as well, namely, hegemonization.[28] If homogenization is the throwing of different elements into the pot, hegemonization is the act
of stirring the contents of the pot. Agency is of the essence here. The arm that
stirs the pot is the will and power to dominate. Thus homogenization may be
seen as a first or parallel step in the final goal of global dominance. Mazrui does
not end there. Using the metaphor of space exploration he suggests that even
before it fully comes into being, globalization is overtaken by ventures into outer
space. This constitutes, he thinks, a reaching out beyond the globe. The connotations are those of universalization in the strict sense of encompassing the whole
universe.

   We can spell out some of the implications of this ambition to go beyond the
globe. The will to dominate mentioned above has not been limited to peoples,
cultures, religions, and languages. It has included animals and indeed the earth
and outer space itself. For the present the fear may not yet be what might happen
to space as a result (although this is already a concern) but what might happen to
the earth and its denizens when the hegemonizing gaze is vertical rather than

horizontal. When the downward gaze that is the preserve of the gods becomes an attribute of some humans, what is there to act as a guarantee against excess and folly? In other words, there is something deeply unsettling about the *beyond* in the phrase "beyond the globe." If globe here is taken metaphorically to depict recognized boundaries, be they spatial, social, cultural, scientific, or technological, the seriousness of the threat of a cultural orientation that knows or respects no boundaries becomes amply manifest.

When they want to describe someone who allows no boundaries to stop him from doing what he wants, the Shona say, "He punched the sun with his fist." What this describes is absolute, unstoppable will and willfulness. In the modern project, it seems that only those who are prepared to punch the sun may hope to find a place in the sun. Of course, this drive and singleness of purpose is one thing; the harvest of burns and bruises it incurs is quite another, as the present environmental crisis attests.

A major effect, if not intention, of globalization is the generalization of certain particulars inherent in the orientation that is depicted by the metaphor "a place in the sun," together with the orientation itself. In the almighty name of the information revolution and the magic of advertising, a consciousness-raising campaign is executed that has the audacity of telling people what they want and what they need in order to be fully human and happy. On the strictly religious front proselytization of various kinds offers a spiritual complement to these mundane efforts.

Propagation, whether of goods or gods, seems to have become a sacred good in itself, deploying the salesperson and the preacher in a frantic race for the mind of humankind. Recent research shows that even once-local religions are being catapulted into the arena of the global, through such forces as migration, the Internet, and conscious propagation (see Jacob Olupona's contribution in this book). In this global sphere, dominance in the form of insistence on exclusive claims to truth by those who possess certain knowledges and ways of knowing seems only to devalue the meaning of knowledge, as well as debase the meaning of the human. Only commitment to a genuine exchange of knowledges and ways of knowing modulated by an attitude of giving and receiving can lay the foundation of a viable epistemology for a globalizing world.

Conclusion

Since Rudolf Otto presented the numinous as simultaneously, though fluctuatingly, a repelling tremendum as well as a compelling fascinosum, the question has remained that of how this oscillation is played out in religious experience and practice.[29] When, how, and why is the one or the other pole allowed to predominate? It is in an attempt to answer these questions that I offer the typology of a spirituality of distance and a spirituality of closeness. The of a spirituality of distance and a spirituality of closeness. The spirituality of distance is to be found among people who historically have experienced little or no alienation from the sacred. For such people a distant God is not a problem. Their problem may very well be that the sacred is at times too close to them in an unmediated way. As their primary religious response consists in keeping the sacred at a safe distance, and managing its flow toward humans, mediation will accordingly suffuse their rituals.

The spirituality of closeness exists among people who have suffered alienation from the form of the sacred that once held their world together. It may not be surprising that Jewish mysticism emerges at the time of the Second Temple. And while Christianity probably owed its early wave of mysticism to its Jewish roots, this intensifies with the overthrow of Providence in the Enlightenment. The classic response inevitably involves expressions of the people's hunger and thirst for the divine, while pursuit of mystical union with the divine represents an acute form of this spiritual quest.

In this chapter I have attempted to draw attention to the coincidence of the latter spirituality with the materiality of the secular ideology encapsulated in the metaphor "a place in the sun." These in their separate ways feed into a human orientation in the world that makes the metaphor look like a self-fulfilling prophecy in the light of the role of the sun in the present environmental crisis. To the extent that "good religion" has been associated with this spirituality, and to the extent that this combination has formed an unstated but powerful assumption in the academic study of religion, it may be time to revisit this cluster. If at the same time due attention is paid to the spirituality of distance, a redefinition of religion may emerge that might inject new theoretical assumptions into the academic study of religion.

Notes

An earlier version of this chapter, titled "Religion: Quest for a place in the sun or a place in the shade?" was presented to the W.E.B. Du Bois Institute for Afro-American Research, Harvard University, under the auspices of the Mandela Fellowship. I thank the Du Bois Institute for funding and logistical support, and the University of Cape Town for funding and for leave time.

1. For biographical treatment of Rev. Matthew Chigaga Zvimba see Canaan S. Banana, *The Church and the Struggle for Zimbabwe* (Gweru: Mambo Press, 1996); T. Ranger, *The African Voice in Southern Rhodesia, 1898-1930* (London: Heinemann, 1970), 21f; and C. J. M. Zvobgo, *The Wesleyan Methodist Missions in Zimbabwe* (Harare: University of Zimbabwe Publications, 1991), 176f.

2. I have not been able to corroborate this oral anecdote. However, this does not take away from the point I am making about coincidence.

3. George Lakoff and Mark Johnson, *Philosophy in the Flesh: The Embodied Mind and Its Challenge to Western Thought* (New York: Basic, 1999), 47.

4. Paul Gifford, *African Christianity: Its Public Role* (London: Hurst, 1998), 31ff.

5. Rudolf Otto, *The Idea of the Holy*, trans. John Harvey, second edition (Oxford: Oxford University Press, 1958).

6. Robert A. Hinde, *Why Gods Persist: A Scientific Approach to Religion* (London: Routledge, 1999), 82; N. Smart, *The Religious Experience of Mankind* (London: Collins, 1971).

7. Simoni-Wastila, "Unio Mystica and Particularity: Can Individuals Merge with the One?" *Journal of the American Academy of Religion* 68, no. 4 (December 2000): 857-79.

8. Dominique Zahan, "Some Reflections on African Spirituality," in *African Spirituality: Forms, Meanings, and Expressions*, ed. Jacob K. Olupona (New York: Crossroad Publishing Company, 2000), 22-23.

9. Haim Watzman, "The Scholarly and the Ecstatic: Academics Debate How to Approach the Kabalah, the Heart of Jewish Mysticism," *The Chronicle of Higher Education* (January 26, 2001), A16.

10. Watzman, "The Scholarly and the Ecstatic," A17, A18.

11. For a detailed presentation and analysis of these benefits see, inter alia, Anthony Giddens, *The Consequences of Modernity* (Stanford, Calif.: Polity Press, 1990).

12. I am deeply indebted to Fikeni Senkoro of the University of Dar Es Salaam for the insight that while often existing in a dichotomy, heat and coolness are also complementary to each other.

13. Adam Kuper, *Wives for Cattle* (London: Routledge, 1982); Anita Jacobson-Widding, "Notions of Heat and Fever among the Manyika of Zimbabwe," in *Culture, Experience, and Pluralism: Essays on African Ideas of Illness and Healing*, ed. Anita Jacobson-Widding and David Westerlund (Stockholm, Sweden: Upsala, 1989); Megan Biesele, *Women Like Meat: the Folklore and Foraging Ideology of the Kalahari Ju/'hoan* (Johannesburg: Witwatersrand University Press; Bloomington: Indiana University Press, 1993).

14. Jacobson-Widding, "Notions of Heat and Fever," 27, 33.

15. Jacobson-Widding, "Notions of Heat and Fever," 34.

16. Brian Morris, *Animals and Ancestors: An Ethnography* (New York: Oxford University Press, 2000), 229.

17. V. W. Turner, *The Religious Experience of Mankind* (London: Collins, 1971), 10.

18. E. E. Evans-Pritchard, *Nuer Religion* (Oxford: Clarendon Press, 1956), 275; quoted in Richard P. Werbner, *Ritual Passage, Sacred Journey: The Process and Organization of Religious Movement* (Washington: Smithsonian Institution Press; Manchester: Manchester University Press, 1989), 119.

19. Evan M. Zuesse, *Ritual Cosmos: The Sanctification of Life in African Religions* (Athens: Ohio University Press, 1979), 174-76.

20. Werbner, *Ritual Passage*, 119.

21. Gabriel M. Setiloane, *The Image of God among the Sotho-Tswana* (Rotterdam: Balkema, 1976).

22. Francis L. Rakotsoane, *The Southern Sotho's Ultimate Object of Worship: Sky-Divinity or Water-Divinity?* Ph. D. thesis (University of Cape Town, 2001).

23. J. M. Schoffeleers, *River of Blood: The Genesis of a Martyr Cult in Southern Malawi* (Madison: University of Wisconsin Press, 1992), 49-53, 69.

24. Morris, *Animals and Ancestors*, 242.

25. K. Yoshida, "Masks and Transformation among the Chewa of Eastern Zambia." *Senri Ethnological Studies* 31(1991), 203, 241.

26. Ivar Paulson, "The Animal Guardian: A Critical and Synthetic Review," in *History of Religions* 3, no. 2 (1964): 337.

27. George Page, *Inside the Animal Mind* (New York: Doubleday, 1999); Richard D. Ryder, *Animal Revolution: Changing Attitudes toward Speciesism*, revised and updated edition (New York: Berg, 2000); Steven Best, "Animal Rights and Wrongs," *Britannica.com* at wysiwyg://76/http://www.britannica.com/bcom/orig-inal/article/0,5744,1006 6,00.html (accessed August 2000).

28. An eloquent exposition of the essence of hegemony is offered by William Safire, "On Language," *New York Times Magazine* (June 10, 2001): 40, 42. Safire comments that the word *hyperpower* was coined by the French foreign minister Hubert Vedrine in 1999 to describe the power of the United States, which no longer could be adequately described by the term *superpower*. Vedrine is quoted as complaining about such hegemonic power: "We cannot accept a politically unipolar world, nor a culturally uniform world, nor the unilateralism of a single *hyperpower*." It is this aspect of globalization that is connoted by *hegemonization*.

29. Otto, *The Idea of the Holy*.

6

Globalization and African Immigrant Religious Communities

Jacob K. Olupona

In order to adequately explore the relationship between globalization and America's African immigrant religious communities, one must first attempt to define what globalization means. In developing this conceptual framework, one would explore the currents of interaction between the local and the global. For my own purpose in this chapter, this involves an examination of the extent that religion, in the African immigrant context, constitutes a force for adaptation, cultural continuity, and linkage within the African diaspora.

Globalization

The concept of globalization is precarious in that the term as well as the subject matter are both in a state of flux. Previously, various concepts of globalization have been associated with a number of economic and political models that tended to de-emphasize the cultural, traditional, and spiritual effects of modernity. Predominant among these analytical models were the Marxist, socialist, and to some extent dependency scholars who on the one hand criticized the inequities of market capital but on the other tended to accept many of its paradigms of industrial development over indigenous culture.[1] In these past criticisms of global capital as well as their more contemporary advocates, globalization has been under the theoretical hegemony of some variant of the development paradigm. The conceptual focus of this approach centered on examining global theory through its economic aspects of production, trade, colonialism, and imperialism. Only recently have scholars of globalization begun to develop

83

a new methodology to explore "theories of culture, social organization, and identity for global and transnational persons and communities."[2]

We must also note that this new methodology challenges previous notions of both time and space. Within the Marxist/market pedagogy, globalization is linked to a progressive, developmentalist, and what M. Kearney has referred to as a teleological dimension.[3] In other words, under this paradigm, globalization was viewed as a linear and incrementalist trend toward eventual Westernization.

Time in this sense is not only unidirectional towards an eventual homogenization but is also compressed as the capitalist political economy continues to accelerate by increasingly shrinking barriers to capitalism.[4] As a product of modernity, private space gives way to capitalist space as more and more aspects of human life become integrated into the global market. In this sense, globalization consists of a "deterritorialization" as production, consumption, communities, politics, and identities become detached from local places.[5]

I wish to acknowledge that, to some extent, these descriptions of globalization are correct in that the modernity component of globalization has in many cases been a force for standardization, secularization, and hegemony of Westernized values over what we can refer to as the local. However, this scholarship is fundamentally flawed in its assumptions that these processes are inevitable or absolute.[6] The causal arrow is in fact bidirectional with crosscurrents of influence running both ways. We must acknowledge that globalization is a process that includes changes within the Westernized state itself. This global implosion, or what Kearney refers to as the "peripheralization at the Core," recognizes that the hegemony of Westernized languages, traditions, and perceptions of the world is becoming increasingly influenced by the forces of immigration, global communication, and international travel. These forces are introducing and strengthening the local within the global itself.

In redefining the concept of globalization, these new paradigms are generally referred to as reflecting some notion of what has become known as transnationalism or transglobality. Similar yet distinct from the conceptualization of globalism, transnationalism refers more to the question of identity and culture not as components bounded within nations but instead as diasporic space of which nations are a component. As stated by Kearney,

> Transnational calls attention to the cultural and political projects of nation-states as they vie for hegemony in relations with other nation-states, with their citizens and "aliens." This cultural-political dimension of transationalism is signaled by its resonance with nationalism as a cultural and political project, whereas globalization implies more abstract, less institutionalized, and less intentional processes occurring without reference to nations, e.g. technological developments in mass international communication and the impersonal dynamics of global popular and mass culture, global finance, and the world environment.[7]

In this context, scholars are beginning to reject the former paradigms of globalization as a pseudonym for modernity in recognition of the transnational elements of globalization. These diasporic trends of immigration, communication, and travel serve to sustain and strengthen local identities in a global context. Here we see that globalization is no longer defined as a form of class struggle or as a standardizing and secularizing process. It is part of a process of forming overlapping identities that transcend the nation-state.[8] We are no longer looking at culture as something that exists within the state or is limited by its boundaries. We must now look at culture as something that exists in zones of identity. It exists in Miami's "little Havana," Haiti's tenth province and throughout the Santeria and Voodoo traditions of the Afro-Caribbean.[9]

Utilizing a transglobal paradigm, we can examine the resiliency, adaptation and even expansion of the traditions of African Christianity, Islam, and indigenous traditions. These faiths have transplanted themselves in America and are increasingly expanding with the conversion of Americans as well as the continual flow of African immigrants. Already we have seen a number of major U.S. cities such as Washington D.C., Atlanta, and New York begin to undertake a fundamental transformation. Unlike earlier waves of immigration, these new immigrants retain an ability to utilize modern technologies of communication and travel which serve to both expand and strengthen these communities in what some scholars have come to refer to as the age of postmodernism or multiple modernities.

My own research as well as that of other scholars of immigration and religion have demonstrated that the previous paradigms of the "great American melting pot" are becoming increasingly rebuked in favor of a "salad bowl" of diversity and resiliency among immigrant populations.[10] Traditions do not disappear, but the relations and the balance between them shifts in the context of globalization. As a consequence, we see a reformation and adaptation of the local into a new cohesion that retains a non-Western memory within a Western environment. These trends are no more prominent than within the African immigrant religious communities.

Globalization and Religion

As I have mentioned, immigration, communication, and travel are some of the medians by which the local is transforming the global. To this we must also add the power and importance of religion. This trend is especially important in the post-Cold War era, as scholars and academics are beginning to question previous maxims that declared that religion was on an eventual decline with the rise of the modern secular state.

In examining this point, my colleague Mark Juergensmeyer states the following in his recent book, *Torror in the Mind of God: The Global Rise of Religi-*

gious Violence,

> Enlightenment modernity proclaimed the death of religion. Modernity signaled
> not only the demise of the Church's institutional authority and clerical control,
> but also the loosening of religion's ideological and inetellectual grip on society.
> Scientific reasoning and the moral claims of the secular social contract replaced
> theology and the Church as the bases for truth and social identity. [11]

Variants of this Weberian paradigm predicted that as states continued to indus-
trialize, modernize, and utilize the new sciences, secularization would continually minimize and mitigate the impact of religion worldwide.

I believe that this assumption is incorrect. Even within the core of Enlightenment Europe, we have seen the rise of a number of spiritual and theological
movements including Methodism in England, Hassidism in Poland, Pietism in
Germany, and the Protestant Great Awakening in the United States. [12] More recent Western movements in the twentieth century as well as the strong influence
of religion within the Latin American and Asian and African diasporas have led
us to question whether we have been misled by a conceptual methodology that
overestimated the power and expansion of the secular state. Only now with the
end of the Cold War are scholars beginning to adequately examine the impact of
the forces of culture, ethnicity, and identity. Only now are scholars beginning to
acknowledge the growing influence of religious institutions in public politics
and cultures around the world. [13] We must acknowledge that the very nature of
secular and political goals themselves can directly influence the formation and
growth of new religious movements such as liberation theology. [14] On this point,
Bennetta Jules-Rosette in her article "The Sacred in African New Religions"
states, "Through this approach, theologians operating within established Catholic and Protestant traditions view the Bible as a revolutionary book, which
documents the processes of religious and political liberation and the goals of
freedom. Their objective is to redefine the sacred as a set of moral principles,
which can be invoked in the wider society to reduce social inequities and injus-
tice." [15]

So strong is the nexus between religion and public politics that often religion
is appropriately viewed as a powerful rival to the state as the source for truth and
authority within the society itself. In many cases, "new religions are seen as potential sources for weakening civic political commitments by virtue of their ability to mobilize masses of people in activities which are not directly supervised
or controlled by the state." [16] This fear of the rising power of religion in the context of globalization is well justified by the intensity of antagonism that is occasionally expressed by its religious activists. Jeurgensmeyer notes that

> resurgent religious activists have proclaimed the death of secularism. They
> have dismissed the efforts of secular culture and its forms of nationalism to re-
> place religion. They have challenged the notion that secular society and the

modern nationstate can provide the moral fiber that unites national communities or the ideological strength to sustain states buffeted by ethical, economic, and military failures. Their message has been easy to believe and has been widely received because the failure of the secular state has been so apparent.

The leadership of the secular state has become increasingly challenged in the last decade of the twentieth century following the end of the Cold War and the rise of the global economy. The Cold War provided contesting models of moral politics—communism and democracy—that have been replaced by the global market that has weakened national sovereignty and is conspicuously devoid of political ideals. The global economy became characterized by transnational businesses accountable to no single governmental authority and with no clear ideological or moral standards of behavior. [17]

Contrary to the notion that religion is on the decline, we are seeing a demonstrable rise in fundamentalist movements, religious violence, and the emergence of new faiths throughout the world. The resiliency and intensity of religion in our contemporary world demonstrate that these faiths retain a certain aspect of adaptability and flexibility. In many cases, religion has been able to co-opt both the mechanisms of modernity as well as its symbols to both enhance its stature as well as spread its presence throughout the world. With this conceptual framework in mind, I address the emerging presence, power, and influence of African immigrant religious communities within the United States.

African Immigrant Religious Communities

As a consequence of globalization, America is beginning to realize the growing impact of a new second wave of migration from Africa. Unlike the experience of Africans in the initial migration of African slavery, the profile of the new African immigrants is different. The last national census indicates that this group is more educated per capita than any other. These new African immigrants are free to establish living religious communities that are indicative of the African mosaic. With substantial talent, resources, and opportunities, this newest wave of immigration is in the process of creating significant religious institutions and movements that are changing societies both within the United States as well as Africa itself. For the purposes of this discussion, one can come to understand these movements as variants of the Christian, Islamic, and African indigenous traditions.

African Immigrant Christianity and the
African Independent Church

Within the African Christian tradition we see not only the presence of main-stream Christian movements but also a new form of Christianity that has become known as the African independent church movement. These churches are unique in that they are indicative of the multiple modernities present in our contemporary era of globalization. Consisting of about 15 percent of the Christian population of sub-Saharan Africa and an ever-greater part of African diaspora movements worldwide, they are autonomous movements with distinct characteristics of both local and global dynamics.[18] In characterizing the growth of this movement, Jules-Rosette writes,

> Historically speaking, the impetus for the growth of new African religious movements may be traced to five basic sources. (1) The disappointment of local converts with the premises and outcomes of Christianity led to the growth of prophetic, Messianic, and millenarian groups. (2) The transition of the Bible into local African vernaculars stimulated a reinterpretation of scripture and a spiritual renewal in Christian groups. (3) The perceived divisions in denominational Christianity and its failure to meet local needs influenced the rise of separatist churches and community-based indigenous churches. (4) The importance of western medicine in the face of personal problems, psychological disorder, epidemics, and natural disasters was a catalyst for concerns with spiritual healing in the new African religious movements. (5) The failure of mission Christianity to break down social and cultural barriers and generate a sense of community has led to the strengthening of social ties in small, sectarian groups.[19]

By looking at the Harrist Church in Cote d'Ivoire, the Aladura Church in Nigeria, Kimbanguism in Zaire, and the Apostolic movements in Zaire, we can see a rich diversity of churches that has reshaped a global faith by integrating it with aspects of indigenous values and traditions.[20]

In the case of the United States, we are seeing the growing stature of many of the most recent and expansionist African independent church movements such as the Celestial Church of Christ, Christ Apostolic Church, and Cherubim and Seraphim. These movements are unique in that they reflect the nexus between African indigenous beliefs and Christianity. They are indicative of a direct linkage between the local and the global.

In order to understand this tradition, we must understand the nature of African Christianity from the colonial era to its modern forms. As in Latin America, this is an evolving process that retains significant aspects of indigenous faith and cultural practice. Many of the first mission converts were social outcasts who later became the new local elites with the rise of colonialism. In reaction to the continued dominance of the mission churches by African Christian elites, African spiritual leaders emerged who claimed they had been called by God to begin authentic African churches. Because of this reversal of status, these African leaders were composed of those who relied upon both Christian and indigenous traditions as the source of truth and authority. It is not surprising therefore that as indigenous Christianity evolved in Africa, the African independent church would retain aspects of indigenous tradition and belief. Images of Jesus as a leader, the Holy Spirit, and the idea of faith healing, for example, allowed many Africans to integrate aspects of their own spirituality into the new faith. African ideas of community, ancestor worship, and revelation continue to persist in the independent church traditions.

As a result of this history, the African independent church has evolved as a means of cultural continuity with African traditions and identities. Often we see individuals engaging in a form of religious pluralism by participating in more than one tradition and one institution at the same time or combining aspects of multiple traditions. This approach constitutes an effort toward accepting aspects of both American and African identity by adapting them both part and parcel. Within the naming ceremonies present in both African Christian and Islamic practices, for example, we see the ceremony become utilized as a means of combining a global faith with local aspects of indigenous and traditional belief. Hymns spoken in African languages can be selected to incorporate indigenous sayings or values. Finally, special or secondary services can be created to supplement or modify existing English sermons.

These crossovers of tradition are not limited to Africans abandoning their indigenous beliefs and traditions in exchange for an African American identity. In other words, the adoption of belief, rituals, and practices can go "both ways" in the sense that not only are African immigrants becoming "Americanized" but also African Americans are at the same time becoming Africanized. Within the research I gathered as part of a Ford Foundation project, I observed numerous examples of traditional practices changing the nature of religion as practiced in the United States.[21] At the Ghanaian Presbyterian-Reformed Church of Brooklyn, for example, Ghanaians are moving away from translated hymns created by German missionaries to ones with African Christian compositions and biblical renditions of praise in the context of more contemporary music and cultural expressions of identity. In the Aladura Celestial Church of Christ in Miami, I counted a number of African American couples wearing the white flowing garments of the church. Some of the women were also spouses of Nigerian members. Likewise, in examining African churches in Los Angeles, I saw many of the same flavors of African tradition such as the Shebshba dance among members of Los Angeles's Ethiopian Christian Fellowship.

African Pentecostal or Charismatic Churches

In addition to the African independent church, we must also examine the African Pentecostal or charismatic churches in the context of globalization. Unlike the previous discussion of African independent churches as the nexus between African tradition and Christianity within the African diaspora, charismatic churches reflect the trend toward modernity within African immigrant Christianity. As previously mentioned, modernity has become commonly viewed as a product of Western culture emphasizing a sense of Western rationalism and scientific/logical reasoning. In the case of these churches, aspects of African spirituality, such as divination, witchcraft, ancestry, and polytheistic beliefs, are strongly discouraged and are even portrayed as products of the devil's influence. However, within these same churches, we see that in many instances views of Holy Spirit possession are officially tolerated and promoted in the tradition of "speaking in tongues."

Pentecostal, or "born again" styles of worship are prominent in African immigrant communities in that they are perceived to allow better incorporation of African beliefs such as spirit possession, fervent prayer, pragmatism, and proximate salvation. For example, Pastor Joseph Dosumu of Gospel Faith Mission International Church in Los Angeles indicated that he converted from Anglican priesthood in Nigeria to a Pentecostal pastor in the United States. Pentecostalism for him was closest to the indigenous systems of worshipping while "evoking the Spirits of the Most High." At Chicago's African United Methodist Church (AUMC) service, I saw that as the church body slowly grew, those who came in while the church was clapping, dancing, and testifying would naturally follow the flow or rhythm of the activity. Some women danced out of their church pews, rejoicing and clapping their hands higher in the air to evoke the Holy One, while others knelt down by their seats, praising God, and still others stayed in their seats jumping and calling out God's name. These situations are not what one would find in "higher Anglicanism."

However, we must be careful to qualify these assertions by "born again" adherents with an understanding that they may in fact place little actual emphasis on the values of African indigenous traditions. Often these "advocates" of spirituality can at the same time be the greatest critics of traditional African beliefs as evil, superstitious, and contrary to the teachings of Christianity. To some extent, the claim that "born again" styles of worship are closer to African styles is an attempt to pull African immigrants away from their indigenous beliefs toward beliefs in conjunction with the values of modernity.

Accommodating Mainstream Churches

I must also mention in discussing the local global dynamic of African Christianity and globalization that even the most traditional and orthodox variants of Christianity are also becoming increasingly changed by the impact of African, Asian, and especially Latin American immigration. In recognition of the new demographic trends, American churches such as the Episcopal, Baptist, or Catholic churches are beginning to offer services that better reflect the interests and concerns of these immigrant communities. These churches in the United States have been steadily developing their "Ethnic Ministries"—ethnically and nationally specific ministries (for example, Irish, Polish, Vietnamese, Haitian, and so on) that minister to a wide range of immigrant communities. The most prominent example of these accommodations focuses on the use of African or indigenous language services. These services can take on various forms, from the use of indigenous language hymns to services conducted entirely in non-English languages. Often these services are Saturday or Sunday evening services conducted after English services. A typical example is reflected in the efforts of Igbo Father Charles Onubogu, who heads the Igbo Catholic Foundation at San Francisco's Sacred Heart Parish. While Father Charles is responsible for leading mass at the Mission Dolores in San Francisco, working with a white and Latino congregation, he also works with the Igbo Catholic Foundation, an ethnic ministry that aims to "reconnect Igbo immigrants in the U.S. to their Igbo culture in Nigeria. By teaching the language and other cultural practices (like dances, music, etc.), the foundation aims to instill in its participants the positive aspects of Igbo and Nigerian life. Celebrating the Igbo language is a great entry into developing an understanding and appreciation for the culture."[22]

The San Francisco Bay Area Igbo community thus comes together during the last Sunday of every month for mass and community support. When we attended the Igbo mass, Father Charles and his associate led the entire mass in Igbo—including songs—except for the sermon, according to a member of the congregation.

Unfortunately, the coordination of these services is difficult; unlike Latin American services where the whole immigrant congregation speaks Spanish, African immigrant communities are substantially divided along linguistic, cultural, and at times political lines. Only in cases where there are significant concentrations of African languages such as Igbo, Yoruba, or certain Ghanaian and Ethiopian communities are there sufficient concentrations of Africans to merit special language services.

Beyond the creation of ethnic and national congregations is another significant trend in African immigrant religion. This involves the increasing number of African priests ministering to American congregations. While this is strongest in the Catholic Church, there is evidence of African priests in Episcopal, Anglican, and Methodist mainstream churches. I was particularly struck by an Igbo father in Miami who ministers to a Catholic Spanish church just a stone's throw from where I lived in the south side of Miami during my field research.

Several African ministers in all these three types of African churches present the notion of a reverse mission to America as a way of justifying their call to minister to American congregations. They argue that Africa has become a center of Christianity developed enough to send missionaries abroad. These ministers hope that these communities will discover their transnational identity in the complex relationships between communities within metropolitan centers, local communities, and the global environment.

African Immigrant Islamic Communities

When one examines the local and global dynamic of America's growing African Islamic communities one is again seeing many of the same patterns that are emerging with the African immigrant Christian communities. Islam, like Christianity, has also been able to adapt, capitalize, and even exploit the technologies of modernity in favor of expanding its own faith as a global religion.[23] Like African Christianity, the growing presence of African Muslims within the United States has begun to change the nature of many of America's largest cities. Islamic mosques that were once dominated by Arabic-speaking and Pakistani communities are now beginning to witness a strong inflow of Islamic Africans from West Africa. Ghanaian Islamic communities, for example, are becoming especially prominent in the cities of New York, Washington D.C., and Atlanta.

However, this mixture of West African Muslims and their own unique local dynamics has caused some tension within the more globally oriented structures of American Islamic mosques. One of the best indicators is the tendency of African Islamic immigrants to detach themselves from existing Islamic mosques in favor of forming their own unique African mosques. This trend is due to a number of factors such as differences in languages of service, culture, and the emphasis placed upon various traditions. In an interview I conducted with a Miami Imam, for example, Imam Majeem referred to difficulties the Africans encountered while sharing a mosque with Pakistanis. Although both groups were Islamic, there were substantial differences in culture, language, and identity between these two groups. As a consequence of these differences, these factors can sometimes lead to issues of trust and association. Imam Majeem states that often "Pakistanis do not want others in their mosques because they feel belongings could be stolen."[24]

Although there are close linkages that help to substantially unite Muslims throughout the world, we cannot ignore the divisive nature of various ethnic and national origins that exist in these immigrant communities. On the other hand, we must also acknowledge that the local aspects of globalization sometimes have a remarkable ability to exist in a transglobal setting. This tendency is nowhere more predominant than in the characteristics of African indigenous traditions and faiths throughout the African diaspora.

Traditional Faiths: African Indigenous Traditions and Faiths

Globalization takes on a different form when it comes to indigenous African religions. Although Christians and Muslims constitute the vast majority of African immigrants, those who are followers of indigenous faiths have had a disproportionate impact. This is due to the fact that globalization has also become a powerful impetus in the expansion of African traditions such as the Yoruba faith of Ile Ife and Oyo into worldwide religions. During a four-day conference I helped to organize, entitled "From Local to Global: Rethinking Yoruba Religious Culture for the New Millennium," at Florida International University, a number of scholars proclaimed that the Yoruba religion can no longer be conceptualized as confined to a provincial ethnic tradition, but has, in fact, attained the status of a "world" religion. Mass education, travel, migration, and communication are forces that have linked the Afro-Atlantic world together over a period of several hundred years. African traditions such as Yoruba or Fon have evolved into the "new" world communities of Santeria, Voodoo, and Brazilian Candomble. In essence many of these variants of African traditions share many of the same core beliefs as their African predecessors but were intentionally modified to retain Christian characteristics to mask their indigenous properties. In her article "Afro-Brazilian Cults and Religious Change in Brazil," Maria Isaura Pereira de Queiroz states that "Catholicism with its numerous saints was employed as a screen to protect the 'barbaric' beliefs, and the slaves went on practicing their rituals. All African groups—Yoruba, Genge, Nago, Bantu, and others—disguised their gods behind the mask of a Catholic divinity, and each African temple had an alter decorated with the image of a patron saint in addition to its pegi.[25]

Under the most oppressive of circumstances, these faiths were able to continue and become worldwide religions due to their remarkable adaptability and resiliency. This tradition continues as these communities continue to expand in the American context, with African immigrants, Afro-Caribbean, and African-Americans, and Americans continuing to show an intense interest in these ancient traditions of African values and ethics. In a number of examples in my research on African immigrant communities, I witnessed an increasing demand for African holy men or medicine persons to travel directly from Africa to the United States to engage in various initiation ceremonies at great expense. This trend could only be possible as a product of the cultural linkages that globalization is in the process of fostering.

This process of globalization of African immigrant traditions is taking on a special meaning for both African Americans and many Caucasian and Latino converts. Increasingly, America is seeing the introduction of priests from Africa such as Nigerian Youruba-Ifa holy men. In the tradition of Ifa, the devotees of Orisha are followers of a religion with expansionist and missionary tendencies that have crisscrossed the Afro-Atlantic world. Indeed a sizable number of Ifa priests have developed a strong clientele and semipermanent homes in many of America's largest cities. Wande Abimbola, for example, is a former chancellor of a Nigerian university and former senator of Nigeria who is now a prominent Ifa priest based in Boston. Another example is Ele buibon, an Ifa priest based in the Nigerian city of Osogbo, who spends close to four months a year with clients in cities such as New York, Los Angeles, and Atlanta. Finally, Chief Bolu Fatumise of Chicago's Ifa Orisha Cultural Center/African Shrine, who is interviewed in a Ford Foundation project pilot study I am conducting, is the son of a highly respected Ifa priest who was William Bascon's principal informant during his famous research trip to Nigeria in 1937. It is also interesting to note that his title, the reverend chief Bolu Fatumise the Gbawoniyi of Ile-Ife, means "the one who gives honor to Ifa," and is an implicit reference to the role he plays in America as the one who gives honor to Ifa in a foreign land. His work assists not only followers of Orisha in the United States but also in Nigeria for close to two months out of the year during Ifa ceremonies and festivals.

It seems that in the globalizing practice of indigenous African religions, we are witnessing the intersection of African immigrant and African American religious nationalism and religion. African immigrants are playing important roles in the revitalization of African indigenous religion in America although the agents of these traditions are in many cases black Americans. The environment of globalization is creating strong linkages between indigenous identities in transnational and global dimensions. Not only have these communities formulated a mythic linkage with ancient traditions such as the Yoruba kingdom of Oyo or the cities of Ile-Ifa, but they communicate regularly with these cultural centers for the purpose of expanding and reinforcing these traditions within the new American society. A major American center for this revitalization, for example, is the Yoruba community of the Oyotungi Village in South Carolina, whose leader and Oba [king] Oseijami has created a pan African-U.S. traditional Orisha society.

I should also mention that these Orisha devotees in America not only regularly visit Nigeria during important celebrations such as the Ifa and Oshun festivals but that indeed, through their financial support, they assist in the expansion and promotion of cultural practices and festivals that paradoxically are on the decline in Africa but are on the increase in the United States.

Conclusion

We have seen from this discussion that globalization entails not the death of religion but in many cases its expansion and promotion. We must realize that globalization is not the end of history or the eventual evolution of all societies toward a final form of the secularized bureaucratic state. It is an innovative and somewhat unpredictable reshuffling of many of the world's cultures, faiths, and traditions. It is a force for change for both Western and non-Western societies. This is nowhere more evident than in the crosscurrents between contemporary America and the African immigrant religious movements in its Christian, Islamic, and various African indigenous-traditional variations. These movements as sources of cultural continuity, stability, and authority are demonstrating a remarkable resiliency and adaptability to American culture. This strength of culture in many ways stems from a several-hundred-year tradition of innovation and diversity within the African diaspora.

Notes

1. I refer here to the various works of Marxism and socialism that advocated industrialization and urbanization as a necessary stage for Marxist development. Later "Marxist" writings that rejected industrialization as a necessary precursor to revolution in the Maoist or "peasant socialist" tradition obviously do not apply here.

2. M. Kearney, "The Local and the Global: The Anthropology of Globalization and Transnationalism," *Annual Review of Anthropology* 24 (1995): 551.

3. Kearney, "The Local and the Global," 550.

4. Kearney, "The Local and the Global," 551.

5. Kearney, "The Local and the Global," 552.

6. Robert Hefner, "Multiple Modernities: Christianity, Islam, and Hinduism in a Globalizing Age," *Annual Review of Anthropology* 27 (1998): 89.

7. Kearney, "The Local and the Global," 548.

8. Fredric Jameson and Masao Miyoshi, eds., *The Cultures of Globalization* (London: Duke University Press, 1998), xii; Kearney, "The Local and the Global," 558.

9. By the "tenth province" I refer to the Haitian immigrant community in the United States.

10. I refer here to a mapping project that I am currently working on in conjunction with the Ford Foundation entitled "African Immigrant Religious Communities: Identity Formation in America's Pluralistic Society."

11. Mark Juergensmeyer, *Terror in the Mind of God: The Global Rise of Religious Violence* (Berkeley: University of California Press, 2000), 225.

12. Hefner, "Multiple Modernities," 87.

13. Hefner, "Multiple Modernities," 85; J. Casinova, *Public Religions in the Modern World* (Chicago: University of Chicago Press 1998); Robert Hefner, *Democratic Civility: The History and Cross-Cultural Possibility of a Modern Political Ideal* (New Brunswick, N.J.: Transaction, 1998).

14. Phillip Berryman, *Liberation Theology* (New York: Pantheon, 1987).

15. Bennetta Jules-Rosette, "The Sacred in African New Religions," in *The Changing Face of Religion*, ed. James Beckford and Thomas Luckman (London: Sage, 1989), 155.

16. Jules-Rosette, "The Sacred in African New Religions," 155.

17. Juergensmeyer, *Terror in the Mind of God*, 225.

18. Jules-Rosette, "The Sacred in African New Religions," 148-49.

19. Jules-Rosette, "The Sacred in African New Religions," 148.

20. Jules-Rosette, "The Sacred in African New Religions," 149.

21. Again, I refer here to the mapping project that I am working on for the Ford Foundation entitled "African Immigrant Religious Communities: Identity Formation in America's Pluralistic Society."

22. Ford Foundation report, "African Immigrant Religious Communities: Identity Formation in America's Pluralistic Society." Interview with Father Onubogu on July 28, 2000.

23. Hefner, "Multiple Modernities," 90.

24. Ford Foundation project, "African Immigrant Religious Communities: Identity Formation in America's Pluralistic Society." Interview, in fall of 2000.

25. Maria Isaura Pereira de Queiroz, "Afro-Brazilian Cults and Religious Change in Brazil," in *The Changing Face of Religion*, ed. James Beckford and Thomas Luckman (London: Sage, 1989), 88.

7

Ogu's Iron or Jesus' Irony: Who's Zooming Who in Diasporic Possession Cult Activity?

Jim Perkinson

Sometime in the last twenty years, a videotape of a black North American Pentecostal preacher was shown to a number of Candombles in Bahia, Brazil. (I am unable to recall the exact place I heard or read of this occurrence, and it will thus have to remain part of that anonymous production of history that is the real thickness of popular culture creativity in the ongoing project of human habituation.) The Bahians watched the video with mute interest until the preacher moved from warm-up to takeoff in his delivery, shifting from simple communication to searing incantation, from quietude to incandescence. Suddenly, they lurched into agitated outburst, "Xango! Xango! Xango!" They did not speak English, nor did they know anything of Pentecostal worship. They simply knew the arrival gestures of this *orixa* in the flesh of human "being," and the body language was all the eloquence they needed.

The forum may have been Christian, but the rhythm was Afro-Bahian. A preaching of Jesus yielded a message of Xango, speaking war and thunder, blood and bloodlines, without asking doctrinal permission or ecclesial affirmation. One wonders what said preacher would say if he was shown a video of those watching the video of his preaching. He had given more than presumably he intended, more than perhaps he would have wished; indeed, something entirely different than his doctrine would have permitted. What here was hallowed, and what bedeviled, and where the line between? Who was zooming who? The structure of Christian relations with creolized traditions historically has clearly been that of the "missionary position," but who was on top in this situation? The conundrum is paradigmatic for the postcolony—the emergence of the *carnivalesque* as the sign of the times: bodies not fully in control of their inhabitants; subjectivities defying their identities; multiple meanings in single ciphers!

Welcome to global culture! Undoubtedly, this way lies pedagogy for the doctri-
naire and the difference-fearing.

But the irony to be elevated in this polyrhythm is even more darkly rooted.
The Brazilian spirits are regal in repute and bearing, demanding discipline and
formality more akin to aristocratic epistemes of what is important and worthy.[1]
Yes, orixas and *caboclos* challenge the logic of proposition from the "left field"
of possession.[2] But they remain relatively more expressive of the hieratic display
and courtly ceremonial characteristic of West African royalty traditions.[3] Once
mounted upon their "horses," these spirits tend to silent pageantry and aloof
affect.

It is rather in Haiti—where the mud oozes and the cock crows, where the
red-eyed spirits look back like an alarm bell waiting to go off, like the veil of
night dropping, like gunpowder with a fuse burning or a prayer the precise shape
of a bullet—that the shadow appears in starkest relief. Here the opacity reveals
by repelling—and repels by revealing—the true political "light" of "Enlightenment" fame, as indeed it does also, the Christian mission game of clarifying by
colonizing. In fact, it is Haiti in history that stands as the most indecipherable
cipher and will thus provide the requisite "deliverance dilemma" in what follows. How shall an American academy, underwritten by an Enlightenment polity, organized in a globalizing economy, originated from a Calvinist cosmogony,
understand itself in the mirror of its poorest and least anticipated Western Hemi-
sphere "other"? Or in more specifically religious terms, Who is Jesus in the eye
of Ogou?

It is appropriately the Haitian *loa* Ogou (or Ogu; in Nigeria, Ogun; in Benin,
Gu; in Brazil, Ogum) who will form the focus of the inquiry in this chapter.[4] Not
only does this Caribbean "god of iron" subsume his fellow Oyo *orisha*, Shango,
in the creole compound spirit, "Ogou Chango," but the "politics of power" he
articulates lies directly at the core of the colonial encounter I am interested in
interrogating.[5] Had the incident of clandestine appearance cited in the opening
paragraph involved *vodun* practioners of urban Haiti, the shout of excitement
would likely have identified an epiphany of Ogou rather than Xango. Had
France, England, and Spain been schooled in an ideology of paradox and possibility such as Ogou encodes—rather than the privilege of plunder these colonial
powers read into and out of their "Christ-bearing" vocation—Haiti might have
emerged in modernity as a tutor of balance rather than a sign of banishment.[6]
Even today, however, that sign remains one of the times. If Western Christianity
were to take its own Last Judgment text seriously, it would sit at the feet of its
most ravaged and impoverished victim to learn the surprise of the outcome.
What it might learn of is a "Son of Man" (Mt 25:31-46) it has never recognized—and of its own impending apocalypse! Haiti has yet to teach.

In 1791, when a Mambo blew a conch shell on the beach of Bois Caymen in
San Domingo launching the only successful "national" slave revolt in history,
vodun loa were summoned to enter the lists of political liberation.[7] In the ensu-

ing decade-long struggle, the iron-making secrets of Ogou—among other skills and powers of the possession-cult pantheon—were marshaled to forge peasant weapons that would effectively repulse and destroy the cavalry of Napoleon's top general.[8] "Haiti," and history-reading in general in the West, have been made to suffer ever since.[9] This seminal moment of historical reversal, leveraged in part by local African knowledges conserved in creolized cults of possession, displays this reversal as a challenge to Western Christian practices that to date remains unanswered and indeed greatly feared.[10]

It is no accident that the mass media image of Haiti in the United States associates the nation virtually unquestioned with irremediable poverty, uncontrollable AIDS infection, and unimaginable demonisim epitomized by dolls impaled by pins or imprisoned in bottles. At the time of its accomplishment, Haitian independence sent shivers of terror up the backsides of American planters and revealed the true subject of "revolutionary" independence both stateside and on the continent.[11] As C. L. R. James has carefully documented, Paris masses and "Negro" slaves caught the same scent of freedom; however, only the slaves managed to defeat the French middle classes.[12] English intriguers such as Pitt meanwhile promulgated "abolition of the slave trade" (but not, be it noted, the end of slavery) as a means of trying to wrestle the "fattest plum of all colonies" away from French control and into service of English bourgeois wealth accumulation; they were only barely repudiated by the political savvy of a Toussaint L'Ouverture.[13] What was not successfully repudiated, however, was the subsequent submergence of history into superstition in the average "American" awareness, or the careful evisceration of the Haitian achievement by capitalist containment on the international scene.[14] The monumentality of the accomplishment was masked in a monstrosity of lie. "Christian" concern for the "beguilements of darkness" faces perhaps no more ironic subversion and condemnation than the fact of its own obfuscations of this singular and brief realization of Exodus vision in the New World.

The political subversion points to a religious surreption. Hidden behind vodun's chromolithographs of Catholic saints are *minkisi* of Kongolese or Nago spirits.[15] Haitians kept African practice alive under the veneer of a Roman surface. But what if the sleight of hand does not stop there? What if beneath the saint mounted by the spirit, we were suddenly to glimpse a profile of Christ? And then in his shaded gaze, the eye of Ogou? How do we punctuate the (post)colonial *mise en abyme?* Who has the right to command the last place, the deepest *rasin* (root) of spirit? Indeed, who is the horse and who the rider?

In general, this chapter offers a reading of diasporic possession cult activities—as found especially in vodun but also as codified in *santeria* and *candomble* (and as transfigured into the dread beat of Rastafari, transported into the dead beat of Brooklyn streets and refigured as rap)—in accordance with the demand of Black theologian Will Coleman in his book *Tribal Talk.* Coleman asserts that black theology worthy of the name today must "seek to establish a relationship with other liberation movements, both Christian and non-Christian, in order to both enhance its own perspective and contribute to these movements."[16] Part and parcel of that search is a necessary struggle to "interpret and discern God's liberating activity within human experience and history from the broader perspective of other oppressed people."[17]

What follows is a theological embrace of diasporic possession practices that places those activities in a modality of reciprocal hermeneusis with Christian self-understanding. In the mix, African American Christian "spirituality" is juxtaposed alongside diasporic initiation practices to highlight both commonalities and differences in bringing the realm of spirit to bear on the materiality of everyday life. At issue will be Coleman's assertion that "spiritual animation, 'Holy Ghost power,' and the formation of religious communities (non-Christian and Christian) in the African Americas revolved around the whirling vortex that originated deep within the abyss of a West African cosmology."[18] Under pressure is white Presbyterian slave owner Charles Colcock Jones's nineteenth century note that Christological affirmation was relatively lacking in slave liturgy.[19]

While Jones's claim may seem to hold for the surface features of slave—and non-Christian postslavery—celebrations, I argue that the depth structures of those ritual practices may push in a different soteriological direction. The general case of polyrhythmic possession and polymorphic "salvation" argued for in conclusion finds its paradigmatic possibility in the juxtaposition of Jesus-Ogou hinted at above and labored over below. Christian vision today may need to allow for the paradox of discovering its own messiah as a *chwal* (a "horse" mounted by the loa during possession), dancing in the shadows of a Jacmel *peristyle* to a Badragi drumbeat! But first we need a frame.

Long's Labyrinth

Historian of religions Charles Long has long asserted that the entire problematic of Western academic epistemology is irreducibly "postcolonial" in character even as its consciousness has remained largely "Enlightenment" in orientation.[20] For Long, every form of postcolonial identity—whether constructed as "white" or "black," Native American or Puerto Rican, suburban heterosexual Christian male or inner-city Islamic lesbian—is already caught in the dynamic dilemma of the aftermath of colonial history.[21] But the effects of this commonly shared history of violent domination show up quite differently in majority and minority cultures. In religious studies, Long contends that "religions of the oppressed" (vodun, Ghost Dance, cargo cults, santeria, and so on) represent a form of signification upon the academy as salient as the academy's comprehension of these same religions in its own discourses of ethnography, history, philosophy, and theology. The problem is whether the academy in particular (or the "West" in

general) is capable of recognizing its own conundrum as one involving a hermeneutic (and material) economy of reciprocity.

More particularly, Long has offered example in his own thinking.[22] While by
training he is the offspring of the likes of Emerson and Otto, Kant and Comte,
Hegel and Husserl, Long has resolutely remained clear that his other genealogy
runs through the broken mythologies of the colonized. In service of the significance of this double root, he has regularly paid homage to the academy, only to
turn the blade of its own concepts back upon itself. Otto is a clear case in point.

The Lutheran religionist's seminal formula of spiritual experience writ large
—the *mysterium tremendum et fascinosum*—is taken up by Long only to be
thrown down on the anvil of colonial history, broken open, and made to reveal a
seminal difference.[23] Where Christian mission and "enlightened" colonization
successfully conquered not only indigenous economies but indigenous typolo-
gies, the experience on the side of success was merely confirmation.[24] Europe
waxed self-confident of its own myth of chosenness in being able to enforce its
"superiority" at the end of a gun barrel. "Christ" was clearly *the* culmination—
after all, there was the native on the ground cowering or already a corpse! The
coiffured and well-powdered head of Absolute Spirit experienced, in response,
no immediate disruption of its own dialectical consummation. In European reflection on the colonial moment, the apex of development was simply confirmed
as "already occupied," and nothing served immediate notice otherwise.

For the *indigene*, on the other hand, the experience was sheer rupture—all
the way down to the bone and back to the beginning! Colonial dominance
"forced" the native (or imported) body into a ruthless economy of profit; colonial hegemony rewrote the local cosmogony into an equally ruthless "science"
of progress.[25] Indigenous myths of origin were peeled back to their primordial
point of genesis in something akin to a reinauguration of the kind of rupture that
"founds worlds."[26] For those undergoing Western takeover, the colonial experience itself was quintessentially religious—a plunge into a level and quality of
chaos and violence that only myth had ever succeeded in containing and codify-
ing in the past.[27] And thus myth had to be made to do its work again in the colonial present, if consciousness and collectivity were to survive at all.[28]

For Long, *vodun veve`* or cargo quay, ghost dance vision or Holy Ghost
shout, all shared a commonality of formation whatever the particularity of their
codification. They had to organize terror into meaning.[29] For local culture, the
remedy was necessarily reconfigured ritual (until revolt was possible). Interest-
ingly for Long, the academy came up with its own "intimation of absolute disintegration" once it began to pay attention to all the extinction that "progress" was
occasioning around the globe.[30] Otto's formula said more than its formulator
imagined. A West choking on its own mythology of control turned with fascinated gaze to the cultures it thought it had tamed. The terror that could irrupt in
an "enlightened consciousness" without seeming rhyme or reason in the cloister
of a bourgeois home (such as Long explores in the writings of Henry and Wil-

liam James) bespoke a mysteriousness underlying human "being" at once seductive and savage.[31]

Otto's formula captured the experience even as it dissembled the history. There is a huge "Something" underwriting or overshadowing human contingency in the world that both titillates and terrorizes.[32] But colonial power itself is, in part, an organization of might and right in an attempt to enhance the fascination while avoiding the fear. It is also a futile attempt, ultimately. It is part of Long's genius to have insisted on holding the psychological codification of middle-class experiences of vertigo accountable to the history of dominance giving rise to that class in the first place—in forcing whole "other" populations into very concrete material experiences of such contigency.[33] Yes, Western culture is constituted in "fascination" (for ever new "objects," spicy tastes, striking tapestries, exotic bodies, glittering minerals, and so on). But the "underneath" of Western culture—literally the rest of the globe—is then constituted in the tremendousness of the terror necessary to secure that fascination for a limited group of people.

Long refuses to allow slave practices in the invisible institution, or native practices in ghost dancing, or indigenous practices of survival around the globe in the face of Western economic and cultural predation, simply to become one more exercise in Western fascination. "Oh, look, the natives blow human tibia-bone horns to call up the spirits! Can I buy one?" No. "Their" experience of the Absolute partakes of its uncanniness as tremendum—something the West "knows" little about, even as it finds itself unable to shake off the incursions of "deep Dread" within its own privilege-saturated psyche. Remediation (if there is such a thing) for the West in general—as for the academy in particular—lies in the direction of encounter with oppressed cultures' elaboration of trememdousness in their own ritual codes. Long (as numerous other "minority" scholars such as Paul Gilroy, Toni Morrison, and so on) has comprehended deeply that below the particularities of religious and cultural practice in modernity, there is (necessarily) this ongoing negotiation with the drama of death and desire in its most grotesque forms of projection and "enforcement" by one group of human beings on another. It is this drama that colonial historiography and postcolonial hermeneutics seek to explain (and explain away). Strangely, it is this drama that indigenous religion and minority ritual *conserve*.[34]

More accurately, what these latter conserve is the memory of such a struggle. The delirium of being overwhelmed, as also the dynamism of finding means of figuring and transfiguring such, are arguably what animate the survival arts of the oppressed. Long's point is that these collective gestures represent profound significations *of*—as well as "on"—history.[35] They are not just "means of overcoming" by way of escape. They are equally (in potential, if not always in fact) memory in the key of folk critique and vernacular creativity. To the degree they encode human innovation articulating the void of nonbeing into a "strange fruit" of terrible beauty (like a haunting song over a horrific deed), they displace the

ultimacy of the violence. They embody the contradiction of an unspeakable annihilation that is both remembered *as* annihilation (and thus terrifying) *and yet
not entirely bowed down to* by the living community that is (in part) constituted
by that very remembering.

Only the present tense of the remembered intensity, however, is capable of
keeping the representation from falling into mere pornography.[36] And here perhaps we border on the power of memory to capitulate itself as a kind of "formal
reincarnation"—ancestral "victims and/or heroes" rehabilitated in the present of
the living community's rhythm in being allowed to occupy time and space ritually.[37] They do so in the form of a living intensity that amounts to a temporary
takeover of living bodies. Colonial history itself here, for Long, is the new laby-
rinth of initiation, conscripting the body that seeks to articulate its "deep" meaning (ritually) into the living contradiction of a death suffered (in the individual)
and yet survived (in the community which carries that individual forward in the
rhythmic intensity of its remembering). The postcolonial body that "has its eyes
open"—that does not refuse this history of terror and its initiation—*is* this contradiction. It is constituted as a social amalgam of life and death that defies all
logic. It embodies an irresistible premonition of "the ultimate" as the absolute-
ness of paradox. Creation refuses to answer to destruction. And vice versa. The
resulting tension is both the vitality of, and the disease within, the body under
oppression. And yet, dilemma of dilemmas, the ethics of such a knowledge remains an ongoing question of responsibility.

Possession Cults

Katherine Dunham went down to Haiti as an anthropology student. She came
back up out of Haiti as an ambassador of the loa in the medium of dance.[38]
When she teaches her students in the United States or Europe the movements
and beats of the *Yenvalo*, does academic pedagogy begin to open itself to tutor-
ship of a different kind? Or is Danballah incarcerated and emptied out in an
instrumentalizing appropriation of shoulder rolls and hip jerks that, a few dance
companies and video productions down the line, only piles up yet more profits
for the entertainment industry? What is a loa? How do we (who inhabit the in-
finitizing cyberspace of instrumental rationality) account for possession cult
activity?

It is not a question about the "other." In an age when the most powerful human institution in history is given over to an absolutely unfettered logic of ag-
grandizement in deference to an ascribed "Invisible Hand" hovering, omniscient
and omnipresent, over its every least action, it is not primarily the loa of Haiti
that need to be explained. In the zeitgeist of the tomahawk-chop-shout in the
stadium, the wave around the green of another Tiger Wood's triumph on the
course, the warehouse rave, the fan war, the binge in the bar, the coke in the car,

the Prozac for the pained, the Ridlin for the unruly, the chill-out screen for the churned up, the video for the bored and big-bellied, "possession" is not a question. It is rather a matter of whose possession, which loa? Adam Smith's market Magnus undoubtedly reigns supreme today, as the ultimate fetish, the ascendant acolyte of the age, lining up all subsidiaries in a relentless regimentation of both mind and spirit. (No serious CEO or MBA can afford even momentarily to ask whether the de facto deification of capitalist dynamism is really a demon in disguise: brown fields and black waters and burned forests and dead bodies and extinct species to the contrary, the practical belief in the God of Infinite Growth remains virtually absolute.) But the question does remain thinkable: Is there yet resistance and rebellion in the ranks of the invisible worthy of attention and exploration? And how do we approach the ribaldry and revolt we do see?

Ogou as Example

Again, it is worth examining Ogou as both a paradigm and sign. Recent scholarship (as, for instance, in the Sandra Barnes-edited *Africa's Ogun: Old World and New*, published in 1997) points out the counterintuitive context of today: Orisha worship in general and Ogou devotion in particular, are growing. Despite the touted triumph of book religions (Christianity, Judaism, Islam, Buddhism, Hinduism, and so forth) over oral carryovers (traditional religious practices of various ilks) from a ruder age and in spite of the withering auspices of scientific advance, West African and Afro-diasporic religious practices are expanding and proliferating rather than receding.[39] Today some seventy million African and New World peoples are religiously familiar with Ogou (or Ogun in Nigeria and Ogum in Brazil), in a globalizing prodigality of religious exploration whose watchword is "pastiche."[40]

Barnes offers a reading of this burgeoning business of cult as primarily a matter of "meaning making."[41] Soliciting Eco's insistence that "unidimensional, unidirectional modernist predictions of how the world is making itself" are too thin to do justice to the fact, she focuses on subjectivity as the locus of "the struggle to make sense of the world and answer the ultimate questions humans face."[42] For the multisensorial means of exegeting and exhibiting experience found in ritualized pursuit of knowledges, Ogou functions as both "deity" and "concept."[43] Traced through local histories of promulgation and use in Nigeria and Benin as well as en route throughout the colonial and postcolonial eras of Caribbean, Brazilian, and North American diasporas, Ogou demonstrates both durability and adaptability. At the same time, as J. D. Y. Peel points out, he can be neither essentialized nor abstracted in isolation from the historical record.[44]

Historically emergent from hunting, iron smithing (and smelting), and soldiering practices, in modern metamorphoses, Ogou emerges in astonishing prolixity (even as other associations, such as with agriculture and snake handling, disappear).[45] He appears in recent provenance as:[46]

- champion of political resistance,
- guardian of the downtrodden,
- patron of new technologies (of iron making as well as of iron itself and thus of any new modern mechanization),
- protector against accidents on the road,
- medicine of the maroon, enabling flight into the forest solitudes to live in freedom,
- quintessence of conservationist concern to relate to nature in respectful reciprocity,
- archetypal "divine tough guy" in cinema and on TV (*The Believers* and *Miami Vice*, respectively),
- god of war and fire mobilized by a citizen's group intent on driving dope peddlers and criminals from a New Orleans neighborhood,
- hip hero of the New Age ghetto on the West Coast,
- Santeria's "ass-kicker" *santo* Santiago,
- St. Jacques of Kreyol configuration in contemporary Haiti,
- St. Peter the "Key-keeper, Way-opener, Road-maker" of Cuban confession,
- John Henry, Stagolee, and High John the conqueror in African American lore,
- St. George in Brazil, drunken macho general reaping havoc in the *barrio,*
- Promethean-pusher of giant gears on *Compania Fumento*'s seal in Puerto Rico,
- High-tech haunt of the Internet in William Gibson's cyperpunk,
- Milo Rigaud's "first blade of the Tarot,"
- Woye Solinka's muse as well as his "Black Butterfly" mythologizing of Muhammed Ali,
- "the rage of the riot" in Los Angeles's 1992 uprising according to a local santero,
- "Door-guarder-in-an-army-boot" for sale for (only!) $1,200 in the *supermercado,*
- or even, in a triple conflation, the San Domingo ex-slave general Dessalines reincarnate as a loa, itself reread as the crucified taken down from the cross in present-day vodun ceremony.

Yet for all this epiphanic shape-shifting, Ogun remains himself according to Barnes. He embodies a theory about life—and indeed, a theory about theorizing.

The latter involves a polythetic take on phenomenon. Ogou underscores the energies of an incessant war of the symbol. As Wuthnow indicates, beneath the totalizing public postures of institutionalized religions and systematized theologies lies paradox.[47] People are relentlessly recombinant in their chosen codes of

identity. Written texts harbor proliferating practices in their shadows. Underneath the unblemished public face of (whatever) the ideology, heteogeneity and
hybridity name the everyday actuality. And "communities reproduce themselves
primarily through oral means," notes Barnes.[48] The so-called smaller traditions
constantly metabolize with the dominant great traditions in an ongoing symbio-
sis of life and meaning. But this also means the method of uncovering those
meanings must attend to the ongoing ferment.

Barnes is clear that when dealing with a "metacultural" or international figure like an Oedipus, or a Shiva, or now, an Ogou, the methodology of choice
needs to be polythetic. The figure hosts a domain of meaning that is broadly
inclusive even though not able to yield a single overarching principle of interpretation (such as "things relating to iron" in the case of our African figure).
Rather than seeking to isolate the one thing that determines all cases, the need is
to establish something like Wittgenstein's chain of family resemblances that
allow for an intuitive drawing of boundaries while permitting a certain level of
porousness or indeterminacy.[49]

On the other hand, Ogou does embody a kind of "philosophy of the human
condition," according to Barnes, that "can be stated as a theoretical proposition."[50] Shining out from the midst of the ongoing permutations of meaning
gathered under his name is a "compelling observation on human nature" dis-
cernible as a kind of baseline.[51] The discernment of such is complicated, however, by the fact that historically Ogou is not a creature of written texts so much
as of living practices.

Margaret Drewal, for instance, describes the way Ogou-mounted performers
"bombard the senses—sight, sound, touch, and in some cases taste—with recur-
ring reminders of their deity's distinctive qualities."[52] In his case, the dance vocabulary is articulated primarily in terms of "explosive release"—repeated
movements that are "quick, direct, and forceful."[53] Performers often brandish
sharp-bladed iron weapons during the dances, or index their undulations to a
species of snake that is quick and deadly.[54] Accompanying poetic chants make
use of "percussive sounds and word images" to evoke the One who "clears the
obstacles" and "opens the road" with swift, concentrated intentionality.[55] Ogou
"kills with one blow" when he is aroused.

At the same time, however, Bade Ajuwon's analysis of Yoruba hunters' fu-
nerals reveals a pacific Ogou. The chants, the actions of the ceremony leaders,
the deceased hunter's implements put on display all together portray not ruthlessness, but an "inspiring social role model."[56] The dirges emphasize "a lion of
the thick forest," a self-reliant solitary, a provider for the village, a policer of
society's morals, a protector who "never runs away on sighting a beggar."[57]
Ogou in the regalia and ritual of his homeland is a heroic leader, full of both
courage and opportunism, self-sacrifice and lust for life.[58]

As a folk articulation of theory, custom yields a rich ambivalence, a profu-
sion of contrasts and contradiction. A thick elaboration of historical experience

like "Ogou" (or indeed, any other major deity of the pantheon) cannot be adequately read from only one context.[59] His many meanings are performatively crystalized in a vast array of practices including public spectacles, rites of passage, and a "bewildering variety of family, occupational and cult group" activities.[60] The performative signs of Ogou's uniqueness—the wearing of iron emblems, the fiery red eyes of possession, and the sword dances that characterize his ritual epiphany—are thematically elaborated across a wide range of ritual, mythic, symbolic, and artistic representations. The emphasis is neither standardized nor solemnized like a text of Western Christianity. Rather, the focus is on emotionality and personality traits manifest in the pragmatic preoccupations of everyday life. Deity here mirrors humanity in a performative reciprocity that constitutes a sustained inquiry into the mystery of meaning in a character at once flawed and inspiring.

Ogou as Metaphor

Ogou (as other major spirits) thus materializes as an ever rearticulated embodiment of contradiction. (And indeed, it is precisely this capacity to figure a "coherent iconography of contradiction" that exercises my interest below.) Neither his apotheosis of violence nor his concretizing of nurture can be allowed to stand as definitive. Ogou both creates and destroys. He is a lonely occupant of the margins,[61] and he is revolutionary force engendering new social forms.[62] A paragon of id-directed behavior, the mythic Ogou is led to an excess of aggression against his own villagers that results in self-cursing and self-directed punishment as a tireless worker for social sustenance.[63] An icon of extremes, he is the reformed felon who reenters society with heightened commitment to high ethical standards.[64] In him, Dionysian rage is bent to Apollonian relentlessness. In him we meet a universal metaphor: "people create the means to destroy themselves."[65] He represents "human attempts to govern, not what is out of control in nature, but what is out of control in culture."[66] He symbolizes human limitations in the exercise of power, the tragic history of the attempt at mastery, the inevitable self-destruction attending self-creation, the "helplessness that comes from self-knowledge."[67] In sum, according to Barnes, "Ogou conventionally presents two images. The one is terrifying specter: a violent warrior, fully armed and laden with frightening charms and medicines to kill his foes. The other is society's ideal male: a leader known for his sexual prowess, who nurtures, protects, and relentlessly pursues truth, equity, and justice."[68]

Ogou as Mentor

Karen McCarthy Brown takes us even further into the conundrum. As a white feminist scholar, not only has Brown had to argue forcefully for her willingness "to marry Ogou" in the midst of her anthropological research on Voudouisants in Brooklyn. Not enough that she endorse an African religion for herself as not just a "participant observer" but an initiate, bringing her own personal crises under the tutelage of the mambo she was studying and the loa she was seeking to explain. But she has also—as a woman—embraced the icon of male aggression and anger. "A male war God! How could you?" feminist colleagues will ask her.[69] She responds that she chose it . . . and it chose her.[70] Hers is a "tragic vision of life," she claims, in which she has become deeply skeptical that war, hierarchy, or "us-against-them thinking" will ever be eliminated from humanity.[71] She does not inveigh against those who embrace more idealistic visions—"women working with traditional Jewish and Christian models, as well as those who have recently reclaimed the Goddess tradition"—but is more energized by what she finds to be a more realistic pursuit.[72] She takes her key from Ogou's ritual appearances themselves. Typically, possessions by Ogou spirits work a threefold "theologizing with the body."[73] They begin with an outward attack around the temple, raging and bellowing and clanging performance swords against the pillars and doorposts. They progress to threatening advances on attendees standing around nearby, swords descending perilously close to buttocks and noses. They culminate, however, with the swords being directed by the Ogou against themselves.

For Brown, this "choreography of war making" raises a stark issue: angry aggression and violent action are not exorcised by avoidance.[74] The feminist critique of war requires the encounter with anger within oneself. In her own life, the moment of creative transformation came when she "married" her aggression as a power to be owned and worked with, in all of its potentialities for both evil and good.

Ogou as Memory

But it is in Ogou's transformation from Yoruban empire builder to Haitian hologram of resistance that we touch the heart of the modern matter. Barnes posits an origin for Ogou as the apotheosis of a concept deriving from "a set of commonly held notions about the mystical properties of iron and the powerful people who made or used it" coupled with the recognition that earlier contributions to the concept may have come from hunters' resocialization rituals, in which water from blacksmith forges was used to purify those polluted by their killing activities.[75] While none of the ideas of Ogou's genesis can be elevated as definitive, by the time of the emergence of the great Guinean coast kingdoms of Benin, Oyo and Dahomey in the fourteenth to the seventeenth centuries, Ogou had become a layered coagulation of historical processes that underwrote political power.

For many Yoruba-speaking groups, Ogou was worshipped as the "way-shower"—a deity of innovation who was "the [bringer] of fire, the first hunter, the opener of roads, the clearer of the first fields, the first warrior, the introducer of iron, the founder of dynasties, towns and kingdoms."[76] As initiator of the new technology of iron, the new economy of agriculture, a new political order through war, and the new way of life of cities, Ogou emerges as *the* symbol of political supremacy.[77] His iron sword condenses a twin significance of aggression and civilization.[78]

The very intensity of the imagery, however, betrays its tenuousness. Underneath the clarity is the memory of conflict. Barnes notes that in eastern Yorubaland and the kingdom of Benin, "ritual reenactments of battles between kings and town leaders have long figured in large civic pageants dedicated to Ogou."[79] Royal power was an uneasy accession over chiefly power, and Ogou's polyvalent image as aggressor did not only ratify the current incumbent's success, but codified the history of conquest of other groups upon which that rule was predicated. The imagery endorsed both kingly power and the powers that royal configuration only partially succeeded in suppressing.

John Pemberton, for instance, clarifies the degree to which the role of Ogou in the ritual cycle in contemporary southwestern Nigeria codifies an annualized re-negotiation of the "essential question in terms of which the problem of violence and culture must be resolved."[80] The "logic of Ogou" and the "realities of political history" are intertwinned in a ritual process in which "deeply felt contradictions regarding culture and violence, political order and disorder, are acted out and, for the moment, resolved."[81] Since the eighteenth and nineteenth century, Yoruba kingdoms have represented neither a "tribal system" with authority vested in a chiefs' council arbitrated by the king nor a "centralized monarchy" with authority concentrated in the king and chiefs acting as advisors.[82] Rather they embody a vision of history shaped by a perpetual struggle for power between kinship and kingship allegiances.[83]

This human conflict is mediated by the ritualization of nonhuman power. In contemporary celebrations, the crown itself serves as the focal point of power in being understood as simultaneously the mythical "gift of the ancestors," "sacrifical bestowal" of the current senior chiefs, "mystical repository" of the medicines prepared by the priests, and actual endowment by the king's senior wife who embodies the covert potencies of "the mothers."[84] When chiefs and people honor the king, they are "salut[ing] the fact that his power is 'next to the gods.'"[85] In repeatedly appearing and dancing before the orisha of iron and war in such festivals, and on behalf of his subjects, "the king [for his part] turns the powerful deity who can divide and destroy into a force upon whom they can rely to perpetuate their society."[86] But the struggle thus muted remains subtly mobile just under the surface of the ritual.

Ogou as Model

When we turn to Haitian history, the mute turns militant. Initially, of course, this is true with respect to the revolution already noted. Haiti is the result of a powerful and persuasive slave insurrection, amalgamating the ideals of the eighteenth-century French Revolution with (the slaves' own) African traditions of freedom, that has been resisted internationally ever since and reinterred inside a repressive hierarchy on the homefront. As noted above, Ogou played a key role of animation and enablement. As rage and resolve, he articulated resistance; as iron and implement, he also underwrote tactics.

Today Ogou is ensconced as a unique mediatorial figure in urban vodun practices, straddling the two major genealogies of loa—the Rada and Petro pantheons—and thus integrating "right-" and "left-"hand traditions of power.[87] Mediating between the gentler communalized nature forces of the Dahomean line and the more belligerent coercive characters of the Kongo *nanchon*, Ogou is a relentless power-broker. He offers a creole ritual tongue in amalgamating the "watery" familial emphasis of the former with the fiery independence associated with the latter. Where Rada revels in ancestral evocations of ancient *Gine*, Petro represents a bombastic expropriation and imitation of slaveholding powers. In consequence, perhaps more than any other loa, Ogou models a manageable way of being in the dilemma of Haitian (post)modernity.

Straddling family and foreigner, home-world and other-world, Ogou organizes what for McCarthy Brown is an essential articulation in the contemporary situation: the paradox that the "same power which liberates also corrupts and inevitably turns on itself."[88] Indeed, there is not just one such Ogou figure for the Haitian, but seven, or twenty one, or several hundred (the exact number is not the point).[89] And unlike the rigid rule keeping of the typical Petro persona, the Ogou power is rooted primarily in the province of feeling, with all of its complexities and rapidly shifting permutations.[90] Yes for Ogou, rage is definitive, but it is a rage that cuts multiple ways at once. The metaphor is not mere figure. In the *ounfo*, Ougo prances through the threefold performance noted above: he aims his slashing "affect" first at the enemy, then at the ally, and finally at his own embodiment.

In Haitian history, Ogou has left behind his associations with hunting and smithing and taken on primary significance as a recapitulation of the military-political complex.[91] He articulates a plethora of historical moments and present possibilities. Ogou as Sin Jak Maje is a sideswipe of the colonial Spanish power, Santiago, in whose name Christian Spain conducted its *reconquista* campaign against the Moors and then carried out its conquest of the New World. Ogou

Feray is the African warrior reincarnate as the pride of the slave revolt, as the ruthlessness of the Haitian political rulers (often enough against their own people), as the courage of demonstrators and activists in the recent change of government associated with Aristide. Ogou Feray the Magnet brings into play the powers of this "iron god" to gather the lost or even protect against false arrest. Ogou Badragi is the one who battles on past even the last limits of energy and hope.

Ogou Achade is the patron of those who *chante pwen*, "sing a point song," at the juncture of impossibility, where anger is the last resource left with which to defy the oppressive circumstance. The sung, or swallowed, or incised (under the skin), or worn (around the neck), or performed *pwen* (as in dances over veve` drawings around the *peristil*) mark moments when the power of a particular loa is condensed and internalized for use by a devotee.[92] Indeed, as Achade Boko, Ogou is available as "underdog-sorcerer," the dangerous "lefthand" work of one who opts for a weapon outside the normal community sanctions. In Ogou Chango, Ogou Yamson, and Ogou Ageou Hanto, we touch upon Haitian explorations of the self-destructive side of power: the anger that hurts one's own, the pain that leads to excessive rum guzzling, the anguish of loneliness in the ghetto. Ogou is also the last line of defense against fate, when there is nothing left to do but to rail against the night as it descends. And in New York City, McCarthy Brown has witnessed a new wrinkle in Ogou anger: the appearance of tears alongside the rage.[93]

McCarthy Brown also specifies the paradigmatic power such a protean figure makes available. In her perspective, possession cult activity in general serves a communal function of probing the possibilities of alternative forms of identity and working with personal tensions and social conflicts creatively and dramatically. With respect to Ogou ritual in particular, not only is the composite of these Ogou impersonations "an almost clinical diagnosis of what happens when people internalize anger" in the throes of oppression.[94] It also offers transformative possibilities. The vodun spirits neither simply "mirror the Haitian people" nor authoritatively "model morally appropriate behavior."[95] Rather, they dramatize options. They "keep the full range of possibilities latent in any way of being-in-the-world before the eyes of the believers."[96] In their antics, they create a kind of psychosocial "theater in the round," probing history, positing potentiality, posturing conflict and its resolution with pinache and perversity. They occasion insight by provocation. They do not pronounce from on high, but pique and problematize (that awful word!) from below. Ogou, in the mix, is the quintessence of the modern dilemma. In him, anger is given license, and the technological "rule of metal" is met with the human capacity to "have mettle." In him, we meet both menace and meaning. Ogou, in a sense, represents a West African and diasporan theology of modernity. He is simultaneously emblem and exegesis.

History as Initiation

The Ogou cult represents a riff on modernity at multiple levels at once. As mobilizing a content of power-organized/power-resisted through anger and its expression, Ogou is an obvious figure for the age. In his association with iron technologies, he is the modern modality of spirit activity par excellence. Today he can be observed shifting his weight from an industrial heavy-metal emphasis to a postindustrial cyber-silicon focus—and doing so with aplomb and adroitness. To the degree urbanization (in both metropole and periphery) is emerging as the overwhelming feature of the social landscape, the ascent of the hardedged Ogou is the clear "word up" of contemporary spirituality. But there is more to be observed here than simply what meets the eye.

Ogou is the current paragon figure for an approach to living that embodies an ancient and perhaps ubiquitous insight about human "being." Traditional cultures the world over have organized their sense of the processual nature of human becoming in terms of rites of passage. Initiation—whatever its particularities of cultural content and ecological context—represents a refocusing of identity at the level of the body-lived-in-community. Alternative consciousness is generally understood to entail alternative embodiment. Young people in general were taken from childhood to adulthood through a ritual process of reprogramming that taught not simply the mind but the muscle. And this was doubly true for youth giving evidence of being particularly selected by the spirits for a role of mediation between the worlds of spirit and matter, the dead and the living, nature and culture. Possession required initiation—a social induction relocating the individual body inside the communal body by way of a "rewriting" of the ecological context on and in the body itself.[97] And transformation required possession—theatrical performance of the "other possibility" rendered real in bodily terms for the gathered community to see, touch, taste, hear, and smell.

Modernity has scarcely lost the need for this kind of ritual theater of change.[98] But increasingly in our own social processes, the search for an alternate consciousness necessary to a changed life circumstance has been incarcerated in the regnant ideology of consumerist individualism. Modern societies manage both the desire for change and its seeming impossibility by marketing experience in the form of substance or entertainment. The body socialized into its various roles in the regime of labor is offered momentary release in the stadium, on the dance floor, through survivalist weekends, in chemical ingestion. But the local communal body has been dismembered and diffused through the economic order of industrial and now postindustrial reorganization of socioecological topographies. The individual body is left starkly dis-incarnate in any palpable sense in its social setting. The machine is the new "surround" that replaces the sensual intimacies of more traditional rites that initiated the body into localized communities and ecologies. Sheila Walker has traced the way that, even in Haiti, urbanization and modernization have eroded the cultural codes of initiation.[99] What in the countryside is culturally interpreted as "being chosen by the spirits" and given social support in the form of a clearly valued role of mediation, in the environs of Port au Prince, increasingly ends up treated as psychic disorientation. Spiritual breakthrough is recast as mental breakdown.

Within such a modernist scenario, Afro-diasporic rites of initiation and possession (such as those encountered in vodun, santeria, and candomble) represent a kind of conjuration on the surface of Western culture. Older memories of other times are "conserved" not so much in texts as in bodies in motion. The immediacy of contact with "living and dying physicalities"—with sweat, with animal blood, with plant potencies, with damp earth or dry dust, with air vibrated by hand on skin, with mineral hardness and feather softness, with a whole range of scents and smells of living and decaying bodies—communicated an immediacy of spiritual contact. The mystery of living/dying energy pored through the pores of one's own living/dying body in sensual contact with other such bodies. In an aphoristic word, meaning-in-the-mind was known by way of muscle-in-motion, spiritual significance by a syntax of scent and sweat and syncopation.

When speaking this way, the dangers are enormous and the demand to warrant the observations overwhelming. In this writing, I can do no more than suggest. The suggestion is that Charles Long's notion of history itself as initiation for indigenous peoples made (forcibly) to undergo Western modes of modernization augurs eloquently before an uncomprehending academy.[100] Long has (as noted above) endured the lengthy processes of initiation into the "academic body" (of intellectual constructs that are simultaneously somatic edifices) in order to bend those rites in service of articulation of a rite not entered into by the academy (to the degree its configuration is "Western"). Among other ways of trying to figure a depth of pain and opacity of experience that are precisely *not* representable in "normal" academic discourse, Long has made tactical use of a "ritual of reversal" like the signifying practices of his own community. He has taken academic concepts such as Otto's *mysterium* and "broken them in two" and used the break thus opened almost as a modernist form of veve` incantation, auguring an unfigurable underworld that might, nonetheless, surreptitiously appear in Long's own bodily gestures as he spoke. (One wonders if the Candombles invoked in the beginning of this writing would not also recognize certain appearances even in some of the academic performances that the AAR witnesses.) Is the thick style of certain kinds of performance mode merely surface coating, an interesting husk that can be left out of the meaning once that meaning is apprehended? Or is it integral to the significance? Here is the question of this writing in a nutshell.

If a verbal preaching of Jesus can yield a somatic meaning of Xango, what is this thing we call "spirit"? In Long's terms, we might venture to say that here a figure of the fascinosum—Jesus of Pentecostal Christianity, all accepting, all forgiving, summoning all to salvation—is itself overtaken by an elocution of the tremendum—a god of war and lightning, gesturing genocide, pulsating with the polyrhythms of an uncontainable anguish and ecstasy. What was too dense and delirious for the traditional "content" organized by the sign, "Jesus," to carry shows up in the second language of the body, "troping" that first content with an "other" content of form. And in venturing such a description I am not simply celebrating black liturgical vivacity.

The question is one both of form and the content that form encodes. Xango, Ogou, Yemaya, Ezuli, and so on, are dramaturgical personas of the spirit world that embody contradiction in irresolvable form. The entire liturgical context and mode of materialization in this manner of meaning-making posits paradox as the inescapable heart of human endeavor. Are they perhaps truer to the reality of the universe we inhabit (think Heisenberg's uncertainty principle, think Derrida's deconstruction, think Charlie Parker's saxophone!) than the more traditional Western approaches to meaning that try to absolutize or essentialize a separation of good from evil, truth from falsehood, creativity from destruction? Without question, they more accurately convey the essential contradictoriness of modernity as a historical process that has irreducibly built progress on the back of annihilation, leveraged enlightenment as a function of benighting ideology, constructed freedom as the epiphenomenon of slavery.

Ogou as the Spiritual Figurement of the Colonial Tremendum

It is, in any case, at least this latter historical essence of contradiction that exercises the argument here. Specifically with respect to Ogou, the reflection runs as follows. Ogou in origin is an evocation of technological advance and hard-edged power in service of survival that is not only capable of both creation and destruction, but that indeed inevitably effects the latter as it pursues the former. In early modernity, on the west coast of Africa, Ogou (Ogun, Gu) is the figuration of Yoruba, Bini and Fon organizations of political power in fraught forms of domination of kingship over kinship, royal rule over chiefly control. In Haiti, Ogou is the incipient license of and figure for slave appropriations of slaveholder power, African iron ideology turning the implements and inspirations of domination back on the heads of their French bearers in hard-fought acts of resistance and revolt.

In the postindustrial diaspora, Ogou is proving almost meteoric in his powers of metaphoric ascendancy. Riding pig ore into the postmodern gleam of office-tower glory, riding pixel into the global reaches of the cyber netherworld, riding spray-can spigots into graffiti glamour, riding lust into literary light and voyeurism into cinematographic sensationalism, on trial as coconspirator in the Matamoros, Mexico cult murders,[101] animating ardent feminist thinkers to do battle in the culture wars, exercising vigilance over accidents on rural highways and urban streets, finding a new emblem in the New York ghetto in the glock added by

Cubans immigrants to their cauldron (*caldera de ogun*) of iron objects,[102] articulating angry retribution in *lavellas* attacks on former *tonton macoute*,[103] Ogou is growing in leverage and relevance in the contemporary postcolony.

To what degree can this modern mobilization be understood as an eloquent "facing" of a historical terror—in Long's terms, a form of African ritual judo performed on the colonial tremendum that engulfed traditional culture in apocalypse? Can Ogou be grasped as, at least in part, the indigenous West African figure most effective in translating relentless aggression from without into an almost irrepressible internal insurgence? Yes, apart from the Haitian revolution, that insurgence is not in clear political evidence. Yet it is also arguable that African modalities of culture and spirituality have everywhere in the Western world constituted an ever-proliferating insurgent influence, until now it is the case, as Robert Farris Thompson says, "that the entire Western world rocks to an African beat."[104]

Ogou in the Body

The question posed here in terms of wedding Long's use of the tremendum to decode colonial experience and Ogou's growing postcolonial popularity is a question that joins discourse to its drama. Ogou as metaphor cannot be embraced as a simple academic exercise. His idiom is rhythm, meaning worked out at the level of muscle. The tongue alone is not adequate to the articulation. The ritual complex that augurs a presence of the Ogou joins explosive bodily expression to purposeful instrumental resolve. "Anger in action without apology" is perhaps one of his apostrophes. But so is "indignation in defiance of non-deliverance." In *Wretched of the Earth*, Frantz Fanon "read" the buildup of muscular tension among the colonized as an omen of revolution, even as he railed against the discharge of such in the fantastic world of superstition.[105] He saw "murder" clearly written inside the body and labored for its exorcism in the rite of violent resistance alone. Perhaps he was right.

Or perhaps the report from the womanist side of revolt must be championed as the better part of the learning: that subtle survivalist employments of the anger generated by oppression form the long-term conditions for the possibility of revolution (when and if such is ever to become practicable). Here the witnesses would be the likes of Toni Morrison in her exploration (in *Beloved*, for instance) of the way women communally figured and transfigured "violence as a haunt" into a possibility of living fecundly, with scars.[106] Or Delores Williams in her examination of Hagar as the real harbinger of biblical salvation as a message from the margins—even of the Bible itself—insisting on a mature ethic of non-substitution.[107]

But whichever the emphasis, the modality is the method. And the message is in the medium. For a West that has yet to undergo initiation into its own lived history, the possessed body confronts with an irreducible challenge. Possession is not an option. The only question is possession by what, under whose tutelage, for which purpose? Karl Marx saw the industrial factory as the quintessence of fetishistic takeover of the human body: workers reduced to the monstrousness of a single active body part, while all the other muscles and the brain atrophied.[108] We could ad lib: the factory was the "possession cult" of Adam Smith's "invisible hand."

Today we are not less possessed by monstrosity, but the monsters have multiplied. And now it is the eyeball rather than the hand that is being ballooned out of all proportion. As Michel Foucault has offered, we are now occupied by the gaze of surveillance and of super-vision.[109] (And, marvel of marvels, the screen is our hope of rescue! Or is it rather opium no longer needing a needle?) What has clearly *not* been cultivated in capitalist mobilizations of ritual, however, is exploration of the void underlying our own inescapable contingency. We are invited into the commodity as escape, not into ourselves as mystery. And today, even the spirits are increasingly for sale. We can watch "possession," live, on *X Files* or *Millennium*.

But undoubtedly part of the attraction to the occultation is subliminal recognition that we live as living paradox. We are unable to split the atom without splitting ourselves. We are a vibrating something inside the vibrations of everything. More than that we are not sure of. Nothing is simply itself but a composite of all else. Identity is difference in a truly strange and unruly vibrancy.

Ogou in Jesus, Jesus in Ogou

But there then is the conundrum for Christianity. The Western imperium has triumphed at the level of language. For now (but not forever), we speak English (or French or Spanish) in much of the postcolony. But there remain reaches of the colonized body that have not been colonized. At least not by the West. There are languages being spoken underneath the language of domination.[110] Historically in modernity, Jesus is a figure of the dominant, a symbolic cipher of the West, whatever else he may be metaphysically and theologically. But it is apparently quite possible for a human being to preach Jesus while dancing Xango. It may be the case that inside the body baptized in the Spirit we find spirits, that the Holy Ghost of the twentieth century Pentecostal movement is itself ghosted by Ogou and Gede. When the body speaks beyond the tongue, and speaks other than the meanings of the words, how shall we understand? Are we here confronted with the possibility of a history of domination and its subversion articulated in double voice in a single body? Is Jesus as content here mounted by Ogou as form?

If Long's formulation—of the religious experience of the oppressed as a kind of baptism into the Absolute encountered as trememdum—is at all credible, then for Christianity, the question emerges, "Where would Jesus be found in such a scenario?" Liberation traditions would answer, "European Christology was part of the organization of the oppression, one of the legitimizing ideologies leveraging the rupture of indigenous myths of origin in the structure of colonial contact."[111] But Jesus comprehended as liberator, incarnating the message of a God of the oppressed, would ironically have to be sought among the colonized indigenous peoples in their struggles to survive. In part that struggle was against Christianity and Jesus, and in part it appropriated these latter in various innovative masquerades and syntheses.

It is quite possible to read the gospels' depiction of Jesus' career of resistance to oppression in his day and his eventual execution as a subversive as itself tracking the kind of experience Long is attempting to articulate. Jesus' final cry of desperation, retained in all of its Aramaic opaqueness, would underscore a similar experience of "ruptured categories of comprehension," a similar plunge into irreducible terror. *"Eloi, Eloi, lama sabbachthani"* is not the tame protest of a serene passing into certain glory, but the scream of a body ripped away from its moorings in meaning, flinging a last fragment into an empty sky. In Long's terms, we would say that the Palestinian Jesus was gradually stripped of the Jewish mythic structures that gave meaning to his suffering, until at the end of the day he was left utterly naked and alone, without hermeneutic support, before his own contingency and violent end. He was initiated into, and finally himself incarnated—in that cry—God as tremendum. The forms and categories of "messianism" ("Christology") articulated in Jewish prophecy—to the degree they were appropriated and mobilized by the ruling elites of first-century Palestine in service of the priestly/scribal hegemony—were part of the structure of oppression. In the gospels, that dominating messianism is finally ruptured by an experience irrecuperable in language and left behind. Jesus falls out of the discourses that would render his suffering intelligible to the authorities and is left screaming his dismemberment in an archaic bit of Aramaic idiom. And when he is given intelligible form again in the reversal of fate that is represented as resurrection, his long-term presence is a matter of ritual forms of Pentecostal possession that appear delirious and deleterious to those outside the oppressed community of followers.

In the colonial and postcolonial histories of conflagration that have engulfed African-heritage peoples, where might we expect to discover the sources for an authentic Christology, rendering the presence and activity of Jesus among the oppressed not so much intelligible for evaluation as available for use? If Ogou, for instance, is an indigenous West African form increasingly efficacious in articulating the experience of the diaspora, first in the grip of enslavement, then in the wars for political freedom, and finally in a postcolony fraught with social struggle and economic entropy, Christianity might need to wonder in our day about Jesus Ogou rather than Jesus Christ. Such a suggestion is not at all a matter of academic finesse. The question is not a matter of the continuity of images, but of the reality of both liberation and survival among the "least" (Mt 25: 31-46). Jesus as dominant and dominating icon could very well be subverted or sidestepped by Jesus as anonymous rhythm. Or even by Jesus as Ogou. In vodun, santeria, and candomble, Christian iconography and African meaning have been amalgamated in a constant process of creative creolization. Folk experimentation in service of survival still awaits its "Christian" theological articulation, even two centuries now after the Liberator of Slaves has once again acted in history. But this is still the view from the top, from the presupposition of a Christian supremacy that is the real root of white supremacy in the modern world.

From the underside, the real deal may well be Ogou-Jesus. Here is the profound issue Long's challenge about reciprocity raises. If our interdependence is indeed radical, then the signifier cannot be arbitrarily halted at the foot of our particular "familiar." The circulation of meanings in language associated with effects in history is never final, but only provisionally and tactically resolved. To the degree the meaning of "Jesus" is still largely a function of a middle-class worldview associated with largely Western interests, Jesus may have to be understood to be other than "Jesus." But that otherness could, at some point, become more profoundly wedded to another name in history, eclipsing the privileged domain reserved to the name "Jesus," or indeed abandoning it altogether as lost to interests that run so counter to its "original" historical meaning as to have rendered it irrecoverable.[112] Here the issue is simply raised. Its ultimate *denouement* is a matter of the politics of spirit in history.

What can be ventured here as well, though, is the supplement a figure such as Ogou in particular (and diaspora possession activity in general) might add to the history of Jesus. That supplement is a form of challenge about the structure of good news.[113] Ogou has emerged in our brief exegesis above as a broader figure than Jesus to the degree he encodes the centrality of contradiction. If Otto is right in figuring the Absolute in paradoxical terms (even if his exact formula is itself contested as inadequate), then Jesus in history cannot be claimed as the full incarnation of God. He lacks something of the element of paradox that we find so damnably, so provocatively, associated with the likes of an Ogou. And yet, much of the history of transmission of ideas about Jesus has, in fact, made use of the mode of irony—from Mark's "messianic secret" to Kierkegaard's *Training*.[114] What if Ogou's iron is Jesus' irony? Or vice versa? The terrain of investigation has scarcely been glimpsed. To the degree peoples of oppression, in our new postmodern millennium, are looked to as the privileged hiding place of the Christian God in the world (as in Matthew's vision of the Last Judgment), then we should expect the possibility of reversal. We may well confess with our lips and believe in our hearts, but then one day discover that it is our bodies that know the real Otherness that rocks this world and opens up the next one! On that day, dancing, not dogma, might be the ticket to admission!

Nonconclusion

In the history of belief systems and religious practices that try to erect an absolute and essential separation between good and evil, the outcome, again and again, is an appropriation and use of the good to legitimize a power that is finally really more about domination than goodness.[115] "Jesus" has never *not* been the subject of such appropriations and uses. Perhaps it is time to work out a different kind of Christian identity more rooted in the experience of those who all too profoundly are made to know the contradictoriness of power in this world. "Christianity" has yet to do serious theology in relationship to the ways it has been creatively appropriated by various diaspora traditions whose classic texts are not written on paper, but in bodily performances directed to surviving in adverse (and often enough, nearly impossible) circumstances.

In the historic meeting between Jesus and Ogou (or Mary and Yemaya, and so forth) that such traditions have worked out in their symbolic practices, there is a basic posture that the former (Jesus) could learn from the latter (Ogou). Jesus has been ever prone to hierarchical appropriation and totalizing images of power (e.g., God as omnipotent). Ogou—while not avoiding similar conscription in the theaters of political struggle in this world, nonetheless embodies, at the level of the symbol itself, an intuition about power not found in Jesus. That is that power is finally about reciprocity and that power is never separable from the reality of its contradictory effects. It may be long past time to reimagine Jesus in terms of an Ogou or a Yemaya—namely, that Christianity's central figure does not so much constitute a solution as a question, one in whom we meet not just hope but also all the unresolvedness of history. It is not God as Fascinosum, but God as Tremendum that we can't tolerate—all the unanswered disappearances and unrequited rapes and unsolved murders and unrelieved famines and unredeemed holocausts and unavenged middle passages! And yet, if there is a God, that is where that God has to be encountered, and wrestled into meaning, and ironically symbolized in a symbol that does not pretend to close off the radicality of the absurdity. Jesus informed by Ogou would offer not an atoning substitute, but a demanding invitation to live, choose, and risk knowing that even our most powerful realizations of good are full of contradiction and paradox and that goodness itself is still an open question *addressed to* the Ultimate by the violated.

The Unfinal Word

At the level of metaphor, Ogou embodies contradiction as meaning. But likewise at the level of the body, Ogou gives meaning to the metaphor of contradiction. Underneath the level of coherence is a muscle full of tension. It augurs contradiction and war. It is excess. It defies the category. It is opaque, black. It is

Africa in diaspora. It is the beat of drum below the surface of sight, the human shadow of clarity. It strikes the eye with percussive foreboding. It promises an ocean in revolt. It is the volcanic future. It is the smoke of the fire. It is the Ogou in the eye of Jesus, just waiting for the right rhythm. It is the belly below the skull bone, the visceral eruption up the spine, coming with all the clairvoyance of blood. It is the cry of blood on the lip of time. No mouth is large enough for its volume. It is the omen underneath the om, the mantra of the arched back, the thigh-borne hum of every lived hell, the speech of the silent curse, the thunder-clap of the trapped, the red-eyed look at the bottom of every rape looking back, bulging with bristle, bulging like an unrepentant bullet, bringing enlightenment from the graveyard of victims refusing the grave. *This* is resurrection. It is also the nonresolution of history. It is LA when the court has failed. It recognizes no allies. It does not read color. It needs no light. It is white-hot night. It rocks all. And it is in you.

Notes

1. Philip Scher, "Unveiling the Orisha," in *Africa's Ogun: Old World and New*, ed. Sandra T. Barnes (Bloomington: Indiana University Press, 1997), 326; Joseph M. Murphy, *Working the Spirit: Ceremonies of the African Diaspora* (Boston: Beacon, 1994), 74.

2. Robert Farris Thompson, "The Flash of the Spirit: Haiti's Africanizing Vodun Art," in *Haitian Art*, ed. Ute Stebich. The Brooklyn Museum (New York: Harry N. Abrams, 1978), 30.

3. Murphy, *Working the Spirit*, 74.

4. Sandra T. Barnes, "The Many Faces of Ogun: Introduction to the First Edition," in *Africa's Ogun: Old World and New*, ed. Sandra T. Barnes (Bloomington: Indiana University Press, 1997), 23.

5. Karen McCarthy Brown, "Systematic Remembering, Systematic Forgetting: Ogou in Haiti," in *Africa's Ogun*, ed. Sandra T. Barnes, 78.

6. Barnes, *Africa's Ogun,* 19-23; C. L. R. James, *The Black Jacobins: Toussaint L'Ouverture and the San Domingo Revolution*, second edition, revised (New York: Vintage and Random House, 1963), 3-5.

7. James, *The Black Jacobins*, ix, 86-87.

8. Thompson, *Haitian Art*, 28-29; Brown, "Systematic Remembering, Systematic Forgetting," 86.

9. Leslie G. Desmangles, *The Faces of the Gods: Vodou and Roman Catholicism in Haiti* (Chapel Hill: University of North Carolina Press, 1992), 40-42; Karen McCarthy Brown, *Mama Lola: A Vodou Priestess in Brooklyn* (Berkeley: University of California Press, 1991), 5; James, *The Black Jacobins*, 393-94.

10. Margarite Fernandez Olmos and Lizabeth Paravisini-Gebert, "Introduction: Religioius Syncretism and Caribbean Culture," in *Sacred Possessions: Vodou, Santeria, Obeah, and the Caribbean*, ed. Margarite Fernandez Olmos and Lizabeth Paravisini-Gebert (New Brunswick, N.J.: Rutgers University Press, 1997), 5-9.

11. James, *The Black Jacobins*, 85-86; 286-87, 356-61; 366-68; 377.

12. James, *The Black Jacobins*, 60, 116, 120, 270, 290.

13. James, *The Black Jacobins*, 52-54, 271, 369.

14. James, *The Black Jacobins*, 393-94; Desmangles, *The Faces of the* Gods, 40-42; Brown, *Mama Lola*, 5.

15. Thompson, "Flash of the Spirit," 30-32; *Flash of the Spirit: African and Afro-American Art and Philosophy* (New York: Vintage, 1983), 169.

16. Will Coleman, *Tribal Talk: Black Theology, Hermeneutics, and African/American Ways of "Telling the Story"* (University Park: Pennsylvania State University Press, 2000), 179.

17. Coleman, *Tribal Talk*, 179.

18. Coleman, *Tribal Talk*, 52.

19. Coleman, *Tribal Talk*, 50.

20. Charles H. Long, *Significations: Signs, Symbols, and Images in the Interpretation of Religion* (Philadelphia: Fortress Press, 1986), 193-95.

21. Long, *Significations*, 110.

22. Long, *Significations*, 9.

23. Long, *Significations*, 137-39.

24. Long, *Significations*, 123.

25. Long, *Significations*, 193.

26. Long, *Significations*, 123-25.

27. Long, *Significations*, 177-78.

28. Long, *Significations*, 170.

29. Long, *Significations*, 166-69.

30. Long, *Significations*, 125.

31. Long, *Significations*, 161-63.

32. Long, *Significations*, 163.

33. Long, *Significations*, 165.

34. Paul Gilroy, *The Black Atlantic: Modernity and Double Consciousness* (Cambridge, Mass.: Harvard University Press, 1993), 37, 55, 77, 217.

35. Long, *Significations*, 9, 14, 196.

36. Paul Gilroy, *There Ain't No Black in the Union Jack: The Cultural Politics of Race and Nation* (London and Melbourne: Hutchinson, 1987; reprint, Chicago: University of Chicago Press, 1991), 227.

37. Coleman, *Tribal Talk*, 47; Gayraud Wilmore, *Black Religion and Black Radicalism: An Interpretation of the Religious History of Afro-American People* (second revised edition, 1973; reprint, Maryknoll, N.Y.: Orbis Books, 1983), 11.

38. Katherine Dunham, *Island Possessed* (Chicago: University of Chicago Press, 1969), 212-35.

39. Barnes, *Africa's Ogun*, 1.

40. Barnes, *Africa's Ogun*, 1; Sandra T. Barnes, "Africa's Ogun Transformed: Introduction to the Second Edition," in *Africa's Ogun*, xiii.

41. Barnes, "Africa's Ogun Transformed," xix.

42. Barnes, "Africa's Ogun Transformed," xix.

43. Barnes, "Africa's Ogun Transformed," xvi, xiii.

44. Barnes, "Africa's Ogun Transformed," xiv.

45. Robert G. Armstrong, "The Etymology of the Word *Ogun*," in *Africa's Ogun: Old World and New*, ed Sandra T. Barnes, 29.

46. Donald J. Consentino, "Repossession: Ogun in Folklore and Literature," in *Africa's Ogun: Old World and New*, ed Sandra T. Barnes, 290-314; Barnes, "Africa's Ogun Transformed," xiii-xxi; John Mason, "Ogun: Builder of the Lukumi's House," in *Africa's Ogun: Old World and New*, ed Sandra T. Barnes, 359.

47. Barnes, "Africa's Ogun Transformed," xviii.

48. Barnes, "Africa's Ogun Transformed," xviii.

49. Barnes, "The Many Faces of Ogun," 13.

50. Barnes, "The Many Faces of Ogun," 13.

51. Barnes, "The Many Faces of Ogun," 13.

52. Barnes, "The Many Faces of Ogun," 15; Margaret Thompson Drewal, "Dancing for Ogun in Yorubalnad and in Brazil," in *Africa's Ogun: Old World and New*, ed. Sandra T. Barnes, 204, 230.

53. Drewal, "Dancing for Ogun, 230; Barnes, "The Many Faces of Ogun," 15.

54. Barnes, "The Many Faces of Ogun," 15.

55. Barnes, "The Many Faces of Ogun," 15.

56. Barnes, "The Many Faces of Ogun," 15; Bade Ajuwon, "Ogun's Iremoje: A Philosophy of Living and Dying," in *Africa's Ogun: Old World and New*, ed. Sandra T. Barnes, 196.

57. Ajuwon, "Ogun's Iremoje," 182, 187.

58. Ajuwon, "Ogun's Iremoje," 196.

59. Barnes, "The Many Faces of Ogun," 16.

60. Barnes, "The Many Faces of Ogun," 2.

61. Armstrong, "The Etymology of the Word *Ogun*," 29-38.

62. Sandra T. Barnes and Paula Girshick Ben-Amos, "Ogun, the Empire Builder," in *Africa's Ogun: Old World and New*, ed Sandra T. Barnes, 39-64.

63. Mason, "Ogun: Builder of the Lukumi's House," 365.

64. Mason, "Ogun: Builder of the Lukumi's House," 365.

65. Barnes, "The Many Faces of Ogun," 17.

66. Barnes, "The Many Faces of Ogun," 17.

67. Barnes, "The Many Faces of Ogun," 18.

68. Barnes, "The Many Faces of Ogun," 2.

69. Karen McCarthy Brown, "Why Women Need the War God," *Women's Spirit Bonding*, ed. J. Kalven and M. Buckley (New York: Pilgrim Press, 1984), 197.

70. Brown, "Why Women Need the War God," 197.

71. Brown, "Why Women Need the War God," 198 (for comparison, see also James, *The Black Jacobins*, 290-92).

72. Brown, "Why Women Need the War God," 198.

73. Brown, "Why Women Need the War God," 197.

74. Brown, "Why Women Need the War God," 197, 199.

75. Barnes, "The Many Faces of Ogun," 5.

76. Barnes and Ben-Amos, "Ogun, the Empire Builder," 57.

77. Barnes and Ben-Amos, "Ogun, the Empire Builder," 57, 59.

78. Barnes and Ben-Amos, "Ogun, the Empire Builder," 57.

79. Barnes, "The Many Faces of Ogun," 6.

80. John Pemberton III, "The Dreadful God and the Divine King," in *Africa's Ogun: Old World and New*, ed. Sandra T. Barnes, 132.

81. Pemberton, "The Dreadful God," 138.

82. Pemberton, "The Dreadful God," 138.

83. Pemberton, "The Dreadful God," 138.

84. Pemberton, "The Dreadful God," 138.

85. Pemberton, "The Dreadful God," 139.

86. Pemberton, "The Dreadful God," 139.

87. Brown, "Systematic Remembering," 65-68.

88. Brown, "Systematic Remembering," 70.

89. Brown, "Systematic Remembering," 196.

90. Brown, "Systematic Remembering," 70.

91. Brown, "Systematic Remembering," 70-82.

92. Brown, "Systematic Remembering," 74.

93. Brown, "Systematic Remembering," 84.

94. Brown, "Systematic Remembering," 86.

95. Brown, "Systematic Remembering," 86.

96. Brown, "Systematic Remembering," 86.

97. George Brandon, *Santeria from Africa to the New World: The Dead Sell Memories* (Bloomington: Indiana University Press, 1993), 148.

98. Brandon, *Santeria from Africa*, 142.

99. Sheila Walker, *Ceremonial Spirit Possession in Africa and Afro-America: Forms, Meanings, and Functional Significance for Individuals and Social Groups* (Leiden, Netherlands: E. J. Brill, 1972), 104-15.

100. Long, *Significations*, 9, 110, 181; in like manner Coleman has apprehended the "dreaded 'Middle Passage'" as "itself a horrendous pathway of initiation through and/or confrontation with an emerging Eurocentric construction of reality that arose throughout the Americas"; Coleman, *Tribal Talk*, 52.

101. Consentino, "Repossession," 298.

102. Barnes, "The Many Faces of Ogun," 6-7.

103. Consentino, "Repossession," 303-04.

104. Robert Farris Thompson, *Flash of the Spirit: African and Afro-American Art and Philosophy* (New York: Vintage, 1983), xiii-xiv; and in a talk given at the African American Museum of Detroit, November 8, 1997.

105. Frantz Fanon, *The Wretched of the Earth*, trans. Constance Farrington (New York: Grove Press, 1967, 1963), 57, 147, 203, 220, 241, 291; see also Walker, *Ceremonial Spirit Possession*, 161-74.

106. Toni Morrison, *Beloved* (New York: Alfred Knopf, 1987), 262; Mae G. Henderson, "Toni Morrison's *Beloved*: Re-Membering the Body as Historical Text," in *Comparative American Identities: Race, Sex, and Nationality in the Modern Text*, ed. Hortense J. Spillars (New York: Routledge, 1991), 81.

107. Delores Williams, *Sisters in the Wilderness: The Challenge of Womanist God-Talk* (Maryknoll, N.Y.: Orbis Books, 1993), 15-33, 60-83.

108. Karl Marx, *Capital: A Critique of Political Economy*, vol. 1, ed. F. Engels, and trans. S. Moore and E. Aveling (New York: International Publishers, 1967), 360.

109. Michel Foucault, *Power/Knowledge: Selected Interviews and Other Writings, 1972-1977*, ed. C. Gordon, and trans. C. Gordon et al. (New York: N.Y.: Pantheon Books), 92-108.

110. Coleman quotes Wilmore to the effect that "the spirits of the ancestral gods, disembodied and depersonalized, invaded the interstices of the objective world and impregnated the imagination with an interminable variety of ghosts, witches, talking ani-

mals, and supernatural phenomena that comprised the folklore of the southern black";
Coleman, *Tribal Talk*, 47; Wilmore, *Black Religion*, 11.

111. Coleman notes, for instance, that one ex-slave oldster deftly clarified "the post-Christian character of North American (non)religiosity" in terms of white folks being nothing more or less to her than "hants." During slavery, she says, "dere wuz moe rale religion mongst a handful of slaves dan all de Niggers and Whites put together now." But post-slavery, this "rale religion" was itself reduced to being a "'cultural hant' . . . search[ing], hauntingly, for a place to either continue its unfinished work or rest"; Coleman, *Tribal Talk*, 88-89.

112. Jim Perkinson, "Soteriological Humility: The Christological Significance of the Humanity of Jesus in the Encounter of Religions," *Journal of Ecumenical Studies* 31, nos. 1-2 (winter-spring, 1994), 23-24.

113. Albert Nolan, *God in South Africa: The Challenge of the Gospel* (Grand Rapids, Mich.: Eerdmans, 1988), 11, 25, 29.

114. Jim Perkinson, "A Canaanitic Word in the Logos of Christ: Or the Difference the Syro-Phoenician Woman Makes to Jesus," *Semeia* 75 (1996), 78; Jim Perkinson, "A Socio-Reading of the Kierkegaardian Self: Or, the Space of Lowliness in the Time of the Disciple," in *Kierkegaard: The Self in Society*, ed. George Pattison and Steven Shakespeare (London: MacMillan, 1998), 156-72; Anthony Rudd, "Kierkegaard's Critique of Pure Irony," in *Kierkegaard: The Self in Society* ed. George Pattison and Steven Shakespeare (London: MacMillan, 1998), 82-96.

115. Brandon, *Santeria from Africa*, 158.

8

The Future of Our World:
Indigenous Peoples, Indigenous Philosophies, and the
Preservation of Mother Earth

Julian Kunnie

The universe is a fabric, a symphony, a tapestry; everything is connected to
everything else and everything is alive and responsible to its relationships in
every way. The human being is not the crowning glory of creation and certainly
not its master. We are but a small but nevertheless vital, part of the universe
and at least part of our task is to serve as a focus for some of the things that
must be done for the universe really to prosper and fulfill itself. Because everything is alive and because we have responsibilities to all living things, we cannot force the rest of nature to do what we want. Indeed, we must respectfully
approach the rest of nature and seek its permission to initiate a course of action.
When we do this in a humble and respectful way, we find that other parts of the
universe take joy in cooperating with us in the production of something new
and important. Natural entities become our friends and we are able to do mar-
velous things together.
—Vine Deloria, *For this Land*

Introduction

We want to pay tribute to the ancestors of Mother Africa and to those of the Indigenous people of Turtle Island (North America) for being able to pen these
words. We also want to acknowledge the momentous work of our elder, brother,
mentor, and teacher, Charles Long, in his adamancy to proclaim the word of
liberation within the Western academy, particularly in championing the perspectives of the repressed, colonized, and exploited peoples of this world, particu-

larly those of a dark hue. In reflecting upon the conquest of Turtle Island (North America) when Europeans supposedly discovered their utopia and idyllic paradise, lest we forget the difference between myth and reality, between civilization and primitivism, Charles Long perspicaciously reminds us:

> The Edenic quality of the New Word is the backdrop and screen onto which the Europeans projected their fantasies of evil in the New World. The Indians are often portrayed as beasts without intelligence; they are absolutely indiscriminate in their sexual relations, they are cannibalistic—eating their own children and relatives. They lack discipline and often make wretched slaves, and if left to their own devices, they wander up and down and return to their old ways. It is indeed ironic that the Indians are accused of wandering by a class of people and a culture that has institutionalized, spiritualized, and commercialized the pilgrimage of curiosity.[1]

One continent's Enlightenment is the rest of the world's enslavement and subjugation. Contrary to what most Eurocentric scholars have constructed in jargon across the academy as "postcoloniality" and "postcolonialism," we would argue is obdurately Eurocentric because it presupposes the decolonization of the world. Following five centuries of Western European colonial conquest, invasion, dispossession, disenfranchisement, genocide, slavery, and ecocide, we would contend that we are still unremittingly living in a world of colonialism, albeit different in character and texture. It is more accurate, from the vantage point of Indigenous peoples, who are people of the six continents who have refused to be assimilated and integrated into the insanity of modern Western European modernity, but instead persisted in maintaining their cosmologies and cultures, to describe our lot as *neocolonialism*, a condition predicted by the titan of Pan Africanist political organizing, Osagyefo Kwame Nkrumah, and the first president of an independent Ghana.[2]

In light of the fundamentally obscuring character of the "Enlightenment" for most of the world's peoples, it is imperative that the academic study and teaching of religio-cultures and religious studies be thoroughly decolonized, deacademicized, and "de-Enlightenized." Scholars of religion can no longer engage in the old Western business of viewing the world from the mono-focal lenses of Western European imperial history and culture; they need to break out of the Babylonian captivity of European epistemologies and extricate themselves from the tutelage of European philosophies that deemed other Indigenous cultures of the world as devoid of civilization and essentially as means to a Western teleological end. By Indigenous, we mean, as M. A. Jaimes Guerrero asserts,

> to be born of a place. Yet Indigenism in a broader scope also has to do with how you live in relationship and reciprocity to that place. This distinction can be made in terms of indigenism with a lowercase 'i' and Indigenism with a capital 'I' . . . by being Indigenous in this context, is not necessarily inherent in

any race or creed among Native peoples. Yet it is about cultures among land-based peoples who lived in reciprocal relationship with their environment, habitat, or Indigenous homeland. This can also be conceptualized as "ecocultures" that respect how culture is derived from bioregions for biodiversity, and which in turn nurture cultural diversity for health and well-being among Indigenous peoples . . . Indigenism is also upheld by the principles of "Native Womanism" in the reverence for places where one's ancestors are buried and where one's children are born. These are often called "the navel of our existence" which is why it is still a traditional practice, among many Native people, to bury a child's birth aftermath near a site where they are born, and preferably to nourish a tree or plant, and for this person to always know their familial origins on her/his life journey.[3]

The study of religions in the academy needs to undergo a revolutionary transformation to realize that, as the Latin American novelist Eduardo Galeano argues, most of the world's scholars (mostly located in the West) have viewed the world downside up, essentially from the vantage point of an imperialistic advantaged colonial European minority.[4]

We are all products of this five-century colonization, genocide, and ecocide, struggling to survive in one form or another. Our thinking has foundationally been influenced by and contaminated by colonial anthropology and ideology, which foolishly classified humanity into three taxonomic categories: Caucasoid, Monhgoloid, and Negroid. The Caucasoids (Indo Europeans) were supposedly derived from a region near the Caucasus Mountains, the Mongoloids (Asian) from Mongolia, and the Negroids (blacks) from Africa. Innocent Onyewuenyi explains:

> The German romantic tendency to emphasize white racial superiority and the Germans as the pure race forced their rejection of the ancients' location of the original home of mankind (sic) in the Nile Valley. The new location was now near the Caucasian mountains. This theory thus placed Germans nearer to the source of humanity than any other European people and justified their claim to be the "pure race," superior to other Europeans, and by deduction, Africans and Asians. Adolph Hitler put this claim into practice during World War II with the extermination of the Jews. His concern for racial purity extended to blacks too, for at the 1938 Olympics, he would not shake the hand of United States Olympic track star Jesse Owens because the athlete was black.[5]

The absurdity of the categorization is borne out by the fact that the people who live near the Caucasus Mountains are not of European stock, but Semitic. There is no scientific basis to race; it is a colonial social construction used to justify the enslavement of Africans and the conquest and dispossession and extermination of various Indigenous peoples by Western European powers. The discovery of the DNA strand in 2000 was not novel news to Indigenous people. They always knew that the color and ethnic community of individuals are no determinants of ability and potential. Yet racism continues to be a torturous experience for the colored majority of the world.

Out of this hegemonic dysfunctional state of affairs emerged "Enlightenment" thinkers who felt that they had revolutionized global thought and culture with the discovery of the ascendancy of reason in human discourse. Philosophers such as Hegel, Kant, and Hume all subscribed to the notion that Indigenous peoples outside Western Europe were primitive, and of inferior mental ability, principally because they did not possess the consciousness of freedom. Hegel, for instance, declared that Africans had never contributed toward human civilization and therefore warranted no earnest study beyond a singular mention.[6] It is important to remember, though, as Enrique Dussel points out, that Hegel was the product of European colonization and subjugation of Indigenous peoples of color, as opposed to the driving ideological force for such racist attitudes.[7] Subsequently, thinkers like Lévi-Strauss and Bruhl would argue that Indigenous peoples were prelogical in their mode of thinking and significantly undeveloped in their intellectual faculties. Many scholars of religion and anthropology, including the likes of Mircea Eliade, E. B. Tyler, and Evans Pritchard, were steeped in this perverted colonialist thinking, defining Indigenous peoples as tribal, and below the status of normative civilized humanity, essentially the nations of Western Europe. These structures of classification and hierarchy continue to vitiate our world, including that of the academy, as Westerners see themselves as supreme on earth, earning the designation from Indigenous people of White supremacists.

Today there is much talk in numerous circles in the West regarding the conservation of the environment and the protection of our fragile ecosystem. Oftentimes, these circles consist of essentially European people whose actions are observed in groups from the Greens Movement to the Sierra Club, leading many to believe that it is the conscience of Western Europeans that has sparked these environmental concerns. Far from it, these persons are recent activists whose actions in sensitizing the world about problems from global warming to deforestation are important, yet who follow in the footsteps of the historical traditions of millennia observed by all of the world's Indigenous peoples. Stan Stevens, a geosciences researcher, notes:

> Native Americans, the Aboriginal peoples of Australia, the Masai and the Maoris, and thousands of other Indigenous peoples control traditional territories from the Canadian and Alaskan arctic to the Amazon and Andes, from Siberia to South Africa, and from the high ground of the Himalaya and Tibet to the atolls of the South Pacific and the outback of Australia. In many parts of the world, these homelands of Indigenous peoples are the best—and often the last remaining places of rich wildness and biological diversity.[8]

The Indigenous peoples of the world are the original conservationists and ecologists of the globe. They live on 19 percent of the earth's surface. They are the peoples who have lived in healthful and civilized ways for millennia, maintaining the natural resource base and diversity of animal and plant species on their lands, and have defended lands being invaded by predatory and colonizing capitalist forces on every continent of the world. They have been responsible for preserving the biologically complex, fecundate, and prolific biological universe in which we all live, which has been and continues to be now threatened by the barbarism of Western European extractive imperialistic systems. Today, so-called protected areas have been established in numerous modern states, often ironically violating the spaces of Indigenous people, who were for millennia the custodians of the earth, not always, but usually caring for it so well that it maintained its natural ecosystems in an unspoiled state. Frequently, when protected areas were established, Indigenous and local residents were moved out, often to the detriment of the land itself.[9]

Indigenous Peoples' Knowledge and Ethical Systems

Contrary to the widely disseminated and propagandistic view that Indigenous peoples (pejoratively referred to as tribal peoples, a term that needs to be expunged from our vocabulary because it implies less than Western European human) possess no ethical framework owing to their "simplistic" cosmologies, Indigenous peoples have always enshrined principles of self-reflection and ethical assessment in their philosophies, traditions, and cultures. The ancient black people of Nubia, Ethiopia, and Egypt, for instance, all embodied traditions of ethics and morality. The notions of justice (*maat*), peace (*hotep*), and love (*mrrwt*) are just three cardinal maxims that established the foundation for the virtues of social justice, mutual cooperation, and respect in ancient Egyptian society, and they prevailed for 3,500 years.[10] The notion of the enjoyment and fulfillment of life (*ankh*) was another ethical virtue, defining attitudes toward life and death. Within the ambit of such principles, the injunction on gender equality was practiced, leading to normative acceptance of women leaders. Not only were women rulers, like Hatshepsut and Nefertiti, but they were also physicians, like Peseshet, a female physician (*swnu*) and an overseer over other female physicians (*imyt-r*) in the world, among one hundred others in the Egypt of 4,000 years ago.[11] All professions in the ancient Egyptian world were open to both women and men, including clergy, administrators, business, and medicine. Egyptian civilizations, like those of ancient China, Korea, India, and Meso-America, all possessed fecundate cultures and prolific philosophical systems. For instance, the Aztec cities of Tenochtitlan (Mexico City today) and Tlatelolco in sixteenth-century Mexico, prior to the Spanish invasion, were clearly centers for intellectual reflection, aesthetic creation, and technological sophistication:

The buildings had flat roofs and were brightly painted with bold murals that would one day inspire Mexican painters of the twentieth century. There were also schools, ateliers, shops with hanging signs, and public lavatories. Unlike European cities of the day, Mexico was clean: wastes were hauled away by barge and composted for fertilizer; a thousand men swept and washed the streets each day. Refined Aztecs, who bathed daily, found it advisable to hold flowers to their noses when they met Europeans, who made a point of being filthy. (Spaniards considered bathing an infidel Moorish custom; to be too clean was to risk the attentions of the Inquisition.)

Most of Mexico's streets were canals, laid out on a grid still followed by the modern city plan. Three great causeways with drawbridges ran north, west, and south to the mainland, an aqueduct brought drinking water from mountain springs, and a long dike kept out briny waters to the east. The Spaniards called Mexico "another Venice."[12]

Indigenous Aztec peoples are hardly uncivilized and devoid of intellectual development and ethical foundations. Even though racist anthropologists have generally defined Aztec cultures as essentially human sacrificing, the evidence points to the acts of human sacrifice as being a recent development around the fifteenth century as resources became scarce, if in fact human sacrifice was a part of Aztec religio-culture.[13] It was apparently a way of appeasing the sun divinity, where enemies of the Aztec nation were offered as a religious sacrifice. Yet, this violence is dwarfed by the systemic violence of European colonialism which eliminated a hundred million people in the Americas, perpetrated the genocide of entire nations, and sacrificed millions more in Africa, Asia, and the Pacific. Modern European warfare sacrificed scores of millions of human beings since the early 1900s. Human sacrifice is institutionalized and systematized under contemporary capitalism, be it through the death penalty in the United States, Western militarism against peoples of color in the underdeveloped world as in Hiroshima, Vietnam, Cuba, Korea, Iraq, El Salvador, and Guatemala; or the enslavement of hundreds of millions of peoples of color by the mammoth Western transnational corporations.

All peoples have contributed toward shaping global civilizations, with Indigenous peoples being the oldest. Constance Hiliard asserts in this regard: "Every society, on every continent, regardless of ethnicity or socio-economic conditions, has contributed its own intellectual products to the collective output of humankind, because the bringing forth of cognitive and creative impulses is as compelling as the springing forth of offspring."[14] Kwasi Wiredu, the African scholar of philosophy, similarly and instructively observes, with particular reference to Africa:

In the changes of and chances of human history some peoples may come to be ahead of others at some particular point in time in some particular area of investigation, but there is nothing to indicate that such situations must be permanent. And there is also no reason why any form of genuine knowledge should be attributed to any peoples in any proprietary sense. And what warrant is there for the pessimism that would permanently debar our imaginations from fore-seeing Africa as an eventual theater of state-of-the-art science and technology, yielding ground to none in the advancement of scientific knowledge for the promotion of human well-being? Imagine how puzzled the Africans of that era would be to learn that some of our ancestors seemed to think that there was something unAfrican about science.[15]

The principle of walking in step with the natural world, even while creating and shaping civilizations, was foundational among most Indigenous peoples. This assertion does not imply some reified romanticized view of Indigenous peoples as devoid of conflict and contradiction. Like all of the human commu-nity, Indigenous peoples' cultures were and are fraught with pain and conflict as they struggled to shape sociocultural environments and live in increasingly com-plex societies. For example, archaeological studies of the Ain Ghazal site in Jor-dan describe a productive village that existed there between 8,000 B.C.E. and 6,000 B.C.E., yet which experienced abandonment of villages. Some scholars ar-gue that such desertion was possibly due to changes in climatic conditions, but also human activities involving use of plaster in building homes, and over-reliance on goat herds. The overuse of lime plaster resulted in extensive con-sumption of energy and burning, far more so than gypsum, for example, accord-ing to these archaeological studies.[16] We cannot say with certainty what precisely caused such abandonment of ancient villages. Yet we can unequivocally argue that there was and is a meticulous respect for the divine power of creation, par-ticularly the Earth, and for the complex and fragile ecological universe in which they lived, among most Indigenous peoples. For instance, among the Tupi-Guarani who live in Brazil, Paraguay, and Argentina, there is the constant striv-ing for perfection, embodied in harmony with the Mother Earth. *Aguyje* is the sign of persons who achieve the desired perfection for which they strive. Guarani virtues, according to contemporary usage, are *teko pora* (goodness), *teko joja* (justice), *ne'e pora* (good words), *ne'e' joja* (just words), joayhu (reciprocal love), *kyre'y* (diligence and availability), *py'a guapy* (deep peace), *teko nem-boro'y* (serenity), and *pya' poti* (inner purity without duplicity).[17] Where Indige-nous peoples have caused environmental damage such as deforestation or over-cultivation, these have always been the effect of Western European colonial in-dustrialism, when such peoples have been forced to acquiesce to transnational logging or food companies owing to the need for sheer survival after being in-vaded and conquered by European or Euro-American military powers. In the islands of Kosrae and Nauru in the South Pacific, Indigenous Koreans have sur-rendered fishing and the cultivation of fresh fruits and vegetables to imports of canned and processed foods from the United States, the Philippines, and other capitalist havens as a result of being colonized by the United States since World

War II. In Nauru, islanders have abdicated fishing and replaced it with phosphate mining, producing material prosperity for a few and obesity, diabetes, and a life expectancy of fifty-five for the overwhelming majority.[18]

The exercise of ethical self-reflection is encapsulated in both written and oral traditions among Indigenous peoples, through philosophical treatises such as the Meroitic texts of ancient Nubia (collected from the second century B.C.E. to the fourth century C.E., the Ge'ez literature of ancient Ethiopia, the Vai tradition of West Africa, the discourses of ancient Chinese, Korean, Indus Valley, and Meso-American Olmec civilizations, to the oral transmitted traditions of the Aboriginal people of Australia, the Maoris of Ao Te Roa (New Zealand), and those of the Indigenous peoples of the Americas and the Caribbean. The scholarship of African philosophers, such as Ibn Khaldun (died 1406), is worth mentioning, since Khaldun wrote defining treatises such as *al Muqaddimah* (Introduction to History) and is considered the founder of sociology and the philosophy of history in Islam, whose works provide some of the most illuminative reflections on areas like social justice, law, political structures, and individual behavior. Kamal-ad-Din-ad-Damiri (died 1405) wrote distinguished works on the study of animal life such as *Hyat-al-Hwyawan*. Abu Bakr al-Baytar wrote the comprehensive manual *Kamil-as-sina'atayn,* viewed as the greatest work in medieval veterinary medicine.[19]

Another example of formidable Indigenous influence and consequence is the impact of Augustine of Hippo, considered one of the foremost patriarchs of classical Christianity. Augustine was a Berber of North African descent, and his philosophical creativity redounded not to his Latin training but to the complex and dynamic religio-cultural ethos of Carthage and Numidia, where in the intercourse with the vagaries of Berber peasant culture, coupled with the popularity of Manichean dualism popular at the time, new theological currents were spawned.

It is also critical to understand that the biblical ethos was heavily conditioned by the earliest Egyptian literature, an Indigenous literature, reflecting on such themes as despair and disillusion, the value of life over death, and the struggle to live the moral life in a society overwhelmed by immorality. "The Dispute of a Man with His Soul" is one such classical text popularized from the seventh through the eleventh dynasties in Egypt covering the period 2200 to 2050 B.C.E.

Among the Basotho and the Tsetswana in Southern Africa, for example, Indigenous value systems confirm intense self-reflection and ethical mandate. The foremost question of equality was not absent within African legal and moral discourses and practices. For instance, in precolonial societies in Southern Africa, such as among the Sotho,

> the Basotho courts had well recognized principles of equality. One Basotho customary norm (*Lekhotla ha la nameloe*—the court lends itself to no person) recognized that all had equal rights before traditional courts. The complaints of

the poor were heard, and King Moshoeshoe, founder of the Basotho nation, was quoted as declaring that the "law knows no one as a "poor man."[20]

So, too, we know that women were given greater opportunities to express themselves and participate in societal decision making. Abusive men were decried by clans, and women were urged not to marry into such families. Collective sanctions were imposed on abusive men.[21] Kwame Gyekye, the Ghanaian ethicist, opines that Indigenous knowledge systems in Africa consist of moral principles and practices that enshrine social and moral rights, so that for instance, "there is no need to assert one's right of food against society or community, since access to food is a necessary part of the traditional social arrangement."[22]

Paramount in the cosmologies of all Indigenous peoples is the principle of cosmic harmony, as derived from the Creator, the source and basis of all life. Among the Tseltal and the Maya in Central America, it is believed that the soul must be in harmony with the body, so that psychic harmony could be realized. Personal well-being must always be in sync with the community, the rest of the natural world, and the universe. Even though Incan rulers demanded surpluses from the production of laborers during the heyday of the Inca nation, they nevertheless returned portions to the people, so their rule was perceived as legitimate by those ruled. As Ronald Wright notes, contrary to the European colonial and capitalist ethics of confiscation and expropriation from the poor, "Andean societies, like many others in the Americas, were built on the ethic of reciprocity, not rapacity."[23] Disharmony causes disruption of and destruction of the world, and Mayan cultures possess intellectual and social mechanisms to critique disharmony. For instance, a person who is two-faced, indecisive, and deceptive is *cheb yo'tan* (of two hearts), and a suspicious and distrustful person is *ma'spisiluk yo'tan* (one who does not act with moral motivation and his whole heart). A jealous person is *ti'ti o' tantayel*, a crafty heart who does not desire the well-being of others and who causes disintegration of the community. In the family, a man's wife is called *snuhp'jti', snuhp' ko'tan*—the other half of my heart, indicating the unity of word and action. *Utel* in Tseltal culture means "to say," to mean "to do." Indigenous people describe those who break their word as "fork-tongued," as the Indigenous nations of North America referred to the Europeans who constantly broke treaties and massacred communities even after promising protection, like at San Creek in Colorado in 1864 when more than three hundred Cheyenne women and children were killed by the U.S. cavalry. Important, too, there is no word for *apologize* among Indigenous people. Persons or communities who have wronged others are required to make reparations for their deeds, in some material form. This is one area where European settler-colonial cultures in the Americas, Australia, Ao Te Roa (New Zealand), and Palestine can learn from Indigenous peoples' ethical systems. Integrity of word and deed are both equally important and sacred, within the train of Indigenous religio-culture. The rejection by Indigenous peoples of white justice is reflected in the formation of a new

Indigenous political party in Bolivia, announced by leader Felipe Quispe, designed to serve the interests of "Indigenous people oppressed for 500 years by white people."[24] It is for the reason of independence and autonomy from Eurocentric systems that Indigenous peoples declared at the First Continental Meeting of Indian Peoples held in Quito, Ecuador, from July 17-21, 1990, in which the vast majority of Indigenous organizations from the Americas participated:

> Now we are fully conscious that our definitive liberation can only be expressed as the full exercise of self-determination . . . . In exercising our right to self-determination, Indians or Indigenous people struggle to achieve our complete autonomy within national contexts . . . (which means) the right Indian peoples have to control our respective territories, including control and management of all the natural resources of the soil, subsoil, and aerial space, the defense and conservation of nature . . . the ecosystem and the conservation of life . . . [and] the democratic constitution of our own governments (self-governments).[25]

Violation of integrative cosmic and social harmony also informs Indigenous understandings of the problem of evil. Persons considered just may suffer because of the actions of other spiritually evil persons or deeds, which disrupt and affect the balance of the rest of the community. Among the Aymara in the Andes of South America, individuals responsible for crime are expelled from the community, or alternatively, could remain in the community under very strict restraints. In other situations, such as illness, animal sacrifices may be performed, under the concept of *kuti* (a return to the point of departure). A spirit is invoked, to the stir up the evil of affliction in a person and have this transferred to an animal. The point of such observances is the restoration of the sense of equilibrium and balance.

The principle of diversity is valorized among all Indigenous peoples. There is a very real sense of "unity in diversity," where individual, family, and community are viewed as sacred. All Indigenous peoples have a multiplicity of cultural prohibitions and injunctions that proscribe negative behavior, and urge other positive alternatives, in accordance with reverence for diversity. For instance, among the Aymara, individuals and smaller units are never suppressed by those from the upper strata. A person is never depicted as singular, but is viewed as a couple, or always seen in relation to somebody else. A wife who is united with her husband never loses her surname, individuality, or her possessions (instructive for the decimation of women in marital relationships in Western European societies). Each part is respected as part of the whole. This solidarity of persons, of wives and husbands, of families and communities, is extant among those who function as persons (*jaqi*) and not among those with chauvinistic, arrogant, and domineering attitudes and behavior (*q'ara*).

Indigenous peoples have always cherished the principles of respect for individual opinion and rights, always in tandem with the community. The multicolored layers of dress, arts and crafts, dances, sculptures, and ceremonies attest to the embracement of cultural heterogeneity and plurality by Indigenous cultures. The plethora of languages existent in Africa and the Americas, more than one thousand in the former and more than eight hundred in the latter, is indicative of the authentically multi-cultural and intercultural character of Indigenous societies. Though conflicts existed among different Indigenous nations, as with all nations of the world, the principle of unity in diversity was predominant. The First Nation Confederacy of the Muskogee, Cherokee, Chippewa, Chickasaw, and Choctaw, and that of the Iroquois Confederation in the north eastern region of Turtle Island, is demonstrative of the principles of unity in diversity. The Iroquois Constitution (Gayanerekowa)—known as the Great Law of Peace of the Constitution of the Iroquois Confederacy—accorded women great economic, political, and legal power, where decision-making roles were exercised complementarily by both female and male councils of each clan. Women were considered the progenitors of the nations, making women hold traditional titles of chieftainship.[26]

Euro-American women need to pay tribute to the Iroquois nations for the institutionalization of all human rights, including women's rights, since the U.S. Constitution (which excluded the rights of Indigenous people, Africans, and women) was patterned upon the Iroquois Confederacy.[27] So, too, among the Nnobi culture of Nigeria, women played foundational roles as far as decision making was concerned in areas of social and political importance, evincing the value placed on gender diversity and complementarity in that culture. Ifi Amadiume, the Nigerian scholar, has done some excellent pioneering work in this regard.[28]

Participatory democracy among Indigenous people is of primordial significance. Diversity of perspective is always encouraged by the presence of persons, not necessarily the vocalization of a vote as in the West. The *kgotla* (council of participants) among the Tsetswana elaborated in the saying *La seke la mo thlakola pele a fetsa go nyela*, literally meaning the unclean anus of someone defecating may not be cleaned until the person has completed the process![29] Even nonsensical perspectives and unpopular views must be heard and cannot be summarily dismissed. The kgotla functions as a pivotal forum for discussing and discerning communal solutions to specific existing problems.

Indigenous Peoples as Original Conservationists, Ecologists, and Future Preservers of Our Ecosystem

Indigenous peoples are the world's original conservationists and ecologists because of the reverence of the Mother Earth. The attachment to land is preponderant because land signifies the place where the ancestors have been buried and reunited with Mother Earth. The Earth is viewed as a living being, alive, whose spirit radiates and responds to human activity, so that all life could exist in harmony. The Earth is a sacred being, cocreator, like a mother, who nourishes all life in her womb. In the Akan tradition of Ghana, Ala is the Earth goddess. Among the Yoruba, Odudua is the Earth goddess who with Orisa-Nla, is supreme and responsible for the creation of beings. Wirjina is the Mother Earth goddess among the Aymara. Among the Butchulla people of Fraser Island in Australia, it is Beeral, the Creator, who sent his messenger, Yindingie, down to make the land, with his helper, K'gari (pronounced *Gurri*), a spirit from the sky. K'gari fell in love with the creation of Yindingi, the bay, beaches, islands, rivers, and mountains, and wanted to stay there forever. Yet since she was spirit, she had to lie down on the rocks in the sea, and when she had done this, she was changed into a beautiful island, clothed with trees, shrubs, ferns, and lovely orchids; lakes were her eyes, and her voice was the sound of the swiftly flowing streams. Then animals, birds, forest creatures, and other people were made—all to live in cosmic harmony with each other.[30]

Indigenous philosophies, thus, in contradistinction to Euro-American and European dominant philosophies, are not human constructed, but in fact, "reflect the land herself speaking through the people of the land."[31] It is not individualistically defined as in classical European philosophy, nor abstract, but always communally grounded and transformative in its objective. In a discussion on the social and cultural customs of the Mossi nation in contemporary Burkina Faso in West Africa, Alan Fiske notes in this regard: "In their social relations, Mossi (sic) only occasionally exhibit Individualism, egoism, competition, maximizing intentions or operate in a framework of free choice and contractually based obligations . . . Mossi (sic) prefer to share crucial resources."[32]

The Mossi have an openness to sharing land resources, and never sell or rent land, and never attempt to profit from the fact of land scarcity, which is becoming a problem in many parts of Africa as a result of migrations, urbanization, and the foisting of agricultural export crop production on such people by ruling regimes. Yet, as Fiske points out, the cardinal principles of "mutual solidarity, sense of common identity and belonging, unity and kindness" predominate.[33] Doing field studies in Burkina Faso, Fiske joined a Mossi work party, called a *sisoaaga*, where members of the youth group (Jeunesse) dug the soil with small sharp hoes. He found this exhausting, and proceeded to purchase picks and shovels to expedite work so that the catchment basin they were digging would be completed quicker. Yet the workers rejected the innovation, despite the fact that prolonged time for the pond construction would result in continued water shortages. Fiske discovered that it was the "joy of laboring in synchrony, in unison side by side, matching each other in one for-one correspondence, working together" that was primordial.[34] "Equality matching" and "Communal solidarity" were paramount, not efficiency maximization and expediency, so normative in

Western capitalist cultures.[35] Pierre Englebert, a World Bank consultant who discusses Fiske's work and the situation of political economies in Burkina Faso, unconvincingly attempts to discredit Fiske's observations about the Mossi nation by arguing that the Mossi have restrained members of the Peul nation from access to water and by casting a cheap ethnocentric shot, contending that such societies "have developed property rights in the form of slavery."[36] Evidently, Englebert, so enamored with the imperialist and Eurocentric policies of the World Bank and its obsession with profit accumulation and market deification, fails to understand that Indigenous peoples such as the Mossi subscribe to and practice an entirely different system of life ethics and principles. Human nature is not selfishly motivated and individualistically oriented, as so much of Western European social science and economies arrogantly assume.[37] Like other Indigenous peoples, the Mossi embody social harmony and respect for the land. When conflicts do emerge, particularly on issues of grazing access and allocation of resources, they are generally the result of the legacy of colonial regimes which destabilized Indigenous economies through forced taxation and enslavement of Indigenous populations for producing export crops, as the French did in Burkina Faso in the early 1900s, exacerbating a situation of drought and famine in 1908 and 1914.[38]

All Indigenous peoples subscribe to the notion that since all life was created by the Creator, the Great Spirit, each creature has a distinctive spirit, imbued by the Creator. We are all thus related by spirit, as Winona LaDuke illustrates in her latest brilliant work:

> Native American teachings describe the relations all around—animals, fish, trees, and rocks—as our brothers, sisters, uncles, and grandpas. Our relations to each other, our prayers whispered across generations to our relatives, are what bind our cultures together. The protection, teachings, and gifts of our relatives have for generations preserved our families. These relations are honored in ceremony, song, story, and life that keep relations close—to buffalo, sturgeon, salmon, turtles, bears, wolves, and panthers. These are our older relatives—the ones who came before and taught us how to live.[39]

We are all children of the Great Spirit and must respect the Creator, by being in harmony with all life. The ancestors are part of the spirit world, and instruct us and converse with us in our daily activities. Their spirits reside in Mother Earth and manifest themselves in a myriad of ways. It is for this reason of veneration of Mother Earth and in thankfulness to the Creator, that Indigenous peoples perform various ceremonies, reaffirming the connectedness of us all. Among Santeria practitioners in Cuba, for example, the *ceiba* tree is viewed as an *axis mundi*, endowed with spiritual power. The *Iroko* tree or *Eegun Okeere*, sacred to the Yoruba, is possibly signified by the *ceiba* tree in Cuba, renamed *Iroko* by Cuban *Lukumi*, and valorized every November 16, when civic leaders and thousands of people circle a ceiba three times, make wishes, and leave coins as offering, akin to the veneration of the Eegun Okeere in Nigeria, where people bring food and perform sacrifices in their intercessory prayers before the tree.[40] In other Santeria ceremonies, blood from sacrificed animals and chickens is sprinkled on the tree, as a way of invoking the spirits, to harmonize blood, the tree, and their rooted-ness in Mother Earth. Among the Karen people of the highlands of Burma and Thailand, when a child is born, the father takes the placenta and the umbilical cord of the newborn and travels deep into the forest to offer these to a tree, lay-ing them in the crook of a branch. This act is symbolic of the deep life-long bond between the child and the tree, that the health and well-being of both are indis-solubly linked with each other.[41] The Mandaya, who live in the southeastern re-gion of Mindanao in the Philippines, also cherish and greatly revere the areca-nut plant, since the roots of this plant are used for divination. As Aram Yen-goyan explains,

> The roots of the areca-nut plant are used as a form of divination in ascertaining how much must be given to the spirits. Abnormal or stunted roots are viewed as a sign that the spirits must be provided with nuts. The use of plant indicators to guide one's actions suggests the state of the plant world and human behavior and then conceptualized in terms of the relationship of the spirits of the forest and of rice to human problems.[42]

The Aboriginal peoples of Australia, the Aymara of South America, and the Ma-sai of Kenya perform similar ceremonies to reenact this deeply interwoven inter-connectedness.

Finally, Indigenous peoples are the original biodiversity teachers of our world. For instance, among the Lubicon Lake Band of the Cree nation of north-ern Alberta, there is a profound reverence for the moose and the bear, and hunt-ing practices were and are based on conservation, whereby they will not kill moose calves, pregnant cows, or all members of a beaver house. It is kept in mind that these animals must be able to replenish themselves in order to provide food for the Lubicon at a later date. The hunting of moose is particularly impor-tant because it provides the hunter recognition and respect. The ethic of sharing the kill is also central.[43] Among the Khanty, Mansi, and Yamalo-Nenets, abo-riginal peoples of the Russian North and of Siberia, there is a similar respectful relationship with the reindeer, an essential being in the Indigenous economy of these peoples.[44]

M. H. Khalil, reflecting from the Indigenous African context in Kenya, ex-plains:

> The life of a traditional community revolves around forests and vegetation. Its relationship with biological resources permeated every sphere of human en-deavor from the cradle to the grave. Given these imperatives, cultural survival

depended on bio-diversity, and for this reason, a sustainableasai harmony was forged between people, forests, and vegetation. The flow of life of a group depended on the flow of biological resources. Every plant was valued in its own right: trees for firewood were different from trees that provided medicine; those used for rituals were distinctive from those utilized for magical practices. Out of this recognition grew a sense of respect, harmony, and sustainable utilization of forest resources in all their diversity.[45]

Today, 25 percent of all world medicinal products come from traditional Indigenous forests. The thousands of herbs, leaves, roots, and plants that served as medicinal cures for Indigenous people for millennia are now being expropriated, essentially stolen, by the large Western biotech and pharmaceutical corporations—all for maximal profit. This predatory behavior jeopardizes the spiritual foundation and basis of these Indigenous medicines. Unquestionably, this confiscation of Indigenous knowledge solely for enrichment and profit must be viewed as biopiracy and must be challenged by all justice-loving people in the world.

Similarly, the healthy, sensible, and judicious ecologically sensitive cattle-grazing practices of the Masai in East Africa can be instructive for all agriculturalists. The Masai

> make use of both high potential and marginal ensuring yearlong availability of pasture, water, and salt licks, and avoided the current droughts, as Kenya is experiencing. Overgrazing never occurred in the Masai traditional system. . . . Masai cattle also exhibit a grazing behavior that is sensitive to the ecology, utilizing the available vegetal matter most efficiently and economically.[46]

The Masai are among the world's foremost biodiversity farmers. Their methods of grazing can check the wave of destruction wrought by overgrazing of the agro-industries and the accompanying environmental catastrophes, including drought and famine.

In Central Africa, the same responsible and ethical comportment prevails, where livelihoods are maintained in modes that foster sustainable and harmonious ecological environments. Regardless of diversity of vocation and quantity of material resources, the wisdom of Indigenous knowledge promoted holistic economic modes of production. Richard Peterson writes:

> The genius in these Central African ways of making a living from the forest is their total integration into a single system of food procurement. Farming was, and in some cases still is, correlated with trapping, hunting, and gathering in a manner bearing enough flexibility to dramatically decrease the risks (much greater in unintegrated or undiversified systems) of going hungry.
>
> The complex and intricate system of correlating shifting cultivation with trapping developed by Central African forest dwellers over hundreds of years of experiment and experience illustrates the ecological benefits of the holistic system particularly well. Not only did such trapping systems serve to control

animal damage to people's crops; they also allowed farmers to obtain sources of protein close to home, thereby indirectly leaving large tracts of forest further afield unexploited.[47]

Among the Achuar nation of the Amazon in Ecuador, there is a complex taxonomic system of botanical classification, all rooted in a spiritual ethos:

> Their knowledge as naturalists falls short of exhausting reality, for the organic world cannot be reduced to simple taxonomic systems. And so the Achuar identify each plant, each animal as belonging to a class; but they also endow each with human effects and a life of its own. Thus every living being in the world of nature has its own personality, which distinguishes it from the other members of its species to deal with it individually.[48]

The Achuar ethnobotanical knowledge system recognizes 262 different names of plants, identified morphologically and by taste and smell.[49]

The sense of Indigenous knowledge systems in agriculture is distinctively the possession of women in many situations. Among the Shona of Zimbabwe, for example, women predict the weather conditions by observing change in leaf color, shifts in wind direction, and cloud formation, temperature, and relative humidity changes, as well as birds, and beetles' songs and their seasonal migrations. Women use their knowledge of taxonomy and morphology to classify crops by gender, where crops like pumpkins, cowpeas, groundnuts, and millet, which had more diversified uses, were considered "women's crops." Women were also responsible for selecting appropriate seed types, based on color, grain, and size, to determine agronomic stability and suitability to different types of soils and terrain, as well as drought and disease resistance ability. When Gary Nabhan, a researcher with the Arizona Sonora Desert Museum, indicates that evolutionary ecologists are skeptical about acknowledging Indigenous peoples as "the first ecologists" because "these scholars are unaware of any truly ecological knowledge derived from ethnobiological field studies," he and they overlook concrete examples from Indigenous peoples such as the Shona of Zimbabwe.[50] Often, sadly, it reflects a Eurocentric reluctance to accept that Indigenous peoples have survived and thrived on Mother Earth for millennia, utiilzing Indigenous technical, botanical, medicinal, and scientific knowledge, without the input and involvement of Western European peoples. Given the obscene decimation of our beautiful planet and world by the obsession with Western industrial and capitalist "progress" that has left devastation in its wake, from the oil fields of the Niger delta that have destroyed the Ogoni nation, to the genocidal effect of uranium and coal mining in Arizona, Oklahoma, and Nevada on the Dineh, Hopi, and Shoshone nations, there is no need to still test Indigenous knowledge by European "scientific standards" and fall into conditioned imperialistic Eurocentric epistemologies, as Nabhan suggests, but rather to listen to the voices of Indigenous people and accept their wisdom as the only hope for the future.[51]

Conclusion

It is abundantly clear from the preceding illustrations that the future of global societies depends on the direction that the world takes: either on the existing path of insanity and destruction as defined by Western European modernity, or the ways of Indigenous people, the original conservationists and ecologists, the true diversity practitioners. In the final analysis, we are all part of the one global family of creation, we are all children of the Creator. What happens to one affects all. What our children experience will have an impact on generations to come. Our educational curricula in religious studies cannot but be holistic if it is to be relevant to the world. It must infuse Indigenous cosmologies into its academic core. Bigfoot Memorial Rider, a Lakota community leader and cofounder of the Takini Network explains this notion in terms of education and nationbuilding:

> There is really no word for parenting in Lakota. The closest way to say it is *Oyate Ptayela*—which really means taking care of the Nation. And, I think that's what it's going to take—we're going to have to rebuild the Nation. That is our task. That is our challenge—*Oyate Ptayela!* (Birgil Kills Straight, Rapid City, South Dakota, 1996)[52]

Let us hope that the peoples of the world will have enough common sense to pursue the right path. *Siyabonga . . . Mitaku oyasin.*

Notes

The opening quotation is taken from Vine Deloria, *For this Land: Writings on Religion in America*, ed. And with an introduction by James Treat (New York: Routledge, 1999), 148.

1. Charles Long, *Significations: Signs, Symbols, and Images in the Interpretation of Religion* (Philadelphia: Fortress Press, 1986), 102-03.

2. See Kwame Nkrumah's incisive work, *Neo-colonialism: The Last Stage of Imperialism* (London: Heinemann Educational Books, 1965), for an explication of the causes and conditions of neocolonialism in Africa.

3. M. A. Jaimes Guerrero, "Native Womanism: Exemplars of Indigenism in Sacred Traditions of Kinship," in *Indigenous Religions: A Companion*, ed. Graham Harvey (London: Cassell, 2000), 48.

4. See Eduardo Galeano's fascinating work, *Upside Down: A Primer for The Looking-Glass World* (New York: Metropolitan Books, Henry Holt & Co., 1998), for a satirical and trenchant critique of Western modernism.

5. Innocent Onyewuenyi, *The African Origin of Greek Philosophy: An Exercise in Afrocentrism* (Nsukka, Nigeria: University of Nsukka Press, 1993), 91.

6. G. W. F. Hegel, *The Philosophy of History* (New York: Dover Publications, 1956), 91-99.

7. This point is well articulated in Lynda Lange's article, "Burnt Offerings to Rationality: A Feminist Reading of the Construction of Indigenous Peoples in Enrique Dussel's Theory of Modernity," in *Decentering the Center: Philosophy for a Multicultural, Postcolonial, and Feminist World*, ed. Uma Narayan and Sandra Harding (Bloomington: Indiana University Press, 2000), 232.

8. Introduction, *Conservation through Survival: Indigenous Peoples and Protected Areas*, ed. Stan Stevens (Washington D.C.: Island Press, 1997), 1.

9. Elizabeth Kemp, "In Search of a Home: People Living in or Near Protected Areas," in *Indigenous Peoples and Protected Areas: The Law of Mother Earth*, ed. Elizabeth Kemp (London: Earthscan, 1993), 5.

10. Theophile Obenga, the ancient Egyptian historical scholar, discusses these phenomena in his classic work, *A Lost Tradition: African Philosophy in World History* (Philadelphia: Source Editions, 1995), 15.

11. Obenga, *A Lost Tradition*, 26.

12. Ronald Wright, *Stolen Continents: The Americas through Indian Eyes since 1492* (New York: Houghton Mifflin, 1992), 20-21.

13. Wright, *Stolen Continents*, 34-35.

14. Constance Hiliard, *Intellectual Traditions of Pre-Colonial Africa* (New York: McGraw Hill, 1998), 7.

15. Kwasi Wiredu, "Our Problem of Knowledge," in *African Philosophy as Cultural Inquiry*, ed. Ivan Karp and D. A. Masolo (Bloomington: Indiana University Press, 2000), 182.

16. Charles Redman, *Human Impact on Ancient Environments* (Tucson: University of Arizona Press, 1999), 107.

17. Bartomew Melia, "The Guarani Religious Experience," in *The Indian Face of God in Latin America*, ed. Manuel Marzal, Eugenio Maurer, Xavier Albo, and Bartomew Melia (Maryknoll, N.Y.: Orbis Books, 1996), 210.

18. Ellen R. Shell, "New World Syndrome," *The Atlantic Monthly* (June 2001).

19. Obenga, *A Lost* Tradition, 12.

20. David Penn and Patricia Campbell, "Human Rights and Culture: Beyond Universality and Relativism," *Third World Quarterly* 19, no. 1 (1998): 7-27.

21. See, for instance, Brooke Grundfest Schoepf's article, "Gender Relations and Development: Political Economy and Culture," in *Twenty First Century Africa: Towards a New Vision of Self Sustainable Development*, ed. Anne Seidman and Frederick Anang (Trenton, N. J.: Africa World Press, 1997).

22. Kwame Gyekye, *African Cultural Values: An Introduction for Some Secondary Schools* (Philadelphia: Sankofa, 1998), 115.

23. Wright, *Stolen Continents*, 70.

24. Clifford Krauss, "Bolivia Makes Key Sessions to Indians," *New York Times* (October 6, 2000): A8.

25. Cited in Hector Diaz Polanco, *Indigenous Peoples in Latin America: The Quest for Self-Determination* (Boulder, Colo.: Westview, 1997), 129.

26. Martha Mantour, "Matriarchy and the Canadian Constitution: A Double-Barrelled Threat to Indian Women," *Agenda: A Journal about Women and Gender* 13 (1992).

27. See for instance, Bruce Johansen's *Forgotten Founders: How the American Indian Helped Democracy* (Boston: Harvard Common Press, 1982).

28. See Ifi Amadiume's two important works, *African Matriarchal Foundations: The Igbo Case* (London: Karnak House, 1995), and *Reinventing Matriarchy, Religion, and Culture* (London: Zed Books, 1997).

29. M. B. Ramose, *African Philosophy through Ubuntu* (Harare, Zimbabwe: Mond Books, 1999).

30. Olga Miller, "Kgari," in *Indigenous Australian Voices: A Reader,* ed. Jennifer Sabbioni, Kay Schaffer, and Sidonie Smith (New Brunswick, N.J.: Rutgers University Press, 1999), 39-40.

31. See Dennis H. McPherson and J. Douglass Rabb, "Native Philosophy: Western or Indigenous Construct?" in *Indigeneity: Construction and Re/Presentation*, ed. James N. Brown and Patricia M. Sant (Commack, N.Y.: Nova Science Publishers, 1995), for an illumination of the distinctiveness of Indigenous philosophy in Turtle Island (North America), and the manner that it stands on its own, free of dependence on European categories, criteria, and constraints. The quote is from page 283.

32. Alan A. Fiske, *Structures of Social Life—The Four Elementary Forms of Human Relations: Communal Sharing, Authority Ranking, Equality Matching, Market Pricing* (New York: Free Press, 1991), 233.

33. Fiske, *Structures of Social Life*, 268.

34. Fiske, *Structures of Social Life*, 246.

35. Fiske, *Structures of Social Life*, 247, 258-85.

36. Englebert, *Burkino Faso: Unsteady Statehood in West Africa* (Boulder, Colo.: Westview and Harper Collins, 1996), 82.

37. Fiske discusses this in *Structures of Social Life*, 32.

38. Pierre Englebert, *Burkino Faso*, 79.

39. Winona LaDuke, *All Our Relations: Native Struggle for Land and Life* (Boston: South End Press, 1999), 2.

40. Wande Abimbola's *Ifa Will Mend Our Broken World: Thoughts on Yoruba Religion and Culture in Africa and the Diaspora* (Roxbury, Mass.: Aim Books, 1997), 105-106.

41. Seri Thongmak and David Hulse, "The Winds of Change: Karen People in Harmony with World Heritage," in *Indigenous Peoples and Protected Areas: The Law of Mother Earth*, ed. Elizabeth Kemp (London: Earthscan Publications, 1993), 162-63.

42. Aram Yengoyan, "Memory, Myth, and History: Traditional Agriculture and Structure in Mandaya Society," in *Cultural Values and Human Ecology in Southeast Asia*, ed. Karl Hutterer, A. Terry Rambo, and George Lovelace (Ann Arbor: Michigan Papers on South and Southeast Asia, Center for South and Southeast Asian Studies, The University of Michigan, 27, 1985), 170.

43. Aileen A. Esperitu, " 'Aboriginal Nations': Natives in Northwest Siberia and Northern Alberta," in *Contested Arctic: Indigenous Peoples, Industrial States, and the Circumpolar Environment*, ed. Eric A. Smith and Joan McCarter (Russian, East European, and Central Asian Studies Center at the Henry Jackson School of International

Studies, University of Washington, in association with University of Washington Press, Seattle, 1997), 45-47.

44. Aileen A. Esperitu, "Aboriginal Nations," 44.

45. M. H. Khalil, *Indigenous Disenfranchisement and Long-Term Conservation: The Impact of Property Rights, Bioprospecting Agreements, and Global Institutions on Genetic Resources and Indigenous Cultures* (Nairobi: ACES Press, Advanced Center for Environmental Studies, 1996), 3-4.

46. John Mbaria, "Who is Really Breaking Nature's Law?" *World Press Review* (October, 2000); reprint from *The East African* (June 12-18, 2000).

47. Richard B. Peterson, *Conversations in the Rainforest: Culture, Values, and the Environment in Central Africa* (Boulder, Colo.: Westview/Perseus Books, 2000), 90-91.

48. Philippe Descola, *In the Society of Nature: A Native Ecology in Amazonia*, trans. Nora Scott (Cambridge, U.K.: Cambridge University Press, 1994), 77.

49. Descola, *In the Society of Nature*, 78.

50. Gary Paul Nabhan, "Native American Management and Conservation of Biodiversity in the Sonoran Desert Bioregion: An Ethnoecological Perspective," in *Biodiversity and Native America*, ed. Paul Minnis and Wayne Elisens (Norman: University of Oklahoma Press, 2000), 32.

51. Nabhan, "Native American Management and Conservation," 33.

52. Maria Yellow Horse Brave Heart, "Oyate Ptayela: Rebuilding the Lakota Nation Through Addressing Historical Trauma among Lakota Parents," in *Voices of First Nations People: Human Services Considerations*, ed. Hilary N. Weaver (New York: Haworth Press, 1999), 124.

9

Cross-cultural Religious Business:
Cocacolonization, McDonaldization,
Disneyization, Tupperization, and
Other Local Dilemmas of Global Signification

David Chidester

"So you've decided to go global!" begins the popular manual for doing cross-cultural business, *Kiss, Bow, or Shake Hands: How to Do Business in Sixty Countries*. In his preface to the book, Hans Koehler, director of the Wharton Export Network, clearly explains that "global" in this instance means doing international business. "Globalization, by definition, requires you to deal with, sell to, and/or buy from people in other countries." Entering the global marketplace, trading with foreign partners, negotiating with foreign competitors, or managing foreign workers requires a basic knowledge about foreign cultures. "Multicultural awareness," Koehler notes, "is a vital component of any global marketing strategy, providing "the knowledge a U.S. executive needs in order to operate overseas."[1] In achieving this multicultural awareness, the U.S. executive will need to know something about foreign history and geography, languages and customs, business practices and negotiating techniques, cultural orientations and cognitive styles. Successful global executives might even have to know something about foreign religions, especially if they want to avoid the mistake reportedly made by the Thom McAn Company when it overlooked the possibility that its nearly illegible logo, printed inside every shoe, might turn out to look like the Arabic script for Allah, which it apparently did, thus causing Muslims to risk desecrating the name of God by walking on it.[2]

Among all of these areas of specialized knowledge, the most immediate, accessible form of "multicultural awareness" can be gained by learning the appropriate physical gestures within different cultures. A vast literature in the field of international business communication recommends careful attention to local body languages. Addressed primarily to American entrepreneurs, or, more specifically, to Euroamerican entrepreneurs with little or no experience of cultural diversity within their own country, this literature warns against kissing in China for fear of being mistaken for a cannibal; it recommends bowing frequently in Japan as a sign of respect; and it advises mastering the distinctive African handshake, a "handshake with a twist," when doing business in Africa. Unveiling the mystery of the African handshake, an Internet guide for doing business in South Africa gives detailed instructions. "Use the traditional Western-style handshake, and then without letting go of the person's hand, slide your hand around the other person's thumb, then go back to the original Western position. After a few tries, you'll get it right."[3] Based on these instructions, it is hard to imagine that anyone could get it right, especially if getting it right means demonstrating the communication skills necessary to do business.

Although most of this advice is designed to help American entrepreneurs establish rapport and avoid embarrassment when dealing with foreign people, this attention to body language often reinforces the notion of fundamental cultural differences between Americans and the rest of the world. In the analysis of body language, cultural kinesics, or the "nonverbal channel of communication," the science of international business communication displays a pervasive American exceptionalism. In a review of kinesics and cross-cultural understanding, for example, one author reproduces an inventory of "postures used to signify humility," but those postures actually seem to be gestures of defeat. The Chinese join hands over their heads and bow, signifying, "I submit with tired hands." Turks and Persians bow, extend their right arm, moving it down, up, and down again, signifying, "I lift the earth off the ground and place it on my head as a sign of submission to you." The African Batokas throw themselves on their backs, roll from side to side, and slap the outside of their thighs, signifying, "You need not subdue me. I am subdued already."[4] Although these signs of submission might be useful to know in global business negotiations, the point of drawing up an inventory of kinesics is to reinforce American exceptionalism. As the author observes, these postures "would either embarrass or disgust most Americans, who are not readily inclined to show humility in any guise."[5]

While compiling a detailed repertoire of cultural kinesics, all of this attention to local body language is advanced under the generalized sign of globalization. What is globalization in this context? Is it a new description of a changing culture or a new and rapidly changing culture of description? On the one hand, as Arjun Appadurai proposed in an influential essay, "Disjuncture and Difference in the Global Cultural Economy," globalization represents a new fluidity in the transnational movement, the global "flows," of people, machines, money, ideas of human solidarity, and images of human possibility.[6] Here globalization appears as a descriptive account of homogeneity and difference, continuity and disjuncture, within the shifting landscapes of the world.

On the other hand, in the literature of international business communication, globalization appears less as a descriptive account of the world than as a mythic narrative, a sacred charter, or a religious mandate for transcending borders and opening new markets all over the world.[7] During the 1990s, according to cultural analyst Thomas Frank, global business interests were opening up a new ideological space, "One Market under God," that excluded "dumb heathens," as Mike Davis observed in a review of Frank's book, who were "unanointed in the ecstatic religion of instant and infinitely increasing wealth."[8] Playfully, but pointedly, these invocations of religion suggest that doing cross-cultural business draws upon sacred symbols, myths, and rituals that operate just like religion. Recently, analysts of successful global businesses—Coca-Cola, McDonald's, Disney, and others—have specifically used the term *religion* in attempting to capture their meaning and power, suggesting that these multinational corporations have assumed symbolic, mythic, and ritualized forms that approximate the forms and functions of world religions. In the context of vast global exchanges and profound local effects, how should we understand these "religious" factors and forces in doing cross-cultural business?

Communication

In the science of international business communication, Edward T. Hall and Geert Hofstede are generally recognized as founders and guiding spirits, even though they produced very different work. For Edward T. Hall, author of an evocative series of books on gestures, time, space, and other forms of "silent language," culture was primarily a matter of context and style. Distinguishing between high context and low context cultures, differentiating between implicit and explicit styles of communication within cultures, Hall seemed less interested in drawing comparisons between or among cultures than in exploring the dynamic relationship between background context and foreground communication in any cultural exchange.[9] By contrast, Geert Hofstede developed a science of comparing cultures that was specifically designed to serve the purposes of doing cross-cultural business; as Hofstede asserted in the title of one essay, "the business of international business is culture."[10] What did Hofstede understand by culture? Basically, he operated on the assumption that culture was a plural category, comprising many distinctive cultures, but that every culture could be reduced to a mentality, the "software of the mind," that established distinctive ways of processing information. Drawing on a database generated from 116,000 questionnaires, distributed in 1968 and 1972 to IBM employees in forty countries, Hofstede distilled four (and, later, five) indicators of cultural differentiation in the ways in which people did business.[11]

Marking out cultural differences as if they could be plotted against a fixed set of binary oppositions in ways of thinking, cultural mentalities, or mental software programs, Hofstede tracked the oppositions between individualism and collectivism, egalitarianism and hierarchy, masculinity and femininity, and risk-taking versus risk-avoidance. Later, bringing China, or at least Hong Kong, into his database, Hofstede added a fifth opposition, the difference between short-term and long-term orientations, supported by observations about the "Confucian dynamics" of upholding cultural obligations of virtue over the long term instead of getting to the truth of the matter in business dealings in the short term. Unavoidably, these oppositions, designed to be useful when doing business in a foreign culture, reflect the cultural interests of business at home. It is easy to suspect that all of these oppositions can be distilled into a fundamental distinction between us and them, especially if we can appear as individualists, in an egalitarian business environment, that is nevertheless masculine in its strength and willing to take risks, while they register as collectivist, hierarchical, feminine, and fearful of taking the kind of risks necessary for gaining profits quickly in the short term. While Hofstede's findings have been open to debate, they have generally set the parameters for cultural analysis in doing cross-cultural business. From prestigious business schools to consultants advertising on the Internet, international business communication has generally followed the lead of Geert Hofstede in translating the complex, bewildering, and perhaps indeterminate diversity of cultural contexts and styles of communication into simple indicators of opposition.

In a representative text for intercultural business communication, the author identifies "Ten Ways Culture Affects Negotiation." At the end of a long discussion of cultural variables in doing cross-cultural business, we end up with a basic opposition between two types of cultures, type A and type B. In business negotiations, type A cultures seek a contract rather than a relationship; they prefer informal rather than formal interaction; they value time instead of disregarding it; they display emotionally expressive rather than emotionally restrained styles; they make specific rather than general agreements; they build agreements from the bottom up rather than from the top down; they form negotiating teams organized around one leader rather than around an implicit group consensus; they are willing to take risks rather than avoiding risks. Although the author warns that no culture entirely fits within either type A or type B, it is difficult to avoid the conclusion that this analysis of international business communication has merely reproduced some of the fundamental cultural stereotypes that Americans hold about others, especially when the author concludes that "Americans may tend to be type A and Japanese type B."[12]

While reifying mentalities, intercultural business communication has failed to recognize the crucial and perhaps determinative role of materiality in human communication. In the science of mediology established by Régis Debray, a field of inquiry that is not cultural studies, communication studies, or media studies, but instead a disciplined investigation of the materiality of culture, communication, and media, we might find a different way of engaging the problem of cross-cultural communication in cross-cultural business. Beginning with his work on the political "logic of the sacred" in his *Critique of Political Reason*, Régis Debray, colleague of Che Guevara, adviser to François Mitterand, and theoretical heretic to the Communist Party, has suggested that an academic study of religion is necessary for interrogating nationalism, exposing its originary myths and ritual repetitions, its sacralizations of space and time, as religious gestures of symbolic efficacy that are required by the material organization of any collectivity. Building on this "religious materialism," *Media Manifestos* profiled Debray's science of mediology, a study of the ways and means of symbolic efficacy that investigated not the meaning but the power of signs, the "becoming-material" forces of symbolic forms. Taking his subject as mediation, Debray has focused on the materiality of signs and signification. Basically, Debray has argued that material organization is necessary for the organization of matter in any transmission of culture. How do signs produce effects? How does saying or showing become doing? In the science of mediology, these are questions of both material and religious importance. Although Debray observes that Marx's problem was that he had not studied the history of religions, the academic study of religion can learn something from this materialist analysis of symbolic efficacy in popular culture.[13]

In the history of religions, Charles Long has also focused attention on the materiality of signification, the materiality of signs, their material transmission, and the modes of human imagination, orientation, and formation that have directly engaged materiality. The imagination of matter, as Long has argued, is not confined to an original, primordial ontology or defined by an enduring, poetic phenomenology.[14] Rather, the imagination of matter is historically situated in the contacts, relations, and exchanges of the colonial era, at work and at stake within colonial situations, whether in America or elsewhere, that provided the material terms for significations of meaning and power. In the intercultural communication of colonial situations, we find arguments arising about the "spirit of matter," the "social life of things," the cultural "promiscuity of objects," the "untranscended materiality" of the fetish, and the deferred promise in the "secret of the Cargo," all increasingly shadowed by the circulation of the commodity, that immaterial materiality, that "very queer thing," as Karl Marx proposed, "abounding in metaphysical subtleties and theological niceties."[15] In a postcolonial, globalizing world, these modes of engaging materiality have continued to generate powerful terms of human signification, which, according to both Régis Debray and Charles Long, fall within the province of the history of religions.

Informed by the work of Debray and Long, I want to propose that international business communication might learn something from the history of religions. In what follows, I hope to demonstrate that cross-cultural business is not essentially a matter of communication, especially not the kind of communication advocated by the science of international business communication, with its stereotypes about body languages, cultural orientations, and styles of cognition. Rather, cross-cultural business is driven by material mediations, significations, and negotiations. For better or worse, cross-cultural business, which is never business as usual, engages materiality through signs and symbols, media and mediations, myths and rituals, personal investments and social formations that bear strange traces of religion. Like imperial, colonizing, and missionizing religions, major transnational corporations have generated new terms for engaging materiality not only within an expanding global economy but also within a changing political economy of the sacred. These globalizing, cross-cultural enterprises have raised any number of local problems in the translation, rationalization, and imagination of materiality, thereby doing a kind of religious work, I will suggest, even if that religious work is mediated and signified by multinational corporations. Briefly, in what follows, I highlight enduring problems of intercultural translation, rationalization, and imagination in the contemporary "religious" business of Coca-Cola, McDonald's, and Disney.

Cocacolonization

As the supreme icon of American cultural imperialism, Coca-Cola has often been rendered in religious terms. Recalling the words of the company's advertising director, Delony Sledge, in the early 1950s, the Coca-Cola Company has operated as if its "work is a religion rather than a business."[16] What kind of religion is this? As I have argued, the religion of Coca-Cola revolves around a sacred object, the fetish of Coca-Cola, that is both desired object and the objectification of desire. "Coca-Cola is the holy grail," as one company executive observed. "Wherever I go, when people find out I work for Coke, it's like being a representative from the Vatican, like you've touched God. I'm always amazed. There's such reverence toward the product."[17] In these potent images of an original holy blood and an enduring sacred tradition, this Coca-Cola executive invoked a religious aspiration for touching what cannot be touched because it is a materiality that is also an icon of holy desire.

The Coca-Cola Company has produced a massive network of global exchanges and local effects that must be regarded as significant forces in any notion of globalization. As company president Roberto Goizueta put it, "Our success will largely depend on the degree to which we make it impossible for the consumer around the globe to escape Coca-Cola." While the vast exchanges that have established and empowered the Coca-Cola empire are obvious, some of the local effects can be surprising. Coca-Cola is not only transnational; it is also translational. Coca-Cola trades on the translation of information, imagery, and desire among vastly different cultural contexts all over the world. In fashioning this worldwide enterprise, foreign governments, trade restrictions, access to supplies, and local competition have often presented problems; but so has cultural

translation. Not only signifying "the global high-sign," Coca-Cola has sometimes generated a chaos of signification in its attempts at global translation. For
example, the Chinese characters that most closely reproduced the sound of
"Coca-Cola" apparently translated as "bite the wax tadpole." In Dutch, "Refresh
Yourself with Coca-Cola" meant "Wash Your Hands with Coca-Cola." French
speakers misheard the French version of the song, "Have a Coke and a Smile,"
as "Have a Coke and a Mouse," while Spanish speakers in Cuba reportedly mis-
read the sky writing for "Tome Coca-Cola" (Drink Coca-Cola) as "Teme Coca-
Cola" (Fear Coca-Cola). Not all translations of Coca-Cola display such blatant
misreadings. Apparently, there were Spanish speakers in Latin America who had
good reasons to fear Coca-Cola. In 1978, Guatemalan union organizer Israel
Marquez informed the company's annual meeting that Coca-Cola's alleged
complicity in state-sponsored terrorism against labor unions had resulted in a
serious image problem. "Coca-Cola's image in Guatemala could not be worse,"
Marquez asserted. "There, murder is called 'Coca-Cola.'"[18]

As a global religious mission, Coca-Cola enters new frontiers, new "contact
zones," and is encountered locally as a problem not only of translation but also
of power relations. In the 1980 South African film *The Gods Must Be Crazy*,
Director Jamie Uys created an absurd allegory for such a local engagement with
the "holy grail" of Coca-Cola. In a Bushman camp in Namibia, a Coca-Cola
bottle, thrown carelessly from an airplane, falls out of the sky to land in the
camp. Gradually, the people find uses for this mysterious object, "one of the
strangest and most beautiful things they have seen," by employing it in working,
preparing food, and even in religious ritual as a musical instrument. As this mysterious object becomes a focus for desire, it also becomes a flash point for competition, dissension, and conflict among individuals in the community, creating a
situation, similar, in some respects, to the cycle of violence analyzed by René
Girard, a cycle of reciprocal revenge that can only be stopped by identifying a
sacrificial victim, a scapegoat, to be expelled from the community. In this case,
the Bushman identifies the single source of violence as the Coca-Cola bottle.
Setting out from the camp, he decides to travel to the end of the earth to return
this mysterious object to the gods. On that sacred journey, however, the Bushman only ends up in modern Johannesburg, initiated into the sordid mysteries of
modernity.[19]

Although this allegory was not produced by the Coca-Cola Company, it nevertheless reinforced the myth of Coca-Cola as the supreme icon of modernity.
John Tomlinson, author of *Cultural Imperialism*, has suggested that if goods are
actually desired by people rather than imposed upon them by force, then their
entry into global markets should not be regarded as cultural imperialism but as
"the spread of modernity."[20] Certainly, this benign reading of the role of a desired commodity, especially the supreme commodity that nobody needs but
everyone desires, the sacred beverage, bottle, and icon of Coca-Cola, misrepre-
sents the power relations in which the translation of desire is precisely what is at

stake. Like the Bible, the Cross, or European styles of housing, clothing, and weapons in other colonial situations of Christian missionary intervention, Coca-Cola marks fundamental oppositions, signifying the slash between primitive and civilized, traditional and modern, or communist and capitalist. In a range of popular imagery, the sacred object of Coca-Cola stands at the frontier of competing religions in a global contact zone. For example, a widely reproduced photographic image from Saudi Arabia shows Muslims bowing in prayer, facing Mecca, but inadvertently also bowing before a bright red soft-drink vending machine, assuming what appears from the photograph to be a posture of religious submission before the sacred logo of Coca-Cola. Visiting the World of Coca-Cola Museum in Atlanta, a group of Tibetan Buddhist monks, wearing robes, were photographed one by one sticking their heads through a cardboard cutout of a waiter pouring a glass of Coca-Cola. They enjoyed making such "modern discoveries," a translator explained.[21] In different ways, these images reinforced stereotypes—Arabian Muslims bowing in blind devotion that made them oblivious to a modernity that was overwhelming them, Tibetan Buddhists encountering that same bewildering modernity with wide-eyed surprise—that elevated Coca-Cola as the crucial sacred object in a frontier zone of interreligious relations.

Following the collapse of the Soviet Union, Coca-Cola operated as a sacred icon not only of modernity but also of a kind of religious initiation into global markets that promised to transform people from "primitive" communism to "modern" capitalism. As the anthropologist Alaina Lemon has observed, "News photos titillate by juxtaposing supposed opposites: for example, fur-hatted soldiers drink Coca-Cola on Red Square." Although Russians had long been familiar with the beverage, Coca-Cola was mobilized to signify both the opposition between communism and capitalism as well as the recent conversion of Russia from one to the other. Recalling a long history of images of "first contact" between European missionaries and startled natives, Lemon concluded, newspapers showed such images of Coke-drinking soldiers to "amuse and astound with images of Russians shaking the invisible hand."[22] As Constance Classen has observed, Coca-Cola operates in a global symbolic economy of "surreal consumerism" in which products "are touted by their advertisers as an eruption of the extraordinary into the everyday."[23] Obviously, Coca-Cola, as the "pause that refreshes," is marketed as precisely such a surrealistic transformation of the ordinary into the extraordinary. If consumer products signify such an eruption of the extraordinary into the ordinary, thereby representing a kind of hierophany, a manifestation of the sacred, reflective consumers will inevitably have to ask, "Where do these things come from?" During her fieldwork in northwestern Argentina, Constance Classen asked people how they felt about drinking a product like Coca-Cola that came from America, bearing the weight of American cultural imperialism, but she found that people generally assumed that Coca-Cola was indigenous. Living with the product and its imagery all their lives, people understood Coca-Cola as a local product. As Classen recounted, "a woman from a Northwestern town asks when I bring up the subject of Coke's status as an import: 'But isn't Coca-Cola Argentine?'"[24] This assumption that Coca-Cola was actually a local product recalled the surrealist story written by Leonora Carrington, a vision of the Mexico of the future in which people valued "bottles of the rare old Indian drink called cocacola."[25]

McDonaldization

In his popular analysis of modernization, sociologist George Ritzer coined the term *McDonaldization* to represent "the process by which the principles of the fast-food restaurant are coming to dominate more and more sectors of American society as well as of the rest of the world."[26] Updating the classic work of Max Weber, who argued that the principles of bureaucratic rationalization, organization, management, and control were the hallmarks of modernization, Ritzer proposed that the fast-food restaurant has extended the scope of those same principles throughout every aspect of personal and social life. Concentrating on McDonald's as the principal model, the ideal type, or the paradigm for this process, Ritzer identified four principles of rationalization—efficiency, calculability, predictability, and control over labor by replacing human with nonhuman technology. Not merely selling burgers, fries, and milkshakes, therefore, McDonald's is actively advancing these principles of rationalization in America and the larger world.

As Ritzer recognized, a social force with such awesome and pervasive power seems to function like a global religion. Certainly, Ray Kroc employed religious language. "The french fry would become almost sacrosanct for me," Kroc reported, "its preparation, a ritual to be followed religiously."[27] But McDonald's was more than a sacrosanct object. "To many people throughout the world," as George Ritzer has observed, "McDonald's has become a sacred institution." As evidence, Ritzer cited a newspaper account of the opening of McDonald's in Moscow "as if it were the Cathedral in Chartres." Reportedly, a Moscow worker described McDonald's as a place to experience "celestial joy."[28] What kind of religion is this? Anchored in a sacred institution, a "cathedral of consumption," McDonaldization might be regarded as a powerful sect within a broader "consumer religion." [29] In that consumer religion, with its sacred places of pilgrimage, sacred times of ritualized gift giving, and sacred objects of holy desire, McDonald's fast-foot restaurant could be regarded as a sect competing for religious market share in the same political economy of the sacred with other sacred institutions, such as the shopping mall, that celebrate the spiritual ecstasy of consumerism. According to Ritzer, however, the "sacred institution" of McDonald's has established a religion that is based not on spiritual ecstasy, despite the Russian worker's claims about experiencing "celestial joy," but on spiritual discipline, a kind of inner-worldly asceticism that regulates desire according to the requirements of bureaucratic rationalization. Unlike the religion of Cocacolonization, with its cross-cultural translation of desire for the sacred object, the religion of McDonaldization represents a cross-cultural rationalization of desire and desire for rationalization. Embedded in the "sacred institution" of McDonald's, but extending through all social institutions, McDonaldization is the religious rationality of modern institutionalized life.

Following Max Weber's dark vision, Ritzer warned about the "iron cage" of rationality, the confining, oppressive structures of bureaucratic rationalization "in which people cannot always behave as human beings—where people are dehumanized."[30] In response to the human irrationality of rationalization, people can reclaim their humanity through local acts of resistance against the global religion of McDonaldization. Increasingly, resistance has become organized. Since the mid-1980s, UN World Food Day, October 16, has been celebrated as Worldwide Anti-McDonald's Day. The fifteenth annual Anti-McDonald's Day in 1999 was marked by 425 local protests in 23 countries. Generally, protests against globalization, especially against the orchestration of the global economy by the International Monetary Fund and the World Bank, have found McDonald's a useful target for opposition. According to some cultural analysts, however, the activity of consumption, even the act of eating a Big Mac, can be an occasion for consumers to mobilize alternative meanings that should also count as acts of resistance to the "iron cage" of McDonaldization. In his semiotic reading of eating at McDonald's, for example, John S. Caputo proposed that consumers are buying not a rationality but a story, a myth, a sacred narrative of "family, food, and fun" in which they can participate in different, personal, and meaningful ways. Nevertheless, Caputo also recognized that this story has a distinctively American flavor. The myth of McDonald's is basically the story of "American culture and consensus—the myth of freedom and equality in which anyone can and does go and eat at McDonald's."[31]

In his argument with Ritzer, Caputo emphasized the importance of *mythos* over *logos*, the meaning of consumption over the machinery of production, and the creativity of human imagination over the routinization of dehumanizing bureaucratic rationalization. Still, given the central role that America plays in both the sociological and the semiotic accounts, how do we understand the global transmission of McDonald's into more than one hundred different countries and their different languages, different cultural orientations, and perhaps even different cognitive styles? By 1996, McDonald's had surpassed Coca-Cola in global brand name recognition. How was that brand actually recognized, consumed, and assimilated in different cultural contexts? As Caputo asked, "How could McDonald's sell a hamburger to the Japanese whose diet consisted primarily of fish and rice?"[32] Anticipating that problem, the founder of McDonald's in Japan, Den Fujita, had an answer. McDonald's promised to effect a dramatic human transformation. "The reason Japanese people are so short and have yellow skins is that they have eaten nothing but fish and rice for 2000 years," Den Fujita reportedly maintained. "If we eat McDonald's hamburgers and potatoes for a thousand years, we will become taller, our skin will become white and our hair blond."[33] Arguably, this promise of human transformation from the image of a traditional Japanese to modern American places Den Fujita as an inside agent of alien American imperialism. "Unlike more traditional conquerors," as Ronald Steel has observed, Americans "are not content merely to subdue others. We insist that they be like us."[34] By this account, Den Fujita was doing the job of American conquerors better than they could ever have done it themselves. McDonald's establishment in Japan, however, did not signify an American conquest and Japanese submission to an alien, American, and globalizing force, not even the pervasive force of rationalization that Ritzer called McDonaldization. Rather, McDonald's emerged as a site of local negotiations over food and foodways, eating and etiquette, age groups and family values, sociality and society. As a result of these ongoing negotiations, as James L. Watson has observed, "the Big Mac, fries, and Coke do not represent something foreign. McDonald's is, quite simply, 'local' cuisine."[35]

Although McDonaldization represents a universalizing rationality of efficiency, calculability, predictability, and control, McDonald's restaurants have had to adapt to local situations and circumstances. Adapting to local tastes, rather than simply imposing a global, homogenized "convergence of taste," McDonald's has produced such culturally specific variations as McSpaghetti in the Philippines, McLaks (grilled salmon sandwich) in Norway, McHuevo (poached egg hamburger) in Uruguay, and MacChao (Chinese fried rice) in Japan. Like Coca-Cola, however, McDonald's has also been actively engaged in interreligious relations, especially when the menu set by its headquarters in the heartland of America, at Hamburger University, Oak Brook, Illinois, conflicts with religious customs, ethics, or laws governing diet. More intimately than Coca-Cola, McDonald's enters into and occasionally comes into conflict with the foodways of the world. Since those foodways are intimately related to religion, the conflicts over food are intensely negotiated. Consistently, although not without conflict, McDonald's has shown a willingness to adapt to local religious requirements. After considerable controversy, McDonald's in Israel agreed to provide hamburgers without cheese, at several outlets, to avoid violating Jewish dietary law. In Malaysia, Singapore, and other countries with a large Muslim presence, McDonald's submitted to inspection by Muslim clerics to ensure the ritual cleanliness, and absence of pork, in the preparation and presentation of meat. In opening new franchises in India, again after considerable controversy, McDonald's introduced a range of new products—mutton-based Maharaja Macs for Hindus who do not eat beef, Vegetable McNuggets and the potato-based McAloo Tikki burger for Hindus who do not eat meat at all—to accommodate religious interests in food, even though Hindu fundamentalists of the Bharatiya Janata Party (BJP) campaigned against McDonald's on religious grounds. In all of these corporate negotiations over the religious significance of food, McDonald's demonstrated an impressive responsiveness to local traditions. Of course, McDonald's was in a strong position to make these local accommodations because it had mastered the art of producing French fries that were universally accepted, from every religious perspective, making them "ever-present," as James Watson has observed, "and consumed with great gusto by Muslims, Jews, Christians, Buddhists, and Hindus."[36] McDonald's could make adjustments for local religious diets, therefore, because it had discovered a dietary constant that was embraced globally by all religions.

As defined by George Ritzer, McDonaldization represents a globalizing steamroller in which the American mastery of the rational arts of efficiency, calculability, predictability, and control is subjecting people in America and the rest of the world to a regime of rationalization that is basically dehumanizing. Certainly, the critical perspective advanced by Ritzer echoed the dehumanizing conditions of colonial situations, except that the imperial, colonizing power, in this case, is ideologically legitimated not by God, country, or manifest destiny but by a Big Mac, fries, and a Coke. As in the case of Coca-Cola, however, McDonald's meaning and power has also been appropriated by consumers all over the world as a local production, as if it were a local, indigenous institution. Reversing the thrust in the classic colonial narratives of "first contact" between Europeans and startled natives, many versions have been told of the story about a child coming from some other part of the world to the United States and expressing astonishment to find a McDonald's restaurant. "Look!" exclaimed the son of a Japanese executive visiting America, "They even have McDonald's in the United States!"[37]

Disneyization

While *McDonaldization* has emerged as a technical term for bureaucratic rationalization, a contrasting, but complementary, term, *Disneyization*, has been advanced to capture the importance of managing, engineering, and molding the human imagination. As defined by sociologist Alan Bryman, Disneyization refers to "the process by which *the principles* of the Disney theme parks are coming to dominate more and more sectors of American society as well as the rest of the world."[38] Those principles—theming, dedifferentiation of consumption, multisector merchandising, and emotional labor—undergird the imagineering of cross-cultural business most clearly exemplified by the Walt Disney Company but increasingly informing the way business is conducted. Taking Disneyland as paradigm, businesses apply the principle of theming to create imaginary worlds that evoke a thematic coherence through architecture, landscaping, costuming, and other theatrical effects to establish a focused, coherent experience. In the process, the activity of consumption is dedifferentiated from entertainment, dissolving the distinction between shopping and playing, so that, as Umberto Eco observed, "you buy obsessively, believing that you are still playing."[39] Reinforcing this coherence of imagination and integration of experience, the merchandising of products depends upon associating goods with logos, with powerful images, such as the Disney characters who sell films, that sell videos, that sell theme parks, that sell consumer products, that sell films, producing "an endless round of self-referential co-advertisements."[40]

In the end, Disneyization is a system of emotional labor that is empowered, not only through the emotional investments made by consumers, but also in the management of emotions by workers at the point of production. As workers, or "cast members" in Disney-speak, perform their scripted interactions with the public—the "friendly smile," the "friendly phrases"—they master a kind of emotional labor that conveys the impression that work is not work but play.[41] In cross-cultural communication, of course, the body language of the "friendly smile" is not always appreciated as a valid form of emotional labor. Although McDonald's also sells a smile with its products, it discovered that throughout most of East Asia, where sales people and service personnel were expected to adopt an expression of seriousness, the "friendly smile" was generally not trusted. For the opening of the first McDonald's in Moscow, where a visible smile can be interpreted as a personal challenge, a McDonald's representative stood outside to explain the meaning of the emotional labor at work in the fast-food restaurant: "The employees inside will smile at you. This does not mean that they are laughing at you. We smile because we are happy to serve you."[42] Selling a "Coke and a Smile," the Coca-Cola Company also operates in the field of emotional labor, participating in the imaginary merger of work, play, and consumption. The Walt Disney Company, however, has set the global standards for imagining happiness, especially through its "classic" animated films and its theme parks, each proclaimed as the "happiest place on earth," where employees and consumers, cast members and guests, both engage in the emotional labor necessary for the success of Disneyization.

It is a cliché of cultural criticism that Disney animated films have been doing a kind of political work. In their classic salvo against American cultural imperialism, *How to Read Donald Duck*, Ariel Dorfman and Armand Mattelart exposed the imperialist ideology encoded in Disney comics and animation, most notoriously in the animated feature *The Three Caballeros* (1945), that explicitly represented and implicitly targeted Latin America.[43] Coinciding with the escalation of the Vietnam War, Disney's *Jungle Book* (1967) altered the geography of Kipling's colonial India—Baloo was transferred from Great Britain to the United States, Mawgli was not an Indian but a "jungle boy"—in ways that have led many critics to read the film as a political allegory for the U.S. "civilizing" mission in the "primitive" jungles of Vietnam. After a long dormant period, Disney animation revived in the Eisner era, producing a series of extremely popular and financially successful films during the 1990s that also have been analyzed as doing a kind of political work.

According to Eleanor Byrne and Martin McQuillan in *Deconstructing Disney*, these films can be read as a strange merger of U.S. and Disney foreign policy. In their deconstructive reading, *The Little Mermaid* (1989) is a story about people of the sea and people of the land, a mermaid who desires human commodities, but incurs a debt that must be paid in order for her to join the humans and gain access to human goods, comprising a political allegory for the fall of the Berlin Wall, the collapse of communism, and indebtedness of Eastern Europe to the West. By contrast to this allegory of debt, *Beauty and the Beast* (1991) is a story about the gift, focusing on the value of hospitality, thereby serving as both legitimation for and invitation to the new Disney theme park and hotels outside Paris. Pursing a global expansion of this Disney politics, *Aladdin* (1992) advances the same U.S. interests in the Arab world that drove the Gulf War, with the genie representing American military advisers. Moving into Africa, *The Lion King* (1994) presents a neoliberal vision of human harmony in response to the demise of apartheid in South Africa. Returning to Europe, *The Hunchback of Notre Dame* (1996) deals with the themes that recall reports of "ethnic cleansing" and calls for "humanitarian intervention" that justified U.S. policy in Bosnia. Finally, extending the scope of the Disney political imagination into the Far East, *Mulan* (1998) responds to the Tiananmen Square massacre by opening relations with China, while also anticipating the establishment of a "major Disney attraction," as Michael Eisner proposed in 1999, "in the world's most populous nation."[44]

As cultivated by the Walt Disney Company, therefore, the emotional labor invested in Disneyization has sustained a kind of political work, the production and reinforcement of a political imagination that had become increasingly global in scope by the end of the twentieth century. Was this political imagination also a kind of religious imagination? Certainly, in calling for a boycott of Disney films, theme parks, and products, the Southern Baptist Convention regarded the Walt Disney Company not only as antireligion, allegedly promoting "immoral ideologies," but as an alternative religion, a pagan religion advanced through its animated features in the New Age harmonial spirituality of the "circle of life" in the *Lion King* or the earth-based indigenous spirituality of *Pocahontas*.[45] In *Pocahontas* (1995), the American centerpiece of the Disney decade of global expansion, a film that also coincided with the company's plans for a new theme park, the aborted Walt Disney's America in Virginia, we find a key moment suggesting that the religious work of Disney animation is the adjudication of human identity and difference. In the scene in which Ratcliff and Pohattan prepare for battle, the leaders stand on either side of the colonial divide between civilization and savagery. Bursting into song, they represent each other. Ratcliff sings, "Here's what you get when races are diverse. Their skins are hellish red, they're only good when dead." In turn Pohattan responds by singing, "This is what we feared, the paleface is a demon. The only thing they feel at all is greed." Instead of resolving this counterpoint in a critique of colonial greed, racism, and violence, however, the film dissolves the differences between European invaders and indigenous Americans by having Ratcliff and Pohattan harmonize on the refrain, "They're savages, savages, barely even human." In this harmony of mutual denial, the audience can only conclude that there was a basic equivalence—mistakes on both sides, misunderstanding on both sides, failure to recognize the humanity of the other on both sides—in intercultural relations between Europeans and Native Americans. Effectively erasing the asymmetries of power, let alone the violence of colonization, this equivalence leaves a human identity, an identity that might be called the human neutral, which stands as a generalized, even universalized basis for dealing with difference.

Throughout the animated films of the 1990s, Disney worked on elaborating this universal construction of human identity. In *The Little Mermaid*, where human beings walk on two legs, but the sea people have no legs, we learn that a sea person can become a human being by paying a debt. In *Beauty and the Beast*, where human beings walk on two legs, but the Beast walks on four legs, we learn that a beast can become human by extending the gift of hospitality. Having sorted out these basic human relations of reciprocity and exchange, the gift and the debt, Disney animation proceeded to broaden its scope by adjudicating human identity and difference in the Muslim world, the African world, and the Asian world. Certainly, these films engaged difference in ways that reproduced stereotypes, risking the reinforcement of religious, cultural, and racial prejudices, but they consistently reinforced a human identity, the human neutral, as an identity defined by its capacity for transcending all differences. If religion is about human identity and difference, human formation and orientation, then Disney animation during the 1990s was definitely engaged in a kind of religious work.

In assessing the religious work of Disney, the theme parks provide a more obvious point of reference. As many cultural analysts have observed, these alternative worlds—Disneyland in Anaheim, Disney World in Orlando, EuroDisney outside of Paris, and Disneyland in Tokyo—have become sacred places of pilgrimage in American and global popular culture. While operating as sacred sites within global tourism, the Disney parks also represent a sacred time, a transcendence of the everyday, ordinary time of the present. Passing through the gates, visitors are informed, "Here you leave today, and enter the world of yesterday, tomorrow, and fantasy."[46] As Walt Disney revealed in 1955, the Disney version of time was both American and global, preserving the American past of yesterday in the interests of a global future for tomorrow, dramatizing the "truths that have created America" so they might be "a source of courage and inspiration to all the world." Critics have argued that the "truths" distilled from the American past and enshrined at Disney theme parks—the complete domination of nature, the unlimited faith in technology, and the uncritical acceptance of the free enterprise system—have not always been a source of hope for the rest of the world. Nevertheless, the Disney theme parks can respond to such criticism by performatively demonstrating that it knows the world better than the world knows itself because "It's a Small World After All."

In analyzing the cross-cultural religious business of the Walt Disney Company, the success of Tokyo Disneyland provides an important test case for theories of globalization and cultural imperialism. Clearly, Tokyo Disneyland is American. "We really tried to avoid creating a Japanese version of Disneyland," spokesperson Toshiharu Akiba recalled. "We wanted the Japanese visitors to feel they were taking a foreign vacation."[47] Nevertheless, Tokyo Disneyland is a particular kind of "America"—a foreign America—that is owned and operated by the Japanese. The success of Tokyo Disneyland has depended entirely upon detailed local negotiations over the processes that we have been considering in reviewing the global dynamics of cross-cultural business—translation, rationalization, and imagination. These dynamics can only briefly be suggested here.

First, the challenge of translation involved not only the task of rendering the English scripts for popular rides into Japanese but also the challenge of mediating the intercultural dynamics of body language. Although the "friendly smile" might fail to translate easily into Japanese, the high-pitched voice of Mickey Mouse curiously resonated with the conventional "service voice" expected from women waiting on customers in department stores.[48]

Second, the principles of bureaucratic rationalization—efficiency, calculability, predictability, and control—exemplified by American management were quickly taken out of the hands of Disney managers from America and mobilized by Japanese managers of Tokyo Disneyland. As sociologist and former Disney cast member John van Maanen observed, "the Japanese have intensified the orderly nature of Disneyland. If Disneyland is clean, Tokyo Disneyland is impeccably clean; if Disneyland is efficient, Tokyo Disneyland puts the original to shame by being absurdly efficient."[49]

Finally, with respect to imagination, especially the temporal imagineering of the past, future, and fantasy, Tokyo Disneyland incorporated important features of the Disney orientation in time, the future of Tomorrowland and the fantasy of Fantasyland, but it fundamentally recast the past. Although its landscape included modified versions of Adventureland and Frontierland (Westernland), Tokyo Disneyland replaced Main Street, USA, with the World Bazaar, which was still an avenue of shops leading from the park's entrance, but it suggested a different past, not a small-town American past, that might lead to a different future. One attraction that was unique to Tokyo Disneyland, "Meet the World," presented the most thorough reworking of the past as an act of Disney imagineering that was presented as thoroughly Japanese. Featuring the traditional White Crane as a guide to the past, initiating two cartoon children into their legacy, "Meet the World" developed a Disneyized version of Japanese history that showed the Japanese people arising from the primordial waters, forming an island nation, and meeting the other people of the world, from the Chinese, but not the Koreans, to the Americans, with all the gains and losses entailed in those encounters, in ways that prepared everyone to sing, "We Meet the World with Love."[50]

Plasticity

As Arjun Appadurai has proposed, *globalization* is a term in our intellectual armory that might advance our ongoing struggles to analyze the shifting terrains of a changing world. At the very least, *globalization* signals our growing awareness that things have changed in the world's landscapes of human, technological, financial, ideological, and media geography. In charting this new global geography, without fixed borders, our attention is directed to global fluidity, fluctuations, circulations, and dispersions of people, machinery, capital, ideas, and images, the global flows that Appadurai has identified as the fluid movement of people through new ethnoscapes, of machinery through new technoscapes, of capital through new financescapes, of ideas of political solidarity through new ideoscapes, and of mass-media-generated images of human possibility through new mediascapes. All of this global fluidity, of course, seems entirely too fluid, divorced from any political economy, but also divorced from the intractable problems posed by the translation, rationalization, and imagination of matter that we have considered with respect to Coca-Cola, McDonald's, and Disney. Materiality might flow, but it might not flow quite so fluidly.

Looking back at the twentieth century, historians in the future could very well find that the world entered the Age of Plastic. In the early decades of the century, plastic was still a metaphor, a figure of speech that signified the opposite of the fixed, the permanent, or the rigid. In the academic work of the pioneering American sociologist Edward Alsworth Ross, for example, everything in human society could be classified as either rigid or plastic. Every social institution—religious, scientific, legal, and so on—had its rigid and plastic sides. As Ross maintained in his classic text *Social Psychology*, published in 1908, the rigid aspects of a society are always at risk, only waiting for destruction, because the rigid "admits only of the replacement of the old by the new." By contrast, the plastic features of social institutions are able to survive change. "Advance on the plastic side," Ross explained, "is much easier than on the rigid side." Instead of risking the fate of being entirely replaced by the new, the plastic side of any social institution "admits of accumulation by the union of the new with the old."[51] While this American sociologist was calculating the stress relations between the rigid and the plastic, the French philosopher Henri Bergson undertook an investigation of laughter, which he also conducted as a sociological study, since he was interested in the ways in which laughter worked "to readapt the individual into the whole," and employed a similar structural opposition between the rigid and the plastic in finding that the function of laughter "is to convert rigidity into plasticity."[52]

During the Age of Plastic, plasticity might have remained a mere metaphor, a figurative, rhetorical opposition to rigidity in cultural analysis, if not for the dramatic transformations in the imagination of matter that attended the chemical engineering of polyethylene. Through this breakthrough in scientific imagination, intervention, and ingenuity, plasticity was transformed into plastic, the polyethylene substance of material plasticity. Around 1942, a frustrated amateur inventor, Earl Silas Tupper, trying to imagine something new, took the industrial waste of black polyethylene slag, a plastic material he called "Poly-T: Material of the Future," and molded that plastic into household products. "Through an act of genius and alchemy," according to Tupperware historian Alison J. Clarke, "Earl Tupper summoned forth a divine creation to benefit humanity."[53] In the Age of Plastic, we must forgive any historian the rhetorical extravagance of invoking divinity or alchemy when talking about a development in plasticity as important as Tupperware. During the Age of Plastic, one of the leading scholars of signs, the semiologist Roland Barthes, realized that plasticity signified everything important in the imagination of matter in the twentieth century. According to Barthes, the production of plastic was an alchemical transformation that mediated exchanges not only between base matter and gold but also between human beings and God. As Barthes described these alchemical transactions, "At one end, raw, telluric matter, at the other, the finished human object; and between these two extremes, nothing; nothing but a transit, hardly watched over by an attendant in a cloth cap, half-god, half-robot."[54] Half God, half robot; part divine, part machine; something superhuman, but also something subhuman—the scientist overseeing the alchemical transformation of earth into plastic was positioned, according to Barthes, at the intersection of these supreme, absolute extremes—divinity above, machines below—that framed the meaning and power of the modern world.

In this way of imagining matter, therefore, plastic seemed to represent a midpoint, a nexus, or an *axis mundi* in creative exchanges, in the sudden, unobserved, and perhaps imperceptible transitions conducted among the more than human, the human, and the less than human. In a plastic age, celebrating its alchemy, plasticity seemed to define the contours of a religious world. Plasticity, however, was not only fluid. Plastic signified not only the alchemical transactions between different levels of reality but also a basic, underlying uniformity. Plastic signified a substantial uniformity of materiality. After all, however it might be produced, plastic was always plastic. Recognizing that homogeneity of plastic, Roland Barthes declared "the hierarchy of substances is abolished: a single one replaces them all: the whole world *can* be plasticized, and even life itself, we are told, they are beginning to make plastic aortas."[55] Replaced, in principle, by plastic, human life and all other values became equivalent. In this plastic imagination of matter, with the abolition of any differentiation of material substances, everything is plastic, even life itself.

At the end of the twentieth century, plasticity continued to be used by cultural analysts as a metaphor. Anthony Giddens, for example, identified "plastic sexuality" as intimate relationships that were independent of the needs of biological reproduction and detached from the bonds of social obligation. "Plastic sexuality," according to Giddens," can be molded as a trait of personality that is intrinsically bound up with the self."[56] During the twentieth century, therefore, plasticity was a multivalent symbol for fluidity, freedom, independence, detachment, change, and transformation. In the case of Tupperware, plasticity even became the basis for a business enterprise, with its sacred object, its sacred rituals, and its myths of redemption through faith, positive thinking, and hard work, which operated as "a kind of religion."[57] At the end of the twentieth century, 85 percent of revenues for Tupperware came from outside of the United States. Of course, all over the world, many bad things were also said about plastic: sampling the cuisine at a McDonald's in India, one customer, Mavli Patel, reported, "I find it all a little plastic tasting"; responding to the incursions of Disney into Europe, the French reportedly reacted against "American imperialism—plastics at its worst."[58] Nevertheless, throughout the twentieth century, plasticity defined the material conditions and imaginative scope for an imagination of matter that informed cross-cultural religious business.

In the shifting terrain that we call globalization, cross-cultural business has generated multinational corporations that operate like religions in providing material organization for the organization of matter, especially for the translation, rationalization, and imagination of matter, in a new political economy of the sacred. Through vast global exchanges, these material signs of the sacred—the sacred object of Cocacolonized desire, the sacred institution of McDonaldized rationality, the sacred, wonderful world of Disneyized imagineering—have produced profound local effects. But they have also marked out new sites of struggle, contact zones, or contested frontiers for renegotiating what it means to be a human person in a human place. As I have tried to suggest, these intercultural negotiations over the sacred are not always controlled by corporate headquarters. Indigenous versions of global signification are constantly being developed through local appropriations of Coca-Cola, McDonald's, Disney, and other transnational forces. As we have seen, many analysts have used the term *religion* for these global exchanges and local appropriations. If religion is about human identity and orientation, then cross-cultural business has been doing a kind of religious work through the material mediations of plastic signs of the sacred.

Notes

1. Terri Morrison, Wayne A. Conaway, and George A. Borden, *Kiss, Bow, or Shake Hands: How to Do Business in Sixty Countries* (Holbrook, Mass.: Adams Media Corporation, 1994), viii.

2. Morrison, Conaway, and Borden, *Kiss, Bow, or Shake Hands*, ix.

3. *Adams Report*, "Global Assignment, Americans Abroad: Doing Business in South Africa," at www.globalassignment.com/10-22-99/southafrica.htm (accessed fall 2000).

4. Genelle G. Morain, "Kinesics and Cross-Cultural Understanding," in *Toward Internationalism: Readings in Cross-Cultural Communication*, ed. Louise Fiber Luce and Elise C. Smith (Boston, Mass.: Heinle & Heinle Publishers, 1987), 120. These postures of humility are derived from Maurice H. Krout, *Introduction to Social Psychology* (New York: Harper, 1942).

5. Morain, "Kinesics," 120.

6. Arjun Appadurai, "Disjuncture and Difference in the Global Cultural Economy," *Modernity at Large: Cultural Dimensions of Globalization* (Minneapolis: University of Minnesota Press, 1996), 27-47.

7. Kalman Applbaum, "Crossing Borders: Globalization as Myth and Charter in American Transnational Consumer Marketing," *American Ethnologist* 27, no. 2 (2000), 257-82.

8. Thomas Frank, *One Market under God: Extreme Capitalism, Market Populism, and the End of Economic Democracy* (New York: Doubleday, 2000); Mike Davis, "The Bullshit Economy," *Village Voice Literary Supplement* (September 2000).

9. Edward T. Hall, *The Silent Language* (New York: Anchor Books and Doubleday, 1959); *The Hidden Dimension* (New York: Anchor Books and Doubleday, 1966); *The Dance of Life: The Other Dimension of Time* (New York: Anchor Books and Doubleday, 1966); *Beyond Culture* (New York: Anchor Books and Doubleday, 1976).

10. Geert Hofstede, "The Business of International Business is Culture," *International Business Review* 3, no. 1 (1994): 1-14.

11. Geert Hofstede, *Culture's Consequences: International Differences in Work-Related Values* (Beverly Hills, Calif.: Sage, 1980*)*; *Cultures and Organizations: Software of the Mind* (New York: McGraw-Hill, 1992).

12. Jeswald W. Salacuse, "Coping with Culture," in *Making Global Deals: Negotiating in the International Marketplace* (New York: Houghton Mifflin, 1991), 71.

13. Régis Debray, *Critique of Political Reason* (London: Verso, 1983); *Media Manifestos: On the Technological Transmission of Cultural Forms*, trans. Eric Rauth (London: Verso, 1996); *Transmitting Culture*, trans. Eric Rauth (New York: Columbia University Press, 2000).

14. Mircea Eliade, *Patterns in Comparative Religion*, trans. Rosemary Sheed (New York: Sheed and Ward, 1958); Gaston Bachelard, *Water and Dreams: An Essay on the Imagination of Matter*, trans. Edith R. Farrell (Dallas: Dallas Institute of Humanities and Culture, 1999).

15. Peter Pels, "The Spirit of Matter: On Fetish, Rarity, Fact, and Fancy," in *Border Fetishisms: Material Objects in Unstable Spaces*, ed. Patricia Spyer (London: Routledge, 1998), 91-121; Arjun Appadurai, ed., *The Social Life of Things: Commodities in Cultural Perspective* (Cambridge: Cambridge University Press, 1986), 3-63; Nicholas Thomas, *Entangled Objects: Exchange, Material Culture, and Colonialism in the Pacific* (Cambridge, Mass.: Harvard University Press, 1991), 27-30; William Pietz, "The Problem of

the Fetish, I," *Res: Anthropology and Aesthetics* 9 (1985): 7; Charles H. Long, *Significations: Signs, Symbols, and Images in the Interpretation of Religion* (Aurora, Colo.: Davies Group, 1999), 129; Karl Marx, *Capital*, 2 vols. trans. Samuel Moore and Edward Aveling (London: Lawrence and Wishart, 1974), 1:81.

16. Mark Pendergrast, *For God, Country, and Coca-Cola: The Unauthorized History of the Great American Soft Drink and the Company That Makes It* (New York: Scribner's, 1993), 261. See David Chidester, "The Church of Baseball, the Fetish of Coca-Cola, and the Potlatch of Rock 'n' Roll," in *Religion and Popular Culture in America*, ed. Bruce Forbes and Jeffrey Mahan (Berkeley: University of California Press, 2000), 219-38.

17. Pendergrast, *For God, Country*, 400.

18. Pendergrast, *For God, Country*, 173, 321.

19. Paul Landau, "Bushmen and Coca-Cola in a Cool World," *Southern African Review of Books* (March/April 1995): 8-9.

20. John Tomlinson, *Cultural Imperialism* (Baltimore: Johns Hopkins University Press, 1991), 173.

21. Pendergrast, *For God, Country*, 401.

22. Alaina Lemon, "'Your Eyes Are Green Like Dollars': Counterfeit Cash, National Substance, and Currency Apartheid in 1990s Russia," *Cultural Anthropology* 13, no. 1 (1998): 35.

23. Constance Classen, "Sugar Cane, Coca-Cola, and Hypermarkets: Consumption and Surrealism in the Argentine Northwest," in *Cross-Cultural Consumption: Global Markets, Local Realities*, ed. David Howes (London: Routledge, 1996), 52.

24. Classen, "Sugar Cane, Coca-Cola," 43.

25. Classen, "Sugar Cane, Coca-Cola," 39; Leonora Carrington, *The Seventh Horse and Other Stories*, trans. Katherine Talbot and Anthony Kerrigan (London: Virago, 1989), 182.

26. George Ritzer, *The McDonaldization of Society* (Thousand Oaks, Calif.: Pine Forge Press, 2000), 1.

27. Ray Kroc and Robert Anderson, *Grinding It Out: The Making of McDonald's* (New York: St. Martins, 1990).

28. Ritzer, *McDonaldization*, 7.

29. William Severini Kowinski, *The Malling of America: An Inside Look at the Great Consumer Paradise* (New York: William Morrow, 1985), 218; Ira G. Zepp, *The New Religious Image of Urban America: The Shopping Mall as Ceremonial Center* (Westminster, Md.: Christian Classics, 1986).

30. Ritzer, *McDonaldization*, 25.

31. John S. Caputo, "The Rhetoric of McDonaldization: A Social Semiotic Perspective," in *McDonaldization Revisited: Critical Essays on Consumer Culture*, ed. Mark Alfino, John S. Caputo, and Robin Wynyard (Westport, Conn.: Praeger, 1998), 49.

32. Caputo, "Rhetoric of McDonaldization," 48.

33. John Love, *McDonald's: Behind the Arches* (New York: Bantam, 1986), 423.

34. Cited in James L. Watson, "Transnationalism, Localization, and Fast Foods in East Asia," in *Golden Arches East: McDonald's in East Asia*, ed. James L. Watson (Stanford, Calif.: Stanford University Press, 1997), 5.

35. Watson, "Transnationalism, Localization," 2. See Emiko Ohnuki-Tierney, "McDonald's in Japan: Changing Manners and Etiquette," in *Golden Arches East*, 161-82.

36. Watson, "Transnationalism, Localization," 24.

37. *Christian Science Monitor* (May 21, 1991), 8.

38. Alan Bryman, "The Disneyization of Society," *Sociological Review* 47 (1999): 26. See Bryman, *Disney and His Worlds* (London: Routledge, 1995).

39. Umberto Eco, *Travels in Hyperreality* (London: Pan, 1986), 43.

40. Stephen M. Fjellman, *Vinyl Leaves: Walt Disney World and America* (Boulder, Colo.: Westview, 1992), 157.

41. John van Maanen, "The Smile Factory: Work at Disneyland," in *Reframing Organizational Culture*, ed. P. J. Frost, L. F. Moore, M. R. Louis, C. C. Lundberg, and J. Martin (Newbury Park, Calif.: Sage, 1991), 58-76.

42. Watson, "Transnationalism, Localization," 24.

43. Ariel Dorfman and Armand Mattelart, *How to Read Donald Duck: Imperialist Ideology in the Disney Comic* (New York: International General, 1975).

44. Eleanor Byrne and Martin McQuillan, *Deconstructing Disney* (London: Pluto Press, 1999).

45. Richard D. Land and Frank D. York, *Send a Message to Mickey: The ABC's of Making Your Voice Heard at Disney* (Nashville, Tenn.: Broadman and Holman, 1998).

46. Brad Prager and Michael Richardson, "A Sort of Homecoming: An Archaeology of Disneyland," in *Streams of Cultural Capital: Transnational Cultural Studies*, ed. David Palumbo-Liu and Hans Ulrich Gumbrecht (Stanford, Calif: Stanford University Press, 1997), 209.

47. Mary Yoko Brannen, "'Bwana Mickey': Constructing Cultural Consumption at Tokyo Disneyland," in *Re-Made in Japan*, ed. Joseph J. Tobin (New Haven, Conn.: Yale University Press, 1992), 216.

48. Brannen, "'Bwana Mickey,'" 221.

49. John van Maanen, "Displacing Disney: Some Notes on the Flow of Culture," *Qualitative Sociology* 15, no. 1 (1992): 17.

50. Aviad E. Raz, *Riding the Black Ship: Japan and Tokyo Disneyland* (Cambridge, Mass.: Harvard University Press, 1999); Mitsuhiro Yoshimoto, "Images of Empire: Tokyo Disneyland and Japanese Cultural Imperialism," in *Disney Discourse: Producing the Magic Kingdom*, ed. Eric Smoodin (London: Routledge, 1994), 181-99.

51. Edward Alsworth Ross, *Social Psychology* (New York: Macmillan, 1908), 331, 335.

52. Henri Bergson, *Laughter: An Essay on the Meaning of the Comic*, trans. Claudesley Brereton and Fred Rothwell (New York: Macmillan, 1911), 35.

53. Alison J. Clarke, *Tupperware: The Promise of Plastic in 1950s America* (Washington, D.C.: Smithsonian Institution Press, 1999), 41.

54. Roland Barthes, *Mythologies* (London: Palladin, 1988), 97.

55. Barthes, *Mythologies*, 99.

56. Anthony Giddens, *The Transformation of Intimacy: Sexuality, Love, and Eroticism in Modern Societies* (London: Polity Press, 1992), 2; Adrian Thatcher, "Postmodernity and Chastity," in *Sex These Days: Essays on Theology, Sexuality, and Society*, ed. Jan Davies and Gerard Loughlin (London: Sheffield Academic Press, 1997), 127-30.

57. Clarke, *Tupperware*, 136.

58. Martin Regg Cohn, "Mumbai: Where's the Beef," *Toronto Star* (November 16, 2000); Bruce Crumley and Dean Fischer, "A Mickey Mouse Operation in Paris," *Time Magazine* (September 12, 1994).

10

Indigenous People, Materialities, and Religion: Outline for a New Orientation to Religious Meaning

Charles H. Long

The Indigenous, the Archaic, and the Primal

John Hollander relates a contemporary story that might serve as an appropriate introduction to the ranges of meanings conveyed by the terms *archaic* and *indigenous*.[1] He tells us that some thirty years ago there was on Third Avenue in the 1950s in New York an Italian restaurant that was simply called Joe's. Joe, the eponymous owner and author of this rather unoriginal name, decided to sell his restaurant—location, lease, stock, and "goodwill"—to another person. Upon the completion of the sale, the restaurant continued to operate under the original name, Joe's, though it was now owned and operated by a person other than the original Joe. After some years of retirement, the original Joe decided to reenter his former profession as a restauranteur and opened another restaurant a few blocks away from the restaurant he had previously sold. He named this restaurant, Joe's also. After a short time the successor at the old place of business—the first Joe's—decided that he should change the name of the restaurant to The Original Joe's. Now in point of fact, the original Joe was no longer at the location of the Original Joe's, that place being run by another person whose name was not even Joe. The original Joe was now proprietor and occupant of a *new* establishment of very recent vintage.

Ambiguities and confusions of this kind point up some of the issues one faces when dealing with any of the notions and meanings that purport to address any form of non-Western culture in the modern period. I have placed all these terms, *indigenous*, *archaic*, and *primal*, within the same linguistic family. They are derivative from older nonmodern languages and cultures of the West. All the terms bear some derivation from the Greek word arche, which carries the following connotation, beginning, starting point, principle, underlying substance as primordial, and ultimate undemonstrable principle.[2] In one way or another all the terms fall within a context that implies something "original." As our little story from John Hollander has shown, it is not at all clear what the original is or where it is located. These sorts of ambiguities become more complex when we are dealing with religious cultural traditions. Is the archaic, primal, or indigenous at the beginning of human existence, at the beginnings of the modern West, or does the archaic refer to "a beginning" as a structure of consciousness?

It is easy to understand why the proprietor renamed his restaurant The Original Joe's. It was a business decision. His customers wanted to know that the restaurant still carried the cuisine and atmosphere that had brought it prosperity when it first opened. Why, however, in the modern period of the West has so much concern and attention on the scholarly as well as the popular level been related to cultures and peoples who have been classified as archaic, primal, or indigenous? It is very clear that these terms did not originate among the cultures and peoples designated by them. They are terms of the modern West's classification and nomenclature of global cultural reality. And in a strange and complex way they represent specific constitutive elements in the creation of the modern West's understanding of itself; in this manner the *indigenous* are necessary aspects of any mode of modernity.

There are thus two dimensions contained in our discussion of the *indigenous*; first it is an element in the stylistics and formative languages of the modern West, and second, the term applies to the non-Western cultures that were encountered during the modern period of colonialism, mercantilism, and imperialism. Now, to be sure, if we take one of the meanings of the term *indigenous*—the original or the first—it is clear that there must be indigenous cultures in all parts of the world, West and non-West. While this is true, the West during the modern period created another term to express its new formation; this was the term *civilization*.[3]

Before continuing along these lines it might be good to rehearse some of the nonmodern meanings of our terms to see in what ways their meanings have shifted. The term *indigenous* has several connotations derived from the Latin: *indigena=native*; *induendo=in or within*; and *gignere=to beget*. These are the same roots from which we derive the English *indigent*. The matter does not stop at this linguistic level; the Romans had a group of deities whom they referred to as *indigetes dii*; the *Sol indiges* was a festival celebrating the completion of sowing; and *Jupiter indiges* was associated with the Torto River. These association of gods with places and activities led an earlier group of scholars to conclude that the Romans had two classes of deities, *di indigetes*, native gods, and *dii novensides*, foreign newcomer gods, but the matter is not quite that simple. The references are probably to another and deeper issue that has to do with the source of the power of being as an inward or inherent power. So while the Romans did venerate some non-Roman gods, the fundamental meaning of *indigenous* had to do with the origins of the power rather than whether they were internal to the Romans or foreign.

As I show in my article dealing with the notions of "primitive" and "civilized" cited above, the notion of "civilization," while descriptive, is a product of the modern West and carried a valuational and normative meaning regarding the nature and status of various human societies. As a matter of fact, many cultures were not referred to as civilizations until after the Second World War. This is because the meaning of civilization, on both the popular and academic levels, emerged as part of a stadial evolutionary history of humankind with the primitives being at the earliest or lowest stages of human evolution. From this perspective the latest or most advanced—and by advanced one always sets forth the notae of technology, science, and rational thinking—should have the prestige of embodying the epitome of "civilization." In many respects, the term *indigenous* was adopted as a "politically correct" way of referring to what had before been called the primitives, or tribal peoples, these names now falling into disgrace. "Indigenous" proved also to be an acceptable name for members of those cultures which had previously been designated by the former terms.

The *Arche* of Modernity: Matter, Exchanges, and the Gods

The modern Western world created its own arche among the peoples it took over through imperialism and within the disciplinary order of the human sciences. In the one sense these archaic cultures were equated with the early beginnings of human life on the face of the earth, and from this academic stylization, contemporary cultures of the peoples of Africa, North and South America, Oceania, Australia, and other non-Western areas of the world thus became populated by the several "backward" cultures of the world. This meant that the distantiation in time as the earliest cultures of human evolution was translated into a distantiation in space—the space defined by the distance of these contemporary cultures from the Western metropoles. In any case, the meaning of these archaic, "primitive," tribal cultures became one of the basic topics of conversation on the popular and sophisticated levels of the West.

Missing in discussions and popularization of these topics are the actual relationships and entanglements of cultures that took place during the imperial and colonial ventures of the modern West. For Europeans and Euro-Americans the cultures of the so-called archaic, primitive, and backward peoples of the world became simultaneously the raw materials for the technological manufacturing industry of the West and the ideological basis for various notions of cultural evolution as well as the necessary substantiation for their notion of civilization. Whether it was land, as in the case of North and South America, or rubber, or indigo, furs, and so on, or from Africa, human beings themselves, the distance that defined the spatiality of these cultures did not prevent the most intimate and necessary relationships to the cultures of conquest. The cultural languages and discourses of the West remain silent regarding this meaning of the modern West. In other words, through academic and popular discourses, the extra-European cultures of the world were relegated to a different temporal sphere, thus isolating and inoculating them the very contact and relationships that played so great a role in the "rise of the modern West."

Since the end of the Second World War and the dismantling of various European empires along with the ensuing "independence" of numerous cultures and peoples throughout the world, there has arisen an academic subfield called "postcolonial theories and studies." In one sense this kind of study might concentrate on the future of these former colonized areas of the world; however, from my perspective, these studies might make their most important contribution by beginning a serious study and discourse about "what really happened" during the colonial period in various parts of the world from the sixteenth through the twentieth centuries. In other words, these studies could give us an alternative understanding of the beginning of the modern world. The period covered by the modern world witnessed the greatest number of diverse cultural contacts with a sustained intensity than any other period of the human history; yet we are, for the most part, blind to these realities when we speak of the meaning of modernity.

The cliche "the West and the Rest" attests to this discursive ideology of the West. It is clear that the propagandists of the West in the guise of beneficent, democratic, liberal, and civilizing rhetorics would rather not confront the gross realities of economic exploitation, tyrannical practices, terrorization, and enslavements, but even more threatening to the West is a serious critical discussion of the linguistic discourses that accompanied their formations in the modern world. For the modern West, modernity represented that period, not only in the life of this culture, but in the life of humankind when religion or any dependence upon transcendent realities was and could be overcome. Religion from this perspective was a relic of the past; it was still present in those cultures defined by the historical evolutionary and stadial theories of the West, in the older and earliest cultures of the archaic, primitive, and barbarous peoples. The study of religion in the modern West thus became almost synonymous with the study of these cultures. E. B. Tylor, the "father" of anthropology as a humanistic and social science discipline, made this identification in his two-volume work, *Primitive Culture*, with one volume, the largest one, devoted to primitive religion. Thereupon followed a tradition in the anthropological sciences of monographs on the religion of several societies and peoples in the world outside the West. It seems as if once the West extirpated any efficacious meaning of religion from its own culture, it became obsessed with the meaning and nature of religion as a human phenomenon as long as this phenomenon could be controlled by placing it in a distant time and place. This obsession also justified imperialism-cum-civilizing-mission, since the authenticity of religion was a very definite sign of those underdeveloped mental capacities that had not yet attained the civilizational status.

In any discussion of the complex beginnings of the modern West one must in one way or another deal with some meaning of religion. Religion did not disappear simply out of the Enlightenment pronouncements. From one point of view, this is clear from the sustaining popularity of Max Weber's thesis regarding the interrelationship of the beginnings of mercantile capitalism and Protestantism. The almost perennial popularity of Weber is tied up with his investigation of the "origin" of capitalism and his explanation of the capitalistic mode in relationship to a specific religious orientation of modern European Christianity. Weber's work, *The Protestant Ethic and the Spirit of Capitalism*, first appeared in 1904 and has since been republished and translated into several languages. Given the scope of my discussion I cannot go into any detailed treatment of this thesis. Suffice to say that Weber attributes the capitalistic mode of production to what he coined as "an inner worldly asceticism" derivative from the reformation tradition in its Calvinist form. Weber, his epigoni, critics, and detractors all see the rise of the capitalistic mode, which is equivalent to the meaning of the Atlantic world as the symbolic and empirical meaning of modernity as arising only out of internal structures of what became known as the modern Western world. Benjamin Nelson has presented a much more cogent argument for the relationship between Protestantism and the beginnings of capitalism. Nelson sees this in a twofold manner: first, Calvin's desacralization of the world and Christian worship; and, second, the ensuing change in the realm of the exchanges between God and the world and within the human community. Thus, by tracing through the theology of exchanges (usury and idolatry) Nelson is able to show how Calvin's theology led to not only a new theory of exchange but equally to a new understanding of the "things" exchanged and the communities created in the exchange structure.[4]

Concealed Entanglements: Materialities, Objects, and Thought

One can observe a characteristic style of concealment and surprise in some of the important inaugurating meanings of Western modernity. Take for example the Cartesian elegant and pithy formula *cogito ergo sum*. In this formula the "I" of the sum emerges almost through a gesture of legerdemain from the ego of the cogito. And again, in Weber's thesis on the beginnings of mercantile capitalism, there is the sense that the good Calvinist Protestants had no idea that the capital accumulated through the practice of an "inner-worldly asceticism" would lead to a universal economy of trade in goods, money, and all other forms of merchandise. We get the sense that they were themselves surprised by this turn of events.

This stylistics of concealment carries implications for a range of other meanings and actions that now must be seen under the broad umbrella of this dynamics of concealment. In the first instance the interrelationship between the imagination of "self" and the meaning of materiality is never discussed and brought to the fore. Second, one gets the sense that there is a continuity between the old Mediterranean meanings of matter, materiality, and exchange and these modes and practices in the Atlantic world, even though scholars have had to resort to new theories of explanation for the Atlantic world.

It is a well-attested fact that every conception of the "self" or "soul," no matter how ethereal or pure, and irrespective of the culture or civilization, *every* conception of a self is related to or presupposes a material object or form as its expressive mode or accompaniment. The notion of a "self" or "soul" requires to a greater or lesser degree the accumulation of objects. These objects or materialities are not adventitious or helter-skelter; they acquire either a personal or societal taxonomy, hierarchy, space, and so on.

This observation is especially instructive in light of the creation of a new mode of humanity in the processes of the Atlantic world. Two contemporary French philosophers, Paul Ricoeur and Merleau-Ponty, have taken up in a critical manner the hermeneutical possibilities of the Cartesian cogito. For Ricoeur the very notion of self-reflection implies the positing of the ego of the cogito. The positing of the "I think" of the cogito is, however, abstract and empty, that is, one must empty oneself of the objects and matter upon which the self depends in an almost intimate relationship to reflect upon the self. The ego of the sum must now reappropriate some forms of substance or matter of the not-self to become an existing existential subject in a life-world.[5]

Merleau-Ponty sees three possible meanings to the cogito: (1) There is the cogito as the psychic fact that "I think." This is an instantaneous constatation and it is possible only under the condition that the experience has no duration. I, therefore, adhere immediately to what I think and cannot doubt it. This is the skeptical understanding which cannot account for the idea of the truth. (2) In the second way, the "I think" of the cogito is combined with the objects which this thought intends. Both the "I think" and the things thought have in this context an ideal existence. (3) Finally, there is the third meaning, "I grasp myself," not as a constituting subject which is transparent to itself and which constitutes the totality of every possible object of thought and experience, but as a particular thought, as a thought engaged with *certain objects*, as a *thought in act*, and it is in this sense that I am certain of myself.[6]

In the most general sense, we might say that the Mediterranean heritage of the West understood God and God's creation as the source of all the objects upon which the human world depended for its specific mode of being. It is precisely in the disavowal of a fundamental efficacious meaning of God and God's creation as the basis for ultimate dependency that the culture and selves of the modern world of the Atlantic created new and different modes of matter, dependence, and exchanges.

Within the same context that fostered the invention and fashioning of the problematics of a new self and a new understanding of exchange and exchanges was the issue of a radically new and different form of matter and materiality. At this juncture we are aided by the seminal researches of William Pietz published in the issues of *RES* between 1985 and 1988.[7] The discussion that follows is derived from my reading of William Pietz's researches on the origin and meaning of the fetish. I turn to the fetish for it is another example of how, in the formation of the Atlantic world, a religious or quasi-religious notion is turned in an almost magical way into another notion that seems to be the opposite of its original meaning. We observed this in the case of the discussion of Calvinism and capitalism and in the Cartesian cogito. A similar procedure might be seen in the career of the fetish.

Let me begin my commentary on Pietz's articles by moving forward and backward from the date 1703, the publication date of William Bosman's *A New and Accurate Description of the Coast of Guinea*. Moving backward, I begin with the voyages of the Portuguese along the African coast in the fifteenth century. One is mindful of the furor regarding the five hundredth anniversary of Columbus's voyages a decade ago, but one often forgets the movement of the Portuguese earlier in that century—first to the Canaries, then to the Cape Verde Islands, then along the coast of West Africa, around the Cape, and into the Indian Ocean and the South Seas; these voyages had as much impact on the world as did those of Columbus. The language of fetishism emerges out of the contact of the Portuguese with the traders along the coast of West Africa.

Trading societies were numerous on the small islands that lie along the West African coast. The inhabitants of these islands appear to have been polyglot—made up of disinherited Africans who were no longer members of a coherent kinship system, quasi Muslims, quasi Jews, and so on—very much like some of the trading groups described by Fernand Braudel in his *The Mediterranean and the Mediterranean*. Unlike the Mediterranean, however, the Portuguese were in an unknown milieu; the Atlantic Ocean along the coast of Africa was new to them and they had no ready-made classifications or categories to make sense of it. They were interested, nevertheless, in trade, especially in the reputed gold that they understood to be in abundance in this area. Now because of this emphasis on trade, the Portuguese as European venturers into terra incognito are not referred to in the language of discovery. We therefore have a rich tradition that refers to practices, observations, and descriptions of what they perceived in these relations of contact. We are not burdened with the rhetoric of curiosity, discovery, and heroic epistemologies as had been the case with the legacy of Columbus. It is precisely because of this difference that Pietz is able to get at one of the productions of this contact—the emergence of the notion of the fetish. The contact with this polyglot creole society along the coast is a specific case of creolization itself, and the processes of creolization expressed within the thickness of description of the economic, erotic, linguistic, and miscegenated structures of both the beginnings of modernity and the origins of a modern meaning of religion.

The fact that the present use and meaning of the fetish lies within the usage of so many disciplines attests to the heterogeneity of its origins. But something more is present in the widespread usage of this term in the several disciplines of the human sciences. Such usage has occurred because, until the work of William Pietz, no one had explored the full meaning of the term in relationship to its origins or its movement into the vocabularies of modernity. The specific usage of the term *fetish* with the several disciplines—economic theory, anthropology, psychoanalysis, history of religions, and so on—really shadows and obscures the full weight of what might be understood regarding the very constitution of these disciplines. More important, the implications of contact as the basis for creative critique is thereby excluded. The term *fetish* enters into contemporary discussion in a rather clean and calm manner, yet always bearing with it a vague and negative connotation. As Pietz himself put it, "Fetish has always been a word of sinister pedigree. Discursively promiscuous and theoretically suggestive, it has always been a word with a past, forever becoming 'an embarrassment' to disciplines in the human sciences that seek to contain and control its sense."[8] I would suggest that this attempt to control and contain the meaning of the fetish within the disciplines is part and parcel of the very constitution of these disciplines—an attempt to contain, control, hide, and obscure a meaning of religion in the modern world that emerges from contact, creolizations, and a highly problematical conception of matter and materiality. Through the archaeology of fetishism opened up by Pietz, the authenticity of all the human sciences requires reexamination. When we add to this the fact that those peoples and cultures who were distanced as the objective sources for the phenomena of religions are now "speaking voices" in the discussion of the very methodological principles upon which such an investigation can and should be made, we are facing a most radical crisis in the constitution of these so-called human science disciplines. The "original Joe" might very well be in some other place than where the sign, "The Original Joe's" is posted.

As I mention above, the Portuguese were interested in trade and to a lesser extent in colonization, but trade and colonization in a world unknown to them. In Pietz's second article on the fetish, he moves into what is one of the most important aspects of his work. What one is forced to realize by reading between the lines of this article is that this new mode of trade in terra incognito presented to the Portuguese traders a kind of analogue to the Cartesian *Meditations*. The Portuguese who were in an unknown country seeking trade were very similar to the Cartesian self that has divested itself of all conventional objects as a basis and possession of selfhood; this means that the traders were at that intermediary of the magical *ergo* that both desires and need objects upon which a new modality of the self must be founded. They have come seeking and desiring gold—an ancient form of matter in a new space. In other words, they find themselves in a strange new world and must come to terms with it in a practical manner, since they have defined their venture as one of practice and not in the language of sheer curiosity or theory. From this theory of practice, the items of actual and possible trade and the relationships and interrelationships of the participants form the epistemological structures of knowledge. So fetishism as a notion and concept emerges out of practical engagements.

It is at this juncture that trade, religion, and eroticism form the basis for the context out of which the notion of the fetish comes forth. A common story told regarding this interrelation goes like this. When the Portuguese trader asked about the god of the inhabitants of these islands, they were often told that their god was a talisman that they wore around their necks or somewhere on their person. This object was often made of gold. The Portuguese, while being able to accept that they worshiped a false god, were taken aback when they found that these inhabitants were willing to trade or barter their "god" for any other object that the Portuguese presented for trade. What fascinated the writers about fetishism was this constellation of a god formed from a precious form of matter (gold), its portability, and its use as an object of exchange.

The Portuguese had a practical interest in religion and gold. We must remember that though the Portuguese are in the Atlantic Ocean they are still bearers of a Mediterranean orientation to the world. Sailing as they did under the flag of a Christian monarch, all their ventures had the implicit necessity to extend the Gospel of Christ. It was thus not out of curiosity that traders and sailors always inquired about the "religion" of those they encountered; the spread of the Gospel was part of a general order of the cosmos. In like manner, the inhabitants of the islands off the west coast of Africa were seen under this double desire—to bring them into the intimacy of the Christian community and to procure gold for themselves and the kingdom of Portugal. Gold as materiality became the empirical and symbolic meaning of this desire as it related to the heterogeneity of exchanges. There is yet another important meaning to this new emergence of matter and materiality.

Pietz provides us with a fascinating history of the Christian theology of matter. He shows us how, through the language and implications of fetishism, a new notion of materiality enters into the Western consciousness. The earlier theological notions of matter were always in one way or another, linked to God's work in creation and in the New Creation initiated by Jesus, the Christ. The discussion of fetishism allowed for an alternate, and quite disparate, notion of matter and materiality. In the words of Pietz, "Out of the very difficulty in grasping the much-used word as a unitary concept, the term [fetish] came to express a novel idea in European theoretical reflection and to thematize a novel general problem: that of the nature and origin of the social value of material objects."[9] Here again we are able to observe the manner in which the Western mode begins with a derision of some distanced others' notion while at the same time taking over what has been perpetrated as an erroneous conception based on ignorance into a new conception in an almost magical gesture. In this manner the Christian theological meaning of matter becomes reconstructed out of the practice of cross-cultural trade and made into a new conception of matter and materiality without confronting any specific ideological or theological debate at the level of an argument. It is remarkable that Enlightenment philosophers such as Kant, Locke, Hume, and Hegel, and political economists such as Adam Smith—and we all remember that Karl Marx coined the term *commodity fetishism*—were all indebted to the fetish discourse. In addition, Pietz tells us that a copy of Bosman's book on the fetish was found in the library of Isaac Newton. So both from the history of modern theology and philosophy the meaning given to fetishism allowed modern Europe to create its progressivistic ideologies while at the same time in a sub-rosa manner adopting the fetish and fetishism as the preeminent meaning of the new forms of matter and materiality in the language of the commodity and monetary systems that undergirded the mercantilism and later capitalism that were coincidental to the beginnings of the modern world system.

One is able to see here that the contact between cultures in the modern period produces a third meaning of culture—the culture of contact. The "culture of contact" is the first locus for the adjudication of meaning and value in the modern world. New "languages" and new orientations to the meaning of "world" take place here. At a later stage, the new "languages" and modes of being derived from this initial contact are stylized into concepts and enter into the languages of both cultures in an important but obscured manner, changing the practices and styles of the cultures without the dominant culture bearing the full and intense responsibility for those meanings generated through the contact as a historical and existential reality.

The other locus for a discussion of the meaning and nature of matter and materiality in the modern world involving indigenous cultures is from the Pacific Rim and is expressed in what has come to be called "cargo cults." The popularity and vogue of cargo cults commenced with the publication of F. E. Williams's *The Vailala Madness and the Destruction of Native Ceremonies in the Gulf District* in 1923. Williams, who was a government anthropologist, attempted to describe and analyze certain disruptive events taking place in the Madang region of New Guinea. Williams described these phenomena as follows:

> Originating in the neighborhood of Vailala, hence it spread rapidly through the costal and certain of the inland villages. This movement involved, on the one hand a set of preposterous beliefs among its victims—in particular the expectation of an early return of deceased relatives—and on the other hand, collective nervous symptoms of sometimes grotesque and idiotic nature. Hence the name Vailala Madness seems apt enough and at least conveys more meaning than any of the various alternatives.[10]

The Vailala Madness and similar such behavior had been occurring in this region for almost a half century before Williams's report. The "Madness" later is referred to as "cargo cults," since a part of the beliefs and behaviors had to do with the return of cargo to the natives of New Guinea. The cargo consisted of the manufactured goods that had been brought from England and Australia to the Melanesians. This was the ordinary stuff found in the average "dry goods" stores of this era—canned foods, knives, hatchets, nails, cloths, and so forth. In the belief of the cargo cultists, these goods which had been brought by the English and Australians had *really* been sent by the Melanesian ancestors. They were either sent directly by them and waylaid enroute by the English and Australians, or the English and Australians were seen as their ancestors who had been transformed in a place of the dead.

K. O. L. Burridge, an anthropologist, has devoted several monographs to the study of the cargo cult phenomenon.[11] He has shown that this phenomenon does not constitute a singular occurrence in these societies. The belief and behavior of the cargo cultist is part of a long transformation taking place in these societies as a result of the contact with Europeans, their goods, matter, beliefs, and behaviors. First, the Melanesians cannot comprehend the Europeans' beliefs and their behaviors: the Europeans claim to believe in a God called Christ who is present in a book called the Bible. They erect a church building in which they venerate this God. The Europeans, however, from the point of view of the Melanesians, in their behavior really venerate the cargo—the commodities—and they never show any relationship between these commodities that they venerate and their God, Jesus Christ.

Second, the Europeans proselytize the Melanesians and many Melanesians are converted to Christianity. They cannot in their conversion make a separation between the sacrality of the conversion to Christ and the sacredness of the materiality of the world or the sacrality of the exchange between the stuff and matter of the world and the inherent meaning of all materiality. In other words, their belief that the cargo, matter, and commodities, were sent by their ancestors is their way of making the exchange of material goods acceptable in their world.

Thus, at the end of the modern period, an era which has been designated by many as "the postmodern," the older so-called primitives, archaic, and indigenous peoples and cultures of the world have not disappeared–as a matter of fact, they have become more prominent. These cultures and peoples should not, however, be looked at or look upon themselves as a throwback or residue of modernity, for they have lived through, in very different ways, the same modern period as those in the West. And, in addition, their lot has been augmented by other cultures and peoples who were colonized and oppressed during this same period of colonialism, the "rise of the West, and the "triumph" of democratic values.

This period allows us to make the following summary statements concerning the meaning of religion and the crisis of the understanding of matter and materiality:

1. The beginnings of the study of religion as an academic discipline must be seen in light of the beginnings of modern globalization and its origins in the formation of the Atlantic world. Religion from this perspective no longer defines an intimacy of meaning but is objectified in time, space, and cultural ideology in various modes of distantiation.

2. Matter and materiality lose their significance as primordial or as having any inherent value.

3. Complexity of meaning is noted in the manner in which a purported religious meaning attributed to a primitive or archaic people (the fetish) becomes the vehicle through which a new notion of objectified matter is transformed into the modern notion of matter as the objectified commodity that has no inherent value.

Reorientation, New Beginning, and the Indigenous

I referred above to Paul Ricoeur's reconstruction of the Cartesian cogito; for Ricoeur, the initial form of the cogito could be seen as an emptying, an evacuation of the self in the modern period. This is not simply metaphorical, for there was in fact a historical connection defined by the stay of Descartes in Holland during the period when the commodity as a new form of matter was in its initial ascendancy as modern materiality.

> In the early merchant clearinghouse of Europe, all these vectors pointed toward Holland, the merchant clearinghouses of Europe, the land of Simon Stevins and the adopted home of Rene Descartes. As Descartes wrote in a letter of 1631, "And thus in the city where I now am, since I seem to be practically the only one here who is not a merchant or in a trade," and it could hardly have been otherwise, since in that era it was the Dutch who were busily occupied with the innovation of the first mercantile culture in Europe.[12]

Ricoeur's characterization might well describe the response and situation of many of the world's population that underwent what from the point of view of the West was the triumph and realization of the epitome of the human mode of being. But precisely in this "rise of the West" there was an emptying and deprivation of the Western "self" or "soul" along with the violence, and deprivations of untold millions in various parts of the world. The existence and memories of these colonized and indigenous populations make it difficult to see the continuation of the West and the extension of its values to all parts of the world as a beneficent meaning to contemplate.

There are other traditions in the world—traditions of indigenous and colonized cultures, and traditions of creolizations, those traditions that I refer to as the "cultures of contact." These cultures, while undergoing and surviving the Western onslaught, created other modes for the understanding of human life and community. If there is to be a recovery, a "filling" again of the self and world, it must return to traditions of this kind as the basis for renewal and critique. This does not mean a return to some mystical and hoary past, for these indigenous, colonized, and ex-colonized people have never gone away. They are the *Joes* of the first restaurant!

The meaning of the indigenous should be seen in two interrelated ways: first, as those peoples, societies, and cultures who were prior to the rise of the West and have in one way or another survived out of "other" traditions the "rise of the West," and second, the indigenous must be understood as the basis for a new epistemological stance in the world. This stance eschews and mounts a critical stance in the face of the Enlightenment sciences. This critical stance does not mean a vulgar dismissal of the Enlightenment orientation, but it means that this orientation cannot assume that it and its traditions are the "only game in town," and therefore the solutions and resolutions of its traditions define the limits of human possibility. In both senses it is the indigenous as the opening again for meaning as the inherent power in life. The Indigenous as empirical reality and hermeneutical epistemological principle lies at the in-betweeness of the all the binaries created in the modern world and it does not opt for any side of these binaries. The meaning of "the indigenous" could define not just a new epistemology but another and alternate stylistics of knowledge that moves us away from the distantiated, objectified, positivistic, and rationalistic styles of knowledge ushered in by the Enlightenment ideologies. The crisis of self and meaning in the contemporary world is at the same time a crisis of the self, and the objects upon which the self must depend, and the exchange of these objects with others. None of these issues can be resolved through a continuation of the ideologies that ushered in the modern world. It is at this point that the indigenous people of the world reveal a resource and invite a contemplation for a form of globalization conducive to a viable human world.

Notes

1. John Hollander, "Originality," *Raritan* 2, no. 4 (Spring 1983).

2. See F. E. Peters, *Greek Philosophical Terms: A Historical Lexicon* (New York: New York University Press, 1967), 23ff.

3. See my discussion of the origin of this term in my essay "Primitive/Civilized: The Locus of a Problem," chapter 6 in *Significations* (Aurora, Colo.: Davies Group Publishers, 1999).

4. See Benjamin N. Nelson, *The Idea of Usury: From Tribal Brotherhood to Universal Otherhood* (Princeton, N.J.: Princeton University Press, 1949). For a fuller discussion of the interrelationship of these Calvinist notions to the meaning of the fetish in the formation of the Atlantic world, see the recent Ph.D. dissertation by Tatsuo Murakami, *Fetishism as the Origin of Religion: A Dissertation Submitted to the Faculty of Religious Studies* University of California, Santa Barbara (December 2000).

5. Paul Ricoeur, *Freud and Philosophy: An Essay on Interpretation* (New Haven, Conn.: Yale University Press, 1970), passim.

6. Maurice Merleau-Ponty, *The Primacy of Perception*, ed. James M. Edie (Evanston, Ill.: Northwestern University Press, 1964), 21-24 passim.

7. William Pietz; all the articles were published in *RES: Anthropology and Aesthetics*. I give the location of each article and respective dates: "The Problem of the Fetish. I, *RES* 9 (Spring 1985): 5-17; "The Problem of the Fetish. II: The Origin of the Fetish," *RES* 13, (Spring 1987); "The Problem of the Fetish. III: Bosman's Guinea and the Enlightenment Theory of the Fetish," *RES* 16 (Autumn 1988), 105-23.

8. Pietz, *RES* (1985): 5.

9. Pietz, *RES* (1988): 109.

10. F. E. Williams, *The Vailala Madness and the Destruction of Native Ceremonies in the Guld District*, Papua Anthropology Report no. 4 (Port Moresby, 1923), 2.

11. See the following by Burridge: *Mambu, A Melanesian Millenarian* (London: Methuen, 1960); *Tangu Traditions* (Oxford, U.K.: Clarendon, 1969); *New Heaven, New Earth: A Study of Millenarian Activities* (Oxford: Basil Blackwell, 1969).

12. Is it simply coincidental that Descartes is residing in Holland where one of the early economists, Simon Stevin, is familiar with his work and that this same Holland is the home of some of the original descriptions of the fetish and fetishism? See Philip Mirowski, *More Heat than Light: Economics as Social Physics, as Nature's Economics* (Cambridge: Cambridge University Press, 1989), 120.

References

Abimbola, Wande. *Ifa Will Mend Our Broken World: Thoughts on Yoruba Religion and Culture in Africa and the Diaspora*. Roxbury, Mass: Aim Books, 1997.

Ada, Michael. *Prophets of Rebellion*. Chapel Hill: University of North Carolina Press, 1979.

Adams Report. "Global Assignment, Americans Abroad: Doing Business in South Africa," at www.globalassignment.com/10-22-99/south africa.htm (accessed fall 2000).

Ajuwon, Bade. "Ogun's Iremoje: A Philosophy of Living and Dying." Pp. 172-98 in *Africa's Ogun: Old World and New*, edited by Sandra T. Barnes. Bloomington: Indiana University Press, 1997.

Albenese, Catherine. *America: Religions and Religion*. Belmont, Calif.: Wadsworth, 1981.

Alfino, Mark, John S. Caputo, and Robin Wynyard, eds. *McDonaldization Revisited: Critical Essays on Consumer Culture*. Westport, Conn.: Praeger, 1998.

Amadiume, Ifi. *African Matriarchal Foundations: The Igbo Case*. London: Karnak House, 1995.

———. *Reinventing Matriarchy, Religion, and Culture*. London: Zed Books, 1997.

Appadurai, Arjun. "Disjuncture and Difference in the Global Cultural Economy." Pp. 27-47 in *Modernity at Large: Cultural Dimensions of Globalization*. Minneapolis: University of Minnesota Press, 1996.

———. ed., *The Social Life of Things: Commodities in Cultural Perspective*. Cambridge: Cambridge University Press, 1986.

Applbaum, Kalman. "Crossing Borders: Globalization as Myth and Charter in American Transnational Consumer Marketing." *American Ethnologist* 27, no. 2 (2000): 257-82.

Armstrong, Robert G. "The Etymology of the Word *Ogun*." Pp. 29-38 in *Africa's Ogun: Old World and New*, edited by Sandra T. Barnes. Bloomington: Indiana University Press, 1997.

Arnold, Philip P. "Diversity in the History of Religions." *Journal of Cultural and Religious Theory*, at www.jcrt.org, 2001 (accessed November 11, 2000). 2001.

———. *Eating Landscape: Aztec and European Occupation of Tlalocan.* Boulder: University Press of Colorado, 1999.

Aschwanden, Herbert. *Symbols of Life: An Analysis of the Consciousness of the Karanga.* Translated by Ursula Cooper. Gweru, Zimbabwe: Mambo Press, 1982.

———. *Symbols of Death: An Analysis of the Consciousness of the Karanga.* Gweru, Zimbabwe: Mambo Press, 1987.

Bachelard, Gaston. *Water and Dreams: An Essay on the Imagination of Matter.* Translated by Edith R. Farrell. Dallas: Dallas Institute of Humanities and Culture, 1999.

Banana, Canaan S. *The Church and the Struggle for Zimbabwe.* Gweru, Zimbabwe: Mambo Press, 1996.

Barnes, Sandra T. "Africa's Ogun Transformed: Introduction to the Second Edition. Pp. xiii-xxi in *Africa's Ogun: Old World and New*, edited by Sandra T. Barnes. Bloomington: Indiana University Press, 1997.

———. "The Many Faces of Ogun: Introduction to the First Edition." Pp. 1-28 in *Africa's Ogun: Old World and New*, edited by Sandra T. Barnes. Bloomington: Indiana University Press, 1997.

Barnes, Sandra T., and Paula Girshick Ben-Amos. "Ogun, the Empire Builder." Pp. 39-64 in *Africa's Ogun: Old World and New*, edited by Sandra T. Barnes. Bloomington: Indiana University Press, 1997.

Barthes, Roland. *Mythologies.* London: Palladin, 1988.

Baudet, Henri. *Paradise on Earth: Some Thoughts on European Images of Non-European Man.* Middletown, Conn.: Wesleyan University Press, 1988 [1959].

Bergson, Henri. *Laughter: An Essay on the Meaning of the Comic.* Translated by Claudesley Brereton and Fred Rothwell. New York: Macmillan, 1911.

Best, Steven. "Animal Rights and Wrongs." *Britannica.co,* 2000, <wysiwyg:// 76:/http://www.britannica.com/bcom/original/article/0,5744,10066,00.html (accessed August 2002).

Biesele, Megan. *Women Like Meat: The Folklore and Foraging Ideology of the Kalahari Ju/'hoan.* Johannesburg: Witwatersrand University Press; Bloomington: Indiana University Press, 1993.

Boisvert, David, and Keith Turnbull. "Who Are the Métis?" *Studies in Political Economy* 18 (Autumn 1985): 107-48.

Bowsfield, H., ed. *Louis Riel: Rebel of the Western Frontier or Victim of Politics and Prejudice?* Toronto: Copp Clark Publishing, 1969.

Brandon, George. *Santeria from Africa to the New World: The Dead Sell Memories.* Bloomington: Indiana University Press, 1993.

Brannen, Mary Yoko. "'Bwana Mickey': Constructing Cultural Consumption at Tokyo Disneyland." Pp. 216-35 in *Re-Made in Japan*, edited by Joseph J. Tobin. New Haven, Conn.: Yale University Press, 1992.

Brave Heart, Maria Yellow Horse. "Oyate Ptayela: Rebuilding the Lakota Nation through Addressing Historical Trauma among Lakota Parents." In *Voices of First Nations People: Human Services Considerations*, edited by Hilary N. Weaver. New York: Haworth Press, 1999.

Brown, Jennifer S. H. "The Métis: Genesis and Rebirth." Pp. 136-47 in *Native People, Native Lands: Canadian Indians, Inuit, and Métis*, edited by Bruce Alden Cox. Ottawa: Carleton University Press, 1988.

Brown, Karen McCarthy. *MaMa Lola: A Vodou Priestess in Brooklyn*. Berkeley: University of California Press, 1991.

———. "SysteMatic Remembering, SysteMatic Forgetting: Ogou in Haiti." Pp. 65-89 in *Africa's Ogun: Old World and New*, edited by Sandra T. Barnes. Bloomington: Indiana University Press, 1997.

———. "Why Women Need the War God." Pp. 190-201 in *Women's Spirit Bonding*, edited by J. Kalven and M. Buckley. New York: Pilgrim Press, 1984.

BryMan, Alan. "The Disneyization of Society." *Sociological Review* 47 (1999): 25-47.

———. *Disney and His Worlds*. London: Routledge, 1995.

Bumsted, J. M. "Crisis at Red River." *The Beaver* 75, no. 3 (June/July 1995): 23-34.

———. "Louis Riel and the United States." *The American Review of Canadian Studies* (Spring 1999): 17-41.

Burridge, K. O. L. *Mambu: A Melanesian Millennium*. London, U.K.: Methuen, 1960.

———. *New Heaven, New Earth: A Study of Millenarian Activities*. Oxford, U.K.: Blackwell, 1969.

———. *Tangu Traditions*. Oxford, U.K.: Clarendon, 1969.

Byrne, Eleanor, and Martin McQuillan. *Deconstructing Disney*. London: Pluto Press, 1999.

Caputo, John S. "The Rhetoric of McDonaldization: A Social Semiotic Perspective." Pp. 39-52 in *McDonaldization Revisited: Critical Essays on Consumer Culture*, edited by Mark Alfino, John S. Caputo, and Robin Wynyard. Westport, Conn.: Praeger, 1998.

Carrington, Leonora. *The Seventh Horse and Other Stories*. Translated by Katherine Talbot and Anthony Kerrigan. London: Virago, 1989.

Chidester, David. "The Church of Baseball, the Fetish of Coca-Cola, and the Potlatch of Rock 'n' Roll." Pp. 219-38 in *Religion and Popular Culture in America*, edited by Bruce Forbes and Jeffrey Mahan. Berkeley: University of California Press, 2000.

————. *Savage Systems: Colonialism and Comparative Religion in Southern Africa*. Charleottesville: University Press of Virginia, 1996.

Clarke, Alison J. *Tupperware: The Promise of Plastic in 1950s America*. Washington, D.C.: Smithsonian Institution Press, 1999.

Classen, Constance. "Sugar Cane, Coca-Cola, and HyperMarkets: Consumption and Surrealism in the Argentine Northwest." Pp. 39-53 in *Cross-Cultural Consumption: Global Markets, Local Realities*, edited by David Howes. London: Routledge, 1996.

Cohn, Martin Regg. "Mumbai: Where's the Beef." *Toronto Star* (November 16, 2000).

Coleman, Will. *Tribal Talk: Black Theology, Hermeneutics, and African/ American Ways of "Telling the Story."* University Park: Pennsylvania State University Press, 2000.

Consentino, Donald J. "Repossession: Ogun in Folklore and Literature." 290-314 in *Africa's Ogun: Old World and New*, edited by Sandra T. Barnes. Bloomington: Indiana University Press, 1997.

Cross, Whitney. *The Burned-Over District: The Social and Intellectual History of Enthusiastic Religion in Western New York, 1800-1850*. Ithaca, N.Y.: Cornell University Press, 1950.

Crumley, Bruce, and Dean Fischer. "A Mickey Mouse Operation in Paris." *Time Magazine* (September 12, 1994).

Davies, Jan, and Gerard Loughlin, eds. *Sex These Days: Essays on Theology, Sexuality, and Society*. London: Sheffield Academic Press, 1997.

Davis, Mike. "The Bullshit Economy." *Village Voice Literary Supplement* (September 2000).

Debray, Régis. *Critique of Political Reason*. London: Verso, 1983.

————. *Media Manifestos: On the Technological Transmission of Cultural Forms*. Translated by Eric Rauth. London: Verso, 1996.

————. *Transmitting Culture*. Translated by Eric Rauth. New York: Columbia University Press, 2000.

Deloria, Vine. *For This Land: Writings on Religion in America*. Edited and with an introduction by James Treat. New York: Routledge, 1999.

Desmangles, Leslie G. *The Faces of the Gods: Vodou and RoMan Catholicism in Haiti*. Chapel Hill: University of North Carolina Press, 1992.

Descola, Philippe. *In the Society of Nature: A Native Ecology in AMazonia*. Translated from the French by Nora Scott. Cambridge, U.K.: Cambridge University Press, 1994.

Dickason, Olive Patricia. *Canada's First Nations: A History of Founding Peoples from Earliest Times*. Toronto: McClelland and Stewart, 1992.

Dorfman, Ariel, and Armand Mattelart. *How to Read Donald Duck: Imperialist Ideology in the Disney Comic*. New York: International General, 1975.

Drewal, Margaret Thompson. "Dancing for Ogun in Yorubalnad and in Brazil." Pp. 199-234 in *Africa's Ogun: Old World and New*, edited by Sandra T. Barnes. Bloomington: Indiana University Press, 1997.

Dunham, Katherine. *Island Possessed*. Chicago: University of Chicago Press, 1969.

Eco, Umberto. *Travels in Hyperreality*. London: Pan, 1986.

Eliade, Mircea. *Patterns in Comparative Religion*. Translated by Rosemary Sheed. New York: Sheed and Ward, 1958.

———. *Patterns in Comparative Religion*. Translated by Rosemary Sheed. Lincoln: University of Nebraska Press, 1999.

———. *The Quest: History and Meaning in Religion*. Chicago: University of Chicago Press, 1969.

Elling, Kurt. *Live in Chicago*. Blue Note, 2000.

———. Kurt Elling lyrics project at www.kurtelling.com/ (accessed November 11, 2000).

Encyclopedia Canadiana. Vol. 7. Toronto: Grolier, 1968.

Englebert, Pierre. *Burkino Faso: Unsteady Statehood in West Africa*. Boulder: Westview, 1996.

Esperitu, Aileen A. "Aboriginal Nations: Natives in Northwest Siberia and Northern Alberta." Pp. 41-67 in *Contested Arctic: Indigenous Peoples, Industrial States, and the Circumpolar Environment*, edited by Eric A. Smith and Joan McCarter. Russian, East European, and Central Asian Studies Center at the Henry Jackson School of International Studies, University of Washington, in association with University of Washington Press, Seattle, 1997.

Evans-Pritchard, E. E. *Nuer Religion*. Oxford, U.K.: Clarendon Press, 1956.

Fanon, Frantz. *Black Skins, White Masks*. Translated by C. L. Markmann, New York: Grove Press, 1967. Reprint, New York: Grove Weidenfeld, 1991.

———. *The Wretched of the Earth*. Translated by Constance Farrington. New York: Grove Press, 1963.

Feuerbach, Ludwig. *The Essence of Christianity*. New York: Harper & Brothers, 1957 [1841].

Fjellman, Stephen M. *Vinyl Leaves: Walt Disney World and America*. Boulder, Colo.: Westview, 1992.

Fiske, Alan A. *Structures of Social Life—The Four Elementary Forms of Human Relations: Communal Sharing, Authority Ranking, Equality Matching, Market Pricing*. New York: Free Press, 1991.

Flanagan, Thomas. *The Diaries of Louis Riel*. Edmonton, Alberta: Hurtig Publishers, 1976.

———. *Louis "David" Riel: "Prophet of the New World."* Revised edition. Toronto: University of Toronto Press, 1996.

————. "Louis Riel: Was He Really Crazy?" Pp. 105-20 in *1885 and After: Native Society in Transition*, edited by Laurie Barron and James B. Waldram. Regina, Sask.: University of Regina, 1986.

————. "On the Trail of the Massinahican: Riel's Encounter with Theosophy." *Journal of the Canadian Church Historical Society* 37 (1995): 89-98.

————. "The Political Thought of Louis Riel." In *Riel and the Métis: Riel Mini-Conference Papers*, edited by A. S. Lussier. Winnipeg: Manitoba Métis Federation Press, 1979.

Forbes, Bruce, and Jeffrey Mahan, eds. *Religion and Popular Culture in America*. Berkeley: University of California Press, 2000.

Foucault, Michel. *Power/Knowledge: Selected Interviews and Other Writings, 1972-1977*. Edited by C. Gordon, translated by C. Gordon et al. Brighton, New York, N.Y.: Pantheon Books.

Frank, Thomas. *One Market under God: Extreme Capitalism, Market Populism, and the End of Economic Democracy*. New York: Doubleday, 2000.

Frost, P. J., L. F. Moore, M. R. Louis, C. C. Lundberg, and J. Martin, eds. *Reframing Organizational Culture*. Newbury Park, Calif.: Sage, 1991.

Galeano, Eduardo. *Upside Down: A Primer for the Looking-Glass World*. New York: Metropolitan Books, Henry Holt Co., 1998.

Giddens, Anthony. *The Consequences of Modernity*. Stanford, Calif.: Polity Press, 1990.

————. *The Transformation of Intimacy: Sexuality, Love, and Eroticism in Modern Societies*. London: Polity Press, 1992.

Gifford, Paul. *African Christianity: Its Public Role*. London: Hurst, 1998.

Gill, Sam. *Native American Religious Action*. Columbia: University of South Carolina Press, 1987.

Gilroy, Paul. *There Ain't No Black in the Union Jack: The Cultural Politics of Race and Nation*. London: Hutchinson, 1987. Reprint, Chicago: University of Chicago Press, 1991.

————. *The Black Atlantic: Modernity and Double Consciousness*. Cambridge, Mass.: Harvard University Press, 1993.

Grottanelli, Cristiano, and Bruce Lincoln. "A Brief Note on (Future) Research in the History of Religions." *CHS Occasional Papers* 4 (1984).

Guerrero, M. A. Jaimes. "Native Womanism: Exemplars of Indigenism in Sacred Traditions of Kinship." In *Indigenous Religions: A Companion*, edited by Graham Harvey. London: Cassell, 2000.

Gyekye, Kwame. *African Cultural Values: An Introduction for Some Secondary Schools*. Philadelphia, Penn.: Sankofa Publishing Company, 1998.

Hall, Edward T. *Beyond Culture*. New York: Anchor Books and Doubleday, 1976.

————. *The Dance of Life: The Other Dimension of Time*. New York: Anchor Books and Doubleday, 1966.

————. *The Hidden Dimension*. New York: Anchor Books and Doubleday, 1966.

————. *The Silent Language*. New York: Anchor Books and Doubleday, 1959.

Harrison, Peter. *"Religion"' and the Religions in the English Enlightenment*. Cambridge: Cambridge University Press, 1990.

Harvey, Van A. *Feuerbach and the Interpretation of Religion*. Cambridge: Cambridge University Press, 1995.

Hegel, G. W. F. *The Philosophy of History*. New York: Dover Publications, 1956.

Henderson, Mae G. "Toni Morrison's *Beloved:* Re-Membering the Body as Historical Text." Pp. 62-86 in *Comparative American Identities: Race, Sex, and Nationality in the Modern Text*, edited by Hortense J. Spillars. New York: Routledge, 1991.

Hiliard, Constance. *Intellectual Traditions of Pre-Colonial Africa*. New York: McGraw Hill, 1998.

Hinde, Robert A. *Why Gods Persist: A Scientific Approach to Religion*. London: Routledge, 1999.

Hofstede, Geert. "The Business of International Business Is Culture." *International Business Review* 3, no. 1 (1994): 1-14.

————. *Culture's Consequences: International Differences in Work-Related Values*. Beverly Hills, Calif.: Sage, 1980.

————. *Cultures and Organizations: Software of the Mind*. New York: McGraw-Hill, 1992.

Hollander, John. "Originality." *Raritan* 2, no. 4 (Spring 1983).

Howes, David, ed. *Cross-Cultural Consumption: Global Markets, Local Realities*. London: Routledge, 1996.

Jacobson-Widding, Anita. "Notions of Heat and Fever among the Manyika of Zimbabwe." Pp. 27-44 in *Culture, Experience and Pluralism: Essays on African Ideas of Illness and Healing*, edited by Anita Jacobson-Widding and David Westerlund. Upsala, 1989.

James, C. L. R. *The Black Jacobins: Toussaint L'Ouverture and the San Domingo Revolution*. Second edition, revised. New York: Vintage and Random House, 1963.

Johansen, Bruce. *Forgotten Founders: How the American Indian Helped Democracy*. Boston: Harvard Common Press, 1982.

Kemp, Elizabeth. "In Search of a Home: People Living in or Near Protected Areas." Pp.3-11 in *Indigenous Peoples and Protected Areas: The Law of Mother Earth*, edited by Elizabeth Kemp. London: Earthscan Publications, 1993.

Khalil, M. H. *Indigenous Disenfranchisement and Long-Term Conservation: The Impact of Property Rights, Bioprospecting Agreements and Global Institutions on Genetic Resources and Indigenous Cultures*. Nairobi: ACES Press, Advanced Center for Environmental Studies, 1996.

Kowinski, William Severini. *The Malling of America: An Inside Look at the Great Consumer Paradise*. New York: William Morrow, 1985.

Krauss, Clifford. "Bolivia Makes Key Sessions to Indians." *New York Times* (October 6, 2000): A8.

Kroc, Ray, and Robert Anderson. *Grinding It Out: The Making of McDonald's*. New York: St. Martin's, 1990.

Krout, Maurice H. *Introduction to Social Psychology*. New York: Harper, 1942.

Kuper, Adam. *Wives for Cattle*. London: Routledge & Kegan Paul, 1982.

LaDuke, Winona. *All Our Relations: Native Struggle for Land and Life*. Boston: South End Press, 1999.

Lakoff, George, and Mark Johnson. *Philosophy in the Flesh: The Embodied Mind and Its Challenge to Western Thought*. New York: Basic, 1999.

Land, Richard D., and Frank D. York. *Send a Message to Mickey: The ABC's of Making Your Voice Heard at Disney*. Nashville, Tenn.: Broadman and Holman, 1998.

Landau, Paul. "Bushmen and Coca-Cola in a Cool World." *Southern African Review of Books* (March/April 1995): 8-9.

Lange, Lynda. "Burnt Offerings to Rationality: A Feminist Reading of the Construction of Indigenous Peoples in Enrique Dussel's Theory of Modernity." Pp. 226-39 in *Decentering the Center: Philosophy for a Multicultural, Postcolonial, and Feminist World*, edited by Uma Narayan and Sandra Harding. Bloomington: Indiana University Press, 2000.

Lanternari, Vittorio. *Religions of the Oppressed: A Study of Modern Messianic Cults*. Translated by Lisa Sergio. New York: Alfred A. Knopf, 1963.

Lemon, Alaina. "'Your Eyes Are Green Like Dollars': Counterfeit Cash, National Substance, and Currency Apartheid in 1990s Russia." *Cultural Anthropology* 13, no. 1 (1998): 22-55.

Long, Charles H. "Cargo Cults as Cultural Historical Phenomena." *Journal of the American Academy of Religion* 42, no. 3 (September 1974): 403-14.

——— "Mircea Eliade and the Imagination of Matter." *Journal for Cultural and Religious Theory* 1, no. 2 (April 2000), at www.jcrt.org/-archives/-01.2/long.shtml (accessed January 15, 2001).

———. "Passage and Prayer: The Origin of Religion in the Atlantic World." Pp. 11-21 in *The Courage to Hope: From Black Suffering to Human Redemption*, edited by Quinton Hosford Dixie and Cornel West. Boston: Beacon, 1999.

———. "Primitive Religion." In *A Reader's Guide to the Great Religions*. Second edition, edited by Charles J. Adams. New York: Free Press, 1977.

———. *Significations: Signs, Symbols, and Images in the Interpretation of Religion*. Philadelphia: Fortress Press, 1986.

———. *Significations: Signs, Symbols, and Images in the Interpretation of Religion*. Aurora, Colo.: Davies Group, 1999.

————. "Silence and Signification: A Note on Religion and Modernity." Pp. 141-150 in *Myth and Symbol: Studies in Honor of Mircea Eliade*, edited by Joseph M. Kitagawa and Charles H. Long. Chicago: University of Chicago Press, 1969.

————. "The West African High God: History and Religious Experience." *History of Religions* 3, no. 2 (1964): 328-42.

Love, John. *McDonald's: Behind the Arches*. New York: Bantam, 1986.

Luce, Louise Fiber, and Elise C. Smith, eds. *Toward Internationalism: Readings in Cross-Cultural Communication*. Boston: Heinle and Heinle, 1987.

Maanen, John van. "Displacing Disney: Some Notes on the Flow of Culture." *Qualitative Sociology*, 15, no. 1 (1992): 5-35.

————. "The Smile Factory: Work at Disneyland." Pp. 58-76 in *Reframing Organizational Culture*, edited by P. J. Frost, L. F. Moore, M. R. Louis, C. C. Lundberg, and J. Martin. Newbury Park, Calif.: Sage, 1991.

Mantour, Martha. "Matriarchy and the Canadian Constitution: A Double-Barrelled Threat to Indian Women." *Agenda: A Journal about Women and Gender* 13 (1992): 59-64.

Martel, Gilles. "L'idéologie messianique de Louis Riel et ses determinants sociaux." *Transactions of the Royal Society of Canada*, series 5, no. 1 (1986): 229-38.

————. *Le Messianisme de Louis Riel*. Waterloo, Ontario: Wilfred Laurier University Press, 1984.

Marx, Karl. *Capital*. 2 volumes. Translated by Samuel Moore and Edward Aveling. London: Lawrence and Wishart, 1974.

————. *Capital: A Critique of Political Economy*. Vol. 1, edited by F. Engels, translated by S. Moore and E. Aveling. New York: International Publishers, 1967.

Mason, John. "Ogun: Builder of the Lukumi's House." Pp. 353-368 in *Africa's Ogun: Old World and New*, edited by Sandra T. Barnes. Bloomington: Indiana University Press, 1997.

Masuzawa, Tomoko. *In Search of Dreamtime: The Quest for the Origin of Religion*. Chicago: University of Chicago Press, 1993.

————. "Reading in the Wake: Supplementary Remarks on the Dreamtime." *Method & Theory in the Study of Religion* 8, no. 3 (1996).

Mauss, Marcel. *The Gift: Forms and Functions of Exchange in Archaic Societies*. New York: W. W. Norton, 1967.

Mazrui, Ali A. "From Slave Ship to Space Ship: Africa between Marginalization and Globalization." *African Studies Quarterly* 2, no. 4 (1999), at web.africa. ufl.edu/asq/ (accessed fall 2000).

Mbaria, John. "Who is Really Breaking Nature's Law?" *World Press Review* (October, 2000); reprint from *The East African* (June 12-18, 2000).

McPherson, Dennis H., and J. Douglass Rabb "Native Philosophy: Western or Indigenous Construct?" Pp. 271-86 in *Indigeneity: Construction and*

Re/Presentation, edited by James N. Brown and Patricia M. Sant. Commack, N.Y.: Nova Science Publishers, 1995.

Melia, Bartomew. "The Guarani Religious Experience." Pp. 169-216 in *The Indian Face of God in Latin America*, edited by Manuel Marzal, Eugenio Maurer, Xavier Albo, and Bartomew Melia. Maryknoll, N.Y.: Orbis Books, 1996.

Merleau-Ponty, Maurice. *The Primacy of Perception*. Edited by James M. Edie. Evanston, Ill., 1964.

Miller, J. R. *Skyscrapers Hide the Heavens: A History of Indian-White Relations in Canada*. Toronto: University of Toronto Press, 1989.

Miller, Olga. "Kgari." Pp. 39-40 in *Indigenous Australian Voices: A Reader*, edited by Jennifer Sabbioni, Kay Schaffer, and Sidonie Smith. New Brunswick, N.J.: Rutgers University Press, 1999.

Mirowski, Philip. *More Heat than Light: Economics as Social Physics, as Nature's Economics*. Cambridge, U.K.: Cambrisge University Press, 1989.

Morain, Genelle G. "Kinesics and Cross-Cultural Understanding." Pp. 117-42 in *Toward Internationalism: Readings in Cross-Cultural Communication*, edited by Louise Fiber Luce and Elise C. Smith. Boston.: Heinle and Heinle Publishers, 1987.

Morris, Brian. *Animals and Ancestors: An Ethnography*. New York: Oxford University Press, 2000.

Morrison, Terri, Wayne A. Conaway, and George A. Borden. *Kiss, Bow, or Shake Hands: How to Do Business in Sixty Countries*. Holbrook, Mass.: Adams Media Corporation, 1994.

Morrison, Toni. *Beloved*. New York: Alfred Knopf, 1987.

Morton, Desmond. "Reflections on the Image of Louis Riel a Century After." Pp. 47-92 in *Images of Louis Riel in Canadian Culture*, edited by Ramon Hathorn and Patrick Holland. Lewiston, N.Y.: Edwin Mellen Press, 1992.

Mossman, Manfred. "The Charismatic Pattern: Canada's Riel Rebellion of 1885 as a Millenarian Protest Movement," *Prairie Forum* 10 (1985): 307-25.

Müller, F. Max. *Lectures on the Origin and Growth of Religion*. Delivered in April, May, and June, 1878. Varanasi, India: Indological Book House, 1964.

Murakami, Tatsuo. *Fetishism as the Origin of Religion*. Ph.D. thesis University of California, Santa Barbara, 2000.

Murphy, Joseph M. *Working the Spirit: Ceremonies of the African Diaspora*. Boston: Beacon, 1994.

Nabhan, Gary Paul. "Native American Management and Conservation of Biodiversity in the Sonoran Desert Bioregion: An Ethnoecological Perspective." Pp. 29-43 in *Biodiversity and Native America*, edited by Paul Minnis and Wayne Elisens. Norman: University of Oklahoma Press, 2000.

Nelson, Benjamin N. *The Idea of Usury: From the Tribal Brotherhood to Universal Otherhood*. Princeton, N.J.: Princeton University Press, 1949.

Nkrumah, Kwame. *Neo-colonialism: The Last Stage of Imperialism.* London: Heinemann Educational Books, 1965.

Nolan, Albert. *God in South Africa: The Challenge of the Gospel.* Grand Rapids, Mich.: William. B. Eerdmans, 1988.

Obenga, Theophile. *A Lost Tradition: African Philosophy in World History.* Philadelphia: Source Editions, 1995.

Ohnuki-Tierney, Emiko. "McDonald's in Japan: Changing Manners and Etiquette." Pp. 161-82 in *Golden Arches East: McDonald's in East Asia,* edited by James L. Watson. Stanford, Calif.: Stanford University Press, 1997.

Olmos, Margarite Fernandez, and Lizabeth Paravisini-Gebert. "Introduction: Religioius Syncretism and Caribbean Culture." Pp. 1-12 in *Sacred Possessions: Vodou, Santeria, Obeah, and the Caribbean,* edited by Margarite Fernandez Olmos and Lizabeth Paravisini-Gebert. New Brunswick, N.J.: Rutgers University Press, 1997.

Onyewuenyi, Innocent. *The African Origin of Greek Philosophy: An Exercise in Afrocentrism.* Nsukka, Nigeria: University of Nsukka Press, 1993.

Otto, Rudolf. *The Idea of the Holy.* Translated by John Harvey. Second edition. Oxford: Oxford University Press, 1958.

Page, George. *Inside the Animal Mind.* New York: Doubleday, 1999.

Pals, Daniel L. "Is Religion a *Sui Generis* Phenomenon?" *Journal of the American Academy of Religion* 55, no. 2 (1987): 259-82.

Palumbo-Liu, David, and Hans Ulrich Gumbrecht, eds. *Streams of Cultural Capital: Transnational Cultural Studies.* Stanford, Ccalif.: Stanford University Press, 1997.

Pannekoek, Frits. *A Snug Little Flock: The Social Origins of the Riel Resistance, 1869-18*70. Winnipeg: Watson and Dwyer, 1991.

Paulson, Ivar. "The Animal Guardian: A Critical and Synthetic Review." *History of Religions* 3, no. 2 (1964): 328-42.

Pels, Peter. "The Spirit of Matter: On Fetish, Rarity, Fact, and Fancy." Pp. 91-121 in *Border Fetishisms: Material Objects in Unstable Spaces,* edited by Patricia Spyer. London: Routledge, 1998.

Pemberton, John III. "The Dreadful God and the Divine King." Pp. 105-46 in *Africa's Ogun: Old World and New,* edited by Sandra T. Barnes. Bloomington: Indiana University Press, 1997.

Pendergrast, Mark. *For God, Country, and Coca-Cola: The Unauthorized History of the Great American Soft Drink and the Company That Makes It.* New York: Scribner's, 1993.

Penn, David, and Patricia Campbell. "Human Rights and Culture: Beyond Universality and Relativism." *Third World Quarterly* 19, no. 1 (1998): 7-27.

Perkinson, Jim. "A Socio-Reading of the Kierkegaardian Self: Or, the Space of Lowliness in the Time of the Disciple." Pp. 156-72 in *Kierkegaard: The Self in Society*, edited by George Pattison and Steven Shakespeare. London: Mcmillan Press, 1998.

———. "A Canaanitic Word in the Logos of Christ: Or the Difference the Syro-Phoenician Woman Makes to Jesus." *Semeia* 75 (1996): 61-86.

———. "Soteriological Humility: The Christological Significance of the Humanity of Jesus in the Encounter of Religions." *Journal of Ecumenical Studies* 31, nos. 1-2 (Winter-Spring 1994): 1-26.

Peters, R. E. *Greek Philosophical Terms: A Historical Lexicon*. New York: New York University Press, 1967.

Peterson, Richard B. *Conversations in the Rainforest: Culture, Values, and the Environment in Central Africa*. Boulder, Colo.: Westview/Perseus Books, 2000.

Pietz, William. "The Problem of the Fetish, I." *Res: Anthropology and Aesthetics* 9 (Spring 1985):5-17.

———. "The Problem of the Fetish II: The Origin of the Fetish." *Res: Anthropology and Aesthetics* 13 (Spring 1987).

———. "The Problem of the Fetish III: Bosman's Guinea and the Englishtenment Theory of the Fetish." *Res: Anthropology and Aesthetics* 16 (Autumn 1988): 105-123.

Polanco, Hector Diaz. *Indigenous Peoples in Latin America: The Quest for Self-Determination*. Boulder, Colo.: Westview, 1997.

Prager, Brad, and Michael Richardson. "A Sort of Homecoming: An Archaeology of Disneyland." Pp. 199-219 in *Streams of Cultural Capital: Transnational Cultural Studies*, edited by David Palumbo-Liu and Hans Ulrich Gumbrecht. Stanford, Calif.: Stanford University Press, 1997.

Preus, J. Samuel. *Explaining Religion: Criticism and Theory from Bodin to Freud*. New Haven, Conn.: Yale University Press, 1987.

Rakotsoane, Francis L. *The Southern Sotho's Ultimate Object of Worship: Sky-Divinity or Water-Divinity?* P.h.D. thesis, University of Cape Town, 2001.

Ramose, M. B. *African Philosophy through Ubuntu*. Harare, Zimbabwe: Mond Books, 1999.

Ranger, T. *The African Voice in Southern Rhodesia, 1898-1930*. London: Heinemann, 1970.

Raz, Aviad E. *Riding the Black Ship: Japan and Tokyo Disneyland*. Cambridge, Mass.: Harvard University Press, 1999.

Redman, Charles. *Human Impact on Ancient Environments*. Tucson: University of Arizona Press, 1999.

Ricoeur, Paul. *Freud and Philosophy: An Essay on Interpretation*. New Haven, Conn.: Yale University Press, 1970.

Riel, Louis. *The Collected Writings of Louis Riel/Les ecrits complets de Louis Riel*. 5 vols. Edited by George F. G. Stanley, Raymond Huel, Gilles Martel, Thomas Flanagan, Glen Campbell, and Claude Rocan. Edmonton: University of Alberta Press, 1985.

Ritzer, George. *The McDonaldization of Society.* Thousand Oaks, Calif.: Pine Forge Press, 2000.

Ronaghen, Allen. "Charles Mair and the North-West Emigration Aid Society." *Manitoba History* 14 (1987): 10-14.

Ross, Edward Alsworth. *Social Psychology.* New York: Macmillan, 1908.

Rudd, Anthony. "Kierkegaard's Critique of Pure Irony." Pp. 82-96 in *Kierkegaard: The Self in Society,* ed. George Pattison and Steven Shakespeare. London: MacMillan Press, 1998.

Ryder, Richard D. *Animal Revolution: Changing Attitudes toward Speciesism.* Revised and updated. New York: Berg, 2000.

Safire, William. "On Language." *New York Times Magazine* June 10, 2001:40-42.

Salacuse, Jeswald W. "Coping with Culture." In *Making Global Deals: Negotiating in the International Marketplace.* New York: Houghton Mifflin, 1991.

Scher, Philip. "Unveiling the Orisha." Pp. 315-31 in *Africa's Ogun: Old World and New,* edited by Sandra T. Barnes. Bloomington: Indiana University Press, 1997.

Schoffeleers, J. M. *River of Blood: The Genesis of a Martyr Cult in Southern Malawi.* Madison: University of Wisconsin Press, 1992.

Setiloane, Gabriel M. *The Image of God among the Sotho-Tswana.* Rotterdam, Netherlands: Balkema, 1976.

Sharpe, Eric J. *Comparative Religion: A History.* Second edition. La Salle, Ill.: Open Court, 1986.

Shell, Ellen R. "New World Syndrome." *The Atlantic Monthly* (June 2001).

Siggins, Maggie. *Riel: A Life of Revolution.* Toronto: Harper-Collins, 1994.

Simon-Wastila. "Unio Mystica and Particularity: Can Individuals Merge with the One?" *Journal of the American Academy of Religion* 68, no. 4 (December 2000): 857-79.

Smart, N. *The Religious Experience of Mankind.* London: Collins, 1971.

Smith , Jonathan Z. *Imagining Religion: From Babylon to Jonestown.* Chicago: University of Chicago Press, 1982.

———. *Map Is Not Territory: Studies in the History of Religions.* Leiden: E. J. Brill, 1978.

Smith, Wilfred Cantwell. *The Meaning and End of Religion.* Minneapolis: Fortress Press, 1991 [1962].

Smoodin, Eric, ed. *Disney Discourse: Producing the Magic Kingdom.* London: Routledge, 1994.

Sprenger, George Herman. "The Métis Nation: Buffalo Hunting Versus Agriculture in the Red River Settlement, 1810-1870." Pp. 120-35 in *Native People, Native Lands: Canadian Indians, Inuit, and Métis,* edited by Bruce Alden Cox. Ottawa: Carleton University Press, 1988.

Spyer, Patricia, ed. *Border Fetishisms: Material Objects in Unstable Spaces.* London: Routledge, 1998.

Stevens, Stan, ed. *Conservation through Survival: Indigenous Peoples and Protected Areas.* Washington D.C.: Island Press, 1997.

Taylor, Victor E., and Charles E. Winquist, eds. *Encyclopedia of Postmodernism.* New York: Routledge, 2001.

Thatcher, Adrian. "Postmodernity and Chastity." Pp. 127-30 in *Sex These Days: Essays on Theology, Sexuality, and Society,* edited by Jan Davies and Gerard Loughlin. London: Sheffield Academic Press, 1997.

Thomas, Nicholas. *Entangled Objects: Exchange, Material Culture, and Colonialism in the Pacific.* Cambridge, Mass.: Harvard University Press, 1991.

Thompson, Robert Farris. *Flash of the Spirit: African and Afro-American Art and Philosophy.* New York: Vintage, 1983.

———. "The Flash of the Spirit: Haiti's Africanizing Vodun Art." Pp. 26-37 in *Haitian Art,* edited by Ute Stebich. The Brooklyn Museum. New York: Harry N. Abrams, 1978.

Thongmak, Seri, and David Hulse. "The Winds of Change: Karen People in Harmony with World Heritage." Pp. 162-68 in *Indigenous Peoples and Protected Areas: The Law of Mother Earth,* edited by Elizabeth Kemp. London: Earthscan Publications, 1993.

Tobin, Joseph J. *Re-Made in Japan.* New Haven, Conn.: Yale University Press, 1992.

Tomlinson, John. *Cultural Imperialism.* Baltimore: Johns Hopkins University Press, 1991.

Turner,V. W. *The Forest of Symbols: Aspects of Ndembu Ritual.* Ithaca, N.Y.: Cornell University Press, 1967.

Wade, Mason. "A Sequel to 1869." Pp. 122-23 in *Louis Riel: Rebel of the Western Frontier or Victim of Politics and Prejudice?* Edited by H. Bowsfield. Toronto: Copp Clark Publishing, 1969.

Wach, Joachim. *Essays in the History of Religions.* Edited by Joseph P. Kitagawa and Gregory D. Alles. New York: Macmillan, 1988.

Walker, Sheila. *Ceremonial Spirit Possession in Africa and Afro-America: Forms, Meanings, and Functional Significance for Individuals and Social Groups.* Leiden, Netherlands: E. J. Brill, 1972.

Wall, Steve, and Harvey Arden. *Wisdom Keepers: Meetings with Native American Spiritual Elders.* Hillsboro, Oreg.: Beyond Words Publishing, 1990.

Watson, James L. "Transnationalism, Localization, and Fast Foods in East Asia." Pp. 1-38 in *Golden Arches East: McDonald's in East Asia,* edited by James L. Watson. Stanford, Calif.: Stanford University Press, 1997.

———. *Golden Arches East: McDonald's in East Asia.* Stanford, Calif.: Stanford University Press, 1997.

Watzman, Hiam. "The Scholarly and the Ecstatic: Academics Debate How to Approach the Kabalah, the Heart of Jewish Mysticism." *The Chronicle of Higher Education* (January 26, 2001).

Werbner, Richard P. *Ritual Passage, Sacred Journey: The Process and Organization of Religious Movement.* Washington, D.C.: Smithsonian Institution Press; Manchester: Manchester University Press, 1989.

Wiebe, Donald. "The Failure of Nerve in the Academic Study of Religion." *Sciences Religieuses/ Studies in Religion* 13, no. 4 (1984): 401-22.

Williams, Delores. *Sisters in the Wilderness: The Challenge of Womanist God-Talk.* Maryknoll, N.Y.: Orbis Books, 1993.

Williams, F. E. *The Vailala Madness and the Destruction of Native Ceremonies in the Gulf District.* Papua Anthropology Report no. 4. Port Moresby, 1923.

Wilmore, Gayraud. *Black Religion and Black Radicalism: An Interpretation of the Religious History of Afro-American People.* Second revised edition (1973). Reprint. Maryknoll, N,Y.: Orbis Books, 1983.

Wiredu, Kwasi. "Our Problem of Knowledge." In *African Philosophy as Cultural Inquiry*, edited by Ivan Karp and D.A. Masolo. Bloomington: Indiana University Press, 2000.

Witvliet, Theo. *A Place in the Sun: Liberation Theology in the Third World.* Translated by John Bowden. Maryknoll, N.Y.: Orbis Books, 1985.

Wolf, Eric R. *Europe and People without History.* Berkeley: University of California Press, 1982.

World Press Review. October 2000.

Wright, Ronald. *Stolen Continents: The Americas through Indian Eyes since 1492.* New York: Houghton Mifflin, 1992.

Yoshida, K. "Masks and Transformation among the Chewa of Eastern Zambia." *Senri Ethnological Studies* 31 (1991): 203-73.

Yoshimoto, Mitsuhiro. "Images of Empire: Tokyo Disneyland and Japanese Cultural Imperialism." Pp. 181-99 in *Disney Discourse: Producing the Magic Kingdom*, edited by Eric Smoodin. London: Routledge, 1994.

Zahan, Dominique. "Some Reflections on African Spirituality." Pp. 3-25 in *African Spirituality: Forms, Meanings, and Expressions*, edited by Jacob K. Olupona. New York: Crossroad Publishing, 2000.

Zepp, Ira G. *The New Religious Image of Urban America: The Shopping Mall as Ceremonial Center.* Westminster, Md.: Christian Classics, 1986.

Zuesse, Evan M. *Ritual Cosmos: The Sanctification of Life in African Religions.* Athens: Ohio University Press, 1979.

————. "Perseverance and Transmutation in African Traditional Religion." Pp. 167-84 in *African Traditional Religions in Contemporary Society*, edited by Jacob K. Olupona. New York: Paragon House, 1991.

Zvobgo, C. J. M. *The Wesleyan Methodist Missions in Zimbabwe.* Harare: University of Zimbabwe Publications, 1991.

Index

Achuar, 140

Akan, 136

Amerian Academy of Religion (AAR), 10, 27

anthropology, 21, 127-28, 172, 176

archaism, 14-15, 169-70, 179

Atlantic Ocean, 22, 175, 177

Atlantic world, 3, 5, 173-75, 179

Augustine of Hippo, 132

axis mundi, 137, 162

Aztec, 45, 129-30

Barthes, Roland, 162

Basho, 31

Baudet, Henri, 21-22

The Bible, 43, 73, 86, 152, 179

Bodin, Jean, 9

Buddhism, 1. *See also* Coca Cola.

Burridge, K. O. L., 179

Calvin, John, 173

Calvinism, 175

Candomble, 93, 97, 113, 118

capitalism, 71, 74, 83-84, 129-32, 152, 173

cargo movements (cargo cults), 8, 52, 101, 149, 178-79

Carrasco, David, 45

ceremony, 41, 45, 89, 93, 105, 137

Christianity, 72, 85, 88-92, 100, 116, 177-79; and God, 72-73, 173, 177; and mysticism, 80; and theology, 11, 177

cipher of religion, 1, 45-46

civilization, 126, 128; and the primitive, 2, 8, 25n46, 126, 152, 157. *See also* Long, Charles H.

Classen, Constance, 152-53

Coca-Cola, 147, 150-53, 157, 161, 163; and Buddhism, 152; and Islam, 152

the Cold War, 86-87

commodities, 58, 116, 149, 178. *See also* religion.

communism, 87, 152, 158

Comte, Auguste, 10, 18

consciousness, 9, 55, 68-69, 170; animal, 77; material structure of, 2, 56, 61. *See* Eliade, Mircea; Feuerbach, Ludwig; Freud, Sigmund; Ricoeur, Paul.

cultural kinesics, 145-46

Darwin, Charles, 7, 16

Debray, Régis, 148-49

Descartes, René, 56, 65n25, 176, 180, 181n12; and cartesian *cogito*, 18, 19, 173-74, 180

Disney. *See* Walt Disney Company.

divination, 138

Durkheim, Emile, 9, 10, 23

Dussel, Enrique, 128

Eden, 22

Eliade, Mircea, 14-16, 23, 56, 128; and consciousness, 2, 17, 55; and materiality, 2, 55; and myth, 14; and the sacred, 44-45, 47; and symbol, 17, 19-20

Elling, Kurt, 47-48

Ellul, Jacques, 30

the Enlightenment, 73, 126, 128, 177, 180; and the study of religion, 21, 23, 56

epistemology, 8, 9-12, 23, 79, 181. *See also* indigeneity.

Erie Canal, 41-42, 47-48

197

Contributors

Philip P. Arnold is Associate Professor of American Religions at Syracuse University. He is the author of *Eating Landscape: Aztec and European Occupation of Tlalocan* (1989) and coeditor with Ann Grodzins Gold of *Sacred Landscapes and Cultural Politics: Planting a Tree* (2001).

Kees W. Bolle is Professor Emeritus of History at the University of California-Los Angeles. He was editor of a series of monographs, *Hermeneutics: Studies in the History of Religions*, from its inception in 1983. He is the author of *The Freedom of Man in Myth* (1968), *The Bhagavadgita: A New Translation* (1979), *Ben's Story: Holocaust Letters, with Selections from the Dutch Underground Press* (2001), and *Enticement of Religion* (2002).

David Chidester is Professor of Comparative Religion at the University of Cape Town, and director of the Institute for Comparative Religion in Southern Africa. He is the author of *Savage Systems: Colonialism and Comparative Religion in Southern Africa* (1996), *Salvation and Suicide: An Interpretation of Jim Jones, the Peoples Temple, and Jonestown* (1988), and *Christianity: A Global History* (2000).

Julian Kunnie is Director and Professor of Africana Studies at the University of Arizona. He is the author of *Models of Black Theology: Issues in Class, Culture, and Gender* (1994) and *Is Apartheid Really Dead? Pan Africanist Working Class Cultural Critical Perspectives* (2000).

Chirevo V. Kwenda is Senior Lecturer of African Indigenous Religions at the University of Cape Town. He is coauthor of *African Religion and Culture Alive* (1997) and *African Traditional Religion in South Africa* (1997).

Charles H. Long is Professor Emeritus of Religious Studies at the University of California-Santa Barbara. He is the author of *Alpha: The Myths of Creation*

(1963) and *Significations: Signs, Symbols, and Images in the Interpretation of Religion* (1986 and 1999).

Tatsuo Murakami is a Research Fellow at Kokushikan University, Tokyo. He received his Ph.D. from the University of California-Santa Barbara in 2001.

Jacob K. Olupona is Professor of African American and African Studies at the University of California-Davis. He is the author of *Kingship, Religion, and Rituals in a Nigerian Community* (1991), *African Traditional Religions in Contemporary Society* (1991), *Religion and Peace in Multi-Ethnic Nigeria* (1992), and *African Spirituality* (2000); and coeditor of *Religious Plurality in Africa: Essays in Honor of John Mbili* (1993).

Jim Perkinson is Associate Professor of Religious Studies/Philosophy at Marygrove College and Ethics at Ecumenical Theological Seminary. He is the author of numerous articles that have appeared in journals such as *Journal of Religion*, *Cross Currents*, and *Semeia*.

Jennifer I. M. Reid is Associate Professor of Religion at the University of Maine at Farmington. She is the author of *Myth, Symbol, and Colonial Encounter: British and Mi'kmaq in Acadia, 1700-1867* (1995).